Writing the Child

CULTURAL MEMORIES

VOL. 18

SERIES EDITOR

Katia Pizzi
Director, Italian Cultural Institute, London

PETER LANG
Oxford · Bern · Berlin · Bruxelles · New York · Wien

Writing the Child

Fictions of Memory in German Postwar Literature

Susanne Baackmann

PETER LANG

Oxford · Bern · Berlin · Bruxelles · New York · Wien

Bibliographic information published by Die Deutsche Nationalbibliothek
Die Deutsche Nationalbibliothek lists this publication in the Deutsche Nationalbibliografie;
detailed bibliographic data is available on the Internet at http://dnb.d-nb.de.

A catalogue record for this book is available from the British Library.

Library of Congress Cataloging-in-Publication Data

Names: Baackmann, Susanne, 1958- author.
Title: Writing the child : fictions of memory in German postwar literature
    / Susanne Baackmann.
Description: Oxford ; New York : Peter Lang, [2022] | Series: Cultural
    memories, 2235-2325 ; vol no. 18 | Includes bibliographical references
    and index.
Identifiers: LCCN 2022034925 (print) | LCCN 2022034926 (ebook) | ISBN
    9781787077225 (paperback) | ISBN 9781787077232 (ebook) | ISBN
    9781787077249 (epub)
Subjects: LCSH: German literature--20th century--History and criticism. |
    Children in literature. | Collective memory in literature. | Psychic
    trauma in literature. | World War, 1939-1945--Literature and the war. |
    LCGFT: Literary criticism.
Classification: LCC PT151.C6 B33 2022 (print) | LCC PT151.C6 (ebook) |
    DDC 830.9/352309045--dc23/eng/20221011
LC record available at https://lccn.loc.gov/2022034925
LC ebook record available at https://lccn.loc.gov/2022034926

Cover image courtesy of Susanne Baackmann.
Cover design by Peter Lang Ltd.

ISSN 2235-2325
ISBN 978-1-78707-722-5 (print)
ISBN 978-1-78707-723-2 (ePDF)
ISBN 978-1-78707-724-9 (ePub)

© Peter Lang Group AG 2022

Published by Peter Lang Ltd, International Academic Publishers,
Oxford, United Kingdom
oxford@peterlang.com, www.peterlang.com

Susanne Baackmann has asserted her right under the Copyright, Designs and Patents Act, 1988,
to be identified as Author of this work.

This publication has been peer reviewed.

For Hannah and David

Zur Kenntnis der mémoire involuntaire: ihre Bilder kommen nicht allein ungerufen, es handelt sich vielmehr in ihr um Bilder, die wir nie sahen, ehe wir uns erinnerten. Am deutlichsten ist es bei jenen Bildern, auf welchen wir – genau wie in manchen Träumen – selber zu sehen sind.

As to the experience of involuntary memory: its images do not come without being solicited. It is much more a matter of images that, prior to recalling them, we never saw. It is the most distinct with those images in which we ourselves can be seen – exactly as in many dreams.

– Walter Benjamin, 'From a Little Speech about
Proust held on my Fortieth Birthday', 1932

Wie schwer es sein muss, hier einen Weg zu finden, kommt vielleicht am deutlichsten in der gängigen Redensart zum Ausdruck, das Vergangene sei noch unbewältigt, man müsse erst einmal daran gehen, die Vergangenheit zu bewältigen. Dies kann man wahrscheinlich mit keiner Vergangenheit, sicher aber nicht mit dieser. Das Höchste, was man erreichen kann, ist zu wissen und auszuhalten, dass es so und nicht anders gewesen ist, und dann zu sehen und abzuwarten, was sich daraus ergibt.

Herein lies the reason for the German's profound awkwardness, which strikes every outsider, in any discussion about the questions of the past. How difficult it must be to find a reasonable attitude is perhaps more clearly expressed by the cliché that the past is still 'unmastered' and in the conviction held particularly by men of good will that the first thing to be done is to set about 'mastering' it. Perhaps that cannot be done with any past but certainly not with the past of Hitler Germany. The best one can achieve is to know and make space for precisely what has been, and then to wait and see what comes of knowing.

– Hannah Arendt, speech on accepting
the Lessing Prize of the Free City of Hamburg, 1959

Contents

CHAPTER 6
'Lore', or the Implicated Subject: Rachel Seiffert's
Postmemory Work   165

EPILOGUE
Memory in a Moment of Danger   195

Bibliography   205

Index   221

Preface

At first, this book seemed to be a purely academic study, designed to engage a larger conversation with colleagues about the vicissitudes of German cultural memory. But it became a much more personal exploration of my relationship to a past I experienced only vicariously. The fiction analysed in this book offers stories about the German child silenced by war or traumatized by silent parents – a child who maintains a tenuous dialogue with the Jewish child, the 'other' child, who in most cases did not survive a war in which they were targeted. These stories forced me to confront childhood silences I grew up with in Germany without having been aware of them at the time. It challenged me to reflect on how, exactly, this war has crossed my own life, my own way of being, my own thinking. How did this war shape me – a white woman born in the Ruhr Valley well after May 1945. Both my father, born one year before the First World War, and my *Kriegskind* mother, born two years after Hitler came to power, were tenaciously silent about their war experiences. During the work on this book, I began to see them with different eyes and found myself wanting to ask them questions I never got to ask. I grew up in a country in which the violence of war had been efficiently covered up by postwar prosperity and the myth of the 'economic miracle'. Yet for the past three decades, I have lived in the United States, a country whose national myth also brackets the violence of racial domination at its core. This core also implicates me – a white woman of European descent with middle-class privileges. How to traverse these intersections of different yet interrelated histories and cultures resting on legacies of systemic persecution, discrimination and domination? How to acknowledge the privileges and opportunities that rest on these legacies and which I benefitted from in both direct and indirect ways? How to understand my own implication in much larger historical textures without finding shelter in convenient historical or theoretical abstractions?

Writing the Child became a book not only about my German family but also about my own child, whose grandparents were among the few children lucky enough to escape Nazi Germany just in time. It became a work of family memory in the broadest sense and reckons with cultural discontinuities I experienced growing up and family discontinuities I married into without fully understanding them. Writing became a labour about unrecognized memory entanglements that settled into my own body after confronting a history I knew only faintly. Hence, I am dedicating it first and foremost to my daughter Hannah. Like her father, David, to whom I owe a lot of gratitude for trying to explain the unexplainable, she will have to find a way to live with what Hannah Arendt – the philosopher she is named after – defined as the best we can do in light of this history: 'Das Höchste, was man erreichen kann, ist zu wissen und auszuhalten, dass es so und nicht anders gewesen ist, und dann zu sehen und abzuwarten, was sich daraus ergibt.' [The best one can achieve is to know and make space for precisely what has been, and then to wait and see what comes of knowing].

Susanne Baackmann
March 2022

Acknowledgements

There are many whom I must thank for their support during the work on this book. The editorial guidance of Mary Child was simply invaluable. Her insightful, clear-headed and ever so tactful suggestions turned the final manuscript into a much more nuanced, coherent and readable text. Her expert knowledge of the Anglophone lexis, grammar and punctuation moderated my Germanic tendencies for long-winded sentences, as well as my preference for repetitions. At this point, I am to blame for any remaining infelicities. Scott Melton also contributed to the final version of the manuscript. His sharp eye for detail added the final polish and allowed me to send it off with a smile on my face. I am so very grateful for Nancy Nenno's help. Her patient support and expert editorial help was a generous and an unexpected gift I greatly appreciated. She continued to believe in this book even when my enthusiasm faltered. Patrick Joseph Hoffman's steady and competent help with every translation, conjunction, preposition, dash and semicolon was equally priceless. Nina Berman, Anja Barr, Mark Smith, Jaime Denison and Joseph Kuster all contributed to this project, albeit in different ways. Their help with initial chapter drafts was another gift that contributed to the final form of this manuscript. I am grateful for the support of colleagues at the University of New Mexico, in particular Pamela Cheek, who throughout the years kept encouraging me to believe in questions to which I had no easy answers; she remained convinced that I would eventually find the answers. I will also never forget the wisdom and support of my mentor and friend Jack Zipes. His urgent and persistent commitment to make this world a better place by taking seriously the power of story not only inspired me deeply, but also sent me on my way into a future of curiosity and exploration that continues on. I owe him immense gratitude.

I must extend a special and heartfelt thanks to John Cousins. His warm and unceasing optimism, uncontainable enthusiasm, patient support, and belief in my work kept me going – particularly when the going got tough.

I am not sure that I would have completed this book without his unfailing readiness to ply me with kind, earnest and heartfelt encouragement, as well as his open-minded and strategic questions about the next chapter, not to mention a never-ending supply of chai and rooibos. Last, but certainly not least, this book is dedicated to my students at the University of New Mexico. Their unceasing curiosity about all things German has kept me curious despite the ambivalence I carry within about a country I left almost four decades ago.

Introduction: Fictions of Memory

The turn of the millennium represents an inflection point in Germany's cultural memory. Rather than receding, the Nazi past uncannily seems ever more present – a paradoxical telescoping of time and space which Anton Kaes observed in 1987. He began his study on the return of history as film with the poignant observation, 'Es scheint unheimlich: Je weiter sich die Vergangenheit zeitlich entfernt, desto näher rückt sie.' [The further the past recedes, the closer it becomes.][1] Twenty years later, this compression of time seems only to have intensified. In 2004, referring to the wake of the 'Supergedenkjahr 1995' [1995, the Year of Super Commemoration], historian Norbert Frei observed: 'Soviel Hitler war nie!'[2] [Never was there so much Hitler!] And in his 2010 study on a new generation of memory, sociologist Michael Heinlein modulates Frei's pithy statement to: 'Soviel Kriegskindheit war nie.' [Never was there so much childhood of war!][3] Through divergent disciplinary lenses, these declarative statements delineate dis/continuities that have shaped (West) German reflections and deflections of the Nazi past. Five decades after the end of the Third Reich Hitler, Hitler's complicated legacy remains palpable in increasingly fictional spaces encoded in cinematic and literary memory work and, more recently, reframed by personal stories told by the German *Kriegskinder* [children of war]. Establishing a dialogue between selected literary memory texts, autobiographical recalls of the Nazi past and the politics of Germany's cultural memory, *Writing the Child*

---

1   Anton Kaes, *Deutschlandbilder. Die Wiederkehr der Geschichte als Film* (Munich: edition text+kritik, 1987), 5. *From Hitler to Heimat. The Return of History as Film* (Cambridge, MA: Harvard University Press, 1989), ix. All German quotes have been adjusted to follow the spelling reform.

2   Norbert Frei, '1945 und wir. Die Gegenwart und die Vergangenheit', in *1945 und Wir. Das Dritte Reich im Bewusstsein der Deutschen* (Munich: Beck, 2005), 7.

3   Michael Heinlein, *Die Erfindung der Erinnerung. Deutsche Kriegskindheiten im Gedächtnis der Gegenwart* (Bielefeld: transcript, 2010), 9.

examines the use of imaginary child witnesses in postwar German literature deployed not only to articulate but also disrupt the traffic between any given moment and an unredeemable past.

The literature examined in this volume was published or gained renewed relevance around the turn of the millennium. Focused on experiences during the last war years or their legacy, the selected texts explore unresolved questions of the present and offer incisive commentary on, as well as interventions in (West) Germany's cultural memory. Dieter Forte's *Der Junge mit den blutigen Schuhen* [*The Boy with the Bloody Shoes*], published in 1995, draws on personal childhood memories and gives voice to a trauma culture which coalesces around the suffering of innocent Germans during the bombing war. Forte's novel represents a new phase in German cultural memory that rests on intersecting autobiographical and fictional narratives, which shape a new memory authorized by the last remaining 'Augenzeugen' [eyewitnesses] – those who witnessed the Third Reich as children. Forte's text is also representative of a wound culture that gains momentum in the 1990s. By contrast, Günter Grass's novel *Die Blechtrommel* [*The Tin Drum*], published four decades earlier in 1959, exposes a culture of memory that in the immediate postwar decades rested on a collective display of faux-innocence and faux-contrition. It garnered renewed attention in 1999 when Grass was awarded the Nobel prize and again in 2006 after the author's belated confession about his SS membership. *Die Blechtrommel* may be the best known and one of the most examined text in the body of material under consideration. It is included here since it is one of the first postwar texts to direct attention to the performativity of autobiographical and literary memory. Gisela Elsner's lesser-known novel *Fliegeralarm* [*Air Raid Alarm*] was published in 1989, just months before the fall of the Berlin Wall. This unusual and satirical text sharply critiques Chancellor Helmut Kohl's memory politics, which sought to normalize the Nazi past and move on. Hans-Ulrich Treichel's *Der Verlorene* [*Lost*], published in 1998, represents yet another phase in Germany's cultural memory: a postmemorial perspective of belatedness. It addresses the transgenerational legacy of the Nazi past and exposes the impact of inherited trauma experienced by succeeding generations. Like *Der Verlorene,* the story collection *The Dark Room* by the British-German author Rachel Seiffert, published in 2001, no longer negotiates first-hand experiences of the Nazi period but instead examines different gradations of complicity and implication in the history of Nazi perpetration. Seiffert's work is written in English yet inscribed by auto-biographical experiences tied to National Socialism, in particular, loving German grandparents who nonetheless remained unreformed Nazis. *The Dark Room* is included here as an example for the resonance of the topic across national, cultural and linguistic borders.

Resting on what Cornelia Blasberg has called 'das markante Einspruchsrecht der Literatur' [the incisive power of objection charac-teristic of literature],[4] a system of signification that not only tolerates but celebrates ambivalence, ambiguity and overdetermination, these texts not only are but also offer insightful witnesses to the Nazi past.[5] They recall ex-periences under Hitler using the voice, gaze or stance of a child to mediate dis/continuities of German identity post-1945 and post-1989. Speaking as, with, or to eyewitnesses of history, they are examined here as 'fictions of memory' in the double sense advanced by Ansgar Nünning. While fic-tion refers most obviously to something 'imaginatively invented' and more specifically to literature concerned 'with the narration of imaginary events and the portraiture of imaginary characters', it has a less commonly known connotation.[6] In law, fiction also refers to a perspective that contests ex-isting conventions, that is, 'a supposition to be at variance with fact but conventionally accepted by reason of practical convenience, conformity with traditional usage, decorum, or the like'.[7] In other words, fiction de-notes both literary, that is, non-referential narratives, as well as underlying theoretical configurations and frameworks. Thus, above and beyond any specific narrative plots and character configurations, literary fictions im-plicitly reveal the work(ings) of overarching memory discourses. They

---

4   Unless otherwise noted, all translations are mine in consultation with Joseph Hoffman and Scott Melton.

5   Cornelia Blasberg, 'Geschichte als Palimpsest. Schreiben und Lesen über die Kinder der Täter', *Deutsche Vierteljahresschrift* 3 (2002): 474.

6   Ansgar Nünning, editorial, 'New Directions in the Study of Individual and Cultural Memory and Memory Cultures', *Journal for the Study of British Cultures* 10, 1/03 (2003): 5.

7   *Oxford English Dictionary* quoted in Nünning, 4.

mediate 'a culturally sanctioned system of ideas, beliefs, presuppositions, and convictions that constitutes [national and collectively curated] mentalities'.[8] *Writing the Child* considers how fictions of memory deploy their heuristic power to expose suppositions and ideological assumptions that have firmly inscribed the myth of innocence into the memory of a perpetrator nation. The texts under consideration in this book use the voice of the child as a capacious aesthetic focalization, a lens which underscores the creative impulse behind every memory narrative. As Walter Benjamin points out, recalls of the past create rather than simply re-present images based on the asynchronous process and poetic nature of remembering. When we remember, we see 'Bilder, die wir nie sahen, ehe wir uns erinnerten'[9] [images that we never saw until we remembered]. In his view, memory is fundamentally fiction, a story that inevitably reframes past experiences and is shaped by retrospective insights. While taking into consideration the autobiographical and generational location of each work, I examine them less as idiosyncratic expressions of individual authors than as contributions to larger cultural, political and social (memory) discourses. *Writing the Child* shares Amir Eshel's conviction that literature looks back in order to look ahead. It strives 'to widen the language and to expand the pool of idioms we employ in making sense of what has occurred while imagining who we may become'.[10] Literature, I argue, does not only have remarkable powers of insight and objection but is also uniquely capable of turning into story unresolved questions of the present by questioning the past in search of a different future.

Based on differing generational and auctorial subject positions, the selected texts describe a mnemonic arc delineated by the perspective of the *Flakhelfer*, Hitler Youth, or more broadly war generation (Günter Grass) – men conscripted into the *Wehrmacht* as juveniles in the last years of the

---

8   Nünning, 5.
9   Walter Benjamin, 'Aus einer kleinen Rede über Proust, an meinem vierzigsten Geburtstag gehalten', in Rolf Tiedemann and Hermann Schweppenhäuser, eds, *Walter Benjamin. Gesammelte Schriften*, II–3 (Frankfurt a.M.: Suhrkamp, 1991), 1064.
10 Amir Eshel, *Futurity: Contemporary Literature and the Quest for the Past* (Chicago, London: University of Chicago Press, 2013), 5.

war; the perspective of the *Kriegskind* generation (Dieter Forte and Gisela Elsner) – German civilians who experienced the last war years as children; and finally the perspective of the *Kriegsenkel* [grandchildren of war] (Hans-Ulrich Treichel, Rachel Seiffert) – children born to parents traumatized by wartime experiences. In critical dialogue with central tenets of Germany's cultural memory, they offer 'fantasies of witnessing' (Weissman). From differing degrees of proximity to an event few contemporary readers have witnessed, the voice of an imaginary German child witness articulates the psychosocial and political reverberations of the Nazi past. Although focused on the effects of state-sanctioned genocide, the selected literature does not directly engage with the Holocaust, nor does it speak from the Jewish perspective. Rather, it unpacks the emotional, political and cultural utility of collective innocence from the perpetrator perspective (in the widest sense). In divergent ways, these fictions of memory reveal what Hannah Arendt has observed with respect to those persecuted under Hitler: '[H]uman beings simply can't be as innocent as they all were in the face of the gas chambers.'[11] In the harsh light of the death camps, innocence has proven to be an absurd epistemological category. However, as a persistent myth that offers palatable screen memories for a fundamentally disrupted national identity, collective innocence has retained its currency, evident most recently in the rhetoric of alt-right parties. This study examines literary works that reframe existing taxonomies of accountability, works that carve out who counts in the continuously growing web of stories about the Nazi past and who does not; who is worthy of recognition and who is not; who can be held accountable and who cannot. While there are certainly seminal East German authors who deploy the child as a witness of the Nazi past, the historical circumstances and ideological tenets to which they are responding represent a radically different memory regime than that of West Germany, including a different understanding of who were the perpetrators and who the victims.[12] I chose to focus on the West

---

11   *Hannah Arendt/Karl Jaspers: Correspondence, 1926–1969*, Lotte Köhler and Hans Saner, eds, Robert and Rita Kimber, trans. (New York: Harcourt Brace Jovanovich, 1992), 54.

12   To name just a few: Bruno Apitz *Nackt unter Wölfen* [*Naked Among Wolves*] (1958), Jurek Becker, *Jakob der Lügner* [*Jacob the Liar*] (1969), Christa Wolf's

German context and its attendant victimologies because it quickly became the dominant memory regime in post-1989 united Germany. Recalling the Nazi past using a child's voice – its limitations and its flexibility, its familiarity and its otherness – means first and foremost to interrogate the traffic between knowledge, denial, complicity and implication. Harnessing the heuristic power of poetic imagination, the critical project of these fictions of memory rests on the vantage point of three interrelated childhood tropes: the innocent, the knowing and the implicated child.

The Child as a Fiction of Memory

The child is never just a child. In this book, the child comes into view as a vicarious witness to the Nazi past – as a discursive surface, not an empirical referent. Itself a potent fiction of memory, the child is used to expose cultural anxieties and desires behind the fantasy of collective innocence.[13] An object of imagination exhibited and celebrated in art for the pleasure of the adult, the child has long been 'naturalized' in the way Roland Barthes describes it in *Mythologies*, his critique of the tropes of mass culture, and *Camera Lucida*, his critique of the language of photography. That is, as an aesthetic icon the child seemingly transcends historical and social specificity; as a memory icon it masks the ideological forces that have shaped and continue to shape it. In a manner similar to the work of myths – narratives which do not offer factual truths but mirror collective desires and aspirations – iconographies of childhood elevate a set of (historically specific) conventions to the category of nature, betraying our implication

---

Kindheitsmuster [*Patterns of Childhood*] (1976), Helga Schütz, *In Annas Namen* [*In Anna's Name*] (1986), *Knietief im Paradies* [*Knee-deep in Paradise*] (2005), and Kurt Bartsch, *Fanny Holzbein* [*Fanny Wooden Leg*] (2004).

13   This aspect of my study builds on the insights of previous work with a similar focus. See for instance Debbie Pinfold, *The Child's View of the Third Reich in German Literature: The Eye Among the Blind* (Oxford: Clarendon Press, 2001) and Nora Maguire, *Childness and the Writing of the German Past: Tropes of Childhood in Contemporary German Literature* (Oxford: Peter Lang, 2013).

as adults in the very process of making the child. Philippe Ariès, one of the early scholars to draw attention to this process, showed the extent to which the modern child is a cultural invention.[14] Commenting on this seminal if unconventional work, literary theorist James R. Kincaid observes that Ariès reveals how 'the modern child is the perceptual frame we have available to us for fitting in just about anything we chose – or nothing. What the child *is* matters less than what we *think* it is and just why we think that way.'[15] In the context of this study, the child is examined as a memory icon that represents a potent trope of innocence.

An imaginary other, the child at once defines, questions and transcends the certainties of adulthood. Similar to the way fictions of memory harness moments of the past in order to define or address uncertainties of the present, the child functions to stabilize the hard-won securities of adulthood. For the Romantics, the child is an aspirational focal point, a glorious memory of a better self irretrievably lost to the adult, a pristine site outside of social norms from which to reassess the social and cultural status quo.[16] As the keeper of poetic insight and utopian promise who reminds us of the possibility of decency, the child is an 'index of civilization' (Jenkins). Yet, as I show in the following chapters, when cast as a witness to violent historical legacies such as National Socialism, the child can also represent an index of barbarism. Lost in(to) a traumatizing history, driven by a savage will-to-know and representing the 'pain of others', the child gains depth as a historical subject implicated in acts of perpetration and discrimination which it neither planned nor authorized, yet nonetheless benefitted from.

The etymological and conceptual roots of the term *innocence* indicate that it refers first and foremost to the impossibility to cause harm. The term is a compound of the prefix *in* (not) and the present participle *nocens* (from *nocere* to be harmful). Accordingly, the innocent child is conceived as a subject who can do no harm. Born helpless into a dangerous and

14　Philippe Ariès, *Centuries of Childhood: A Social History of Family Life*, Robert Baldick, trans. (New York: Vintage, 1962).

15　James R. Kincaid, *Child-Loving: The Erotic Child and Victorian Culture* (New York: Routledge, 1992), 62.

16　For more, see for instance Anne Higonnet, *Pictures of Innocence: The History and Crisis of Ideal Childhood* (London: Thames & Hudson, 1998).

unpredictable world, the child does not (yet) possess historical agency. In fact, the *Oxford English Dictionary* defines innocence as: 'freedom from sin, from guilt or moral wrongdoing in general' as well as 'freedom from cunning or artifice', in short, as a state of foundational guilelessness.[17] While subject *to* the vicissitudes of history, the child is not yet a subject *of* history and thus readily embodies the collective fantasy of being outside of or even exempt from history. Miriam Ticktin notes that innocence works as a 'boundary concept' which 'helps produce and regulate human kinds and their constituent outsides – it helps to imagine "humanity"'.[18] Furthermore, conceived as a state of purity, it is associated with the figure of the victim. As such, the child represents a troubling memory trope. Due to its vulnerability and helplessness, it invites self-identification with Hitler's victims – a fantasy that Ulrike Jureit and Christian Schneider have termed the 'Figur des *gefühlte*n Opfers' [the figure of the *felt* victim] that centres (West) German cultural memory since the mid-1980s. Both individual and collective, this memory trope readily embraces the victims of Nazism, while Nazi perpetrators and their crimes remain obscured and abstract.[19] An icon of vulnerability and victimhood, often unmoored from history and context, the child is the paradigmatic *felt* victim who appeals to protective instincts, mobilizes adult responsibilities and invites heroic fantasies of rescue. Moreover, when standing in for the victim, the child readily represents those deemed worthy of being remembered.

The Knowing Child

The child, however, is also an icon of knowing otherness, at once outside and inside of history. Imbued with the power to make the familiar

---

17   *Oxford English Dictionary*, quoted in Miriam Ticktin, 'A World without Innocence', *American Ethnologist* 44/4 (2017): 578.

18   Ticktin, 578.

19   Ulrike Jureit and Christian Schneider, *Gefühlte Opfer. Illusionen der Vergangenheitsbewältigung* (Stuttgart: Klett-Cotta, 2010), 36.

strange and the strange familiar, it remains close to the fantastical and the unexpected, a voice for asynchronous and enduring continuities (in this case of Nazi mentalities). Walter Benjamin has described the core of the ontological difference between child and adult as resting on a perceptual difference – a perspective not yet delimited by convention and habit. The child, he asserts, can effortlessly grasp connections of seemingly unrelated phenomena and thus find similarities in the unsimilar. In productive contrast with adult logic and judgement, his childhood self, Benjamin remembers, saw the world 'entstellt von Ähnlichkeiten mit allem, was um mich war'[20] [disfigured by similarities with everything around me]. The works under consideration in this study draw on this 'advantage', that is, a way of seeing the world from a 'strange' yet nonetheless deeply insightful perspective. 'Writing the child' as an existential and perceptual strangeness – as precocious perception (Forte), wilful manipulation (Grass), savage destructiveness (Elsner), disarming insightfulness (Treichel), or sober intensity (Seiffert) – the texts under examination here also deploy a more recent trope: 'the knowing child'. I borrow this term from Anne Higonnet, who uses it to describe a representational paradigm shift in photography. Knowing children, she claims, are fully aware of adult desires; they not only witness but expertly mimic that which adults are trying to hide. Aware of the demands of prescriptive family frames, these child subjects know how to efficiently imitate and effectively resist social choreographies of self. Although carefully scrutinized by the eye of the camera and exposed to the viewer, knowing children remain firmly in their own world. These subjects mediate naturalizing projections of childhood; they seemingly offer themselves up, while nonetheless remaining distant and reserved. At times inviting identification, at times rejecting it, their illusive presence frustrates viewers and, I argue, readers alike. They do not demand our empathy; instead of revealing themselves to an audience, they deflect attention, in extreme cases altogether abandoning any dialogue with the viewer or reader.[21]

20   Walter Benjamin, 'Berliner Kindheit um neunzehnhundert', *Walter Benjamin. Gesammelte Schriften*, VII-1, 417.
21   These children are closely related to children in cinema who witness the violence or the after-effects of war and remain resistant to a camera that probes their way

The Implicated Child

The works selected for this study, written by authors of the war time and *Kriegskinder* generations, recall the Nazi past based on personal experiences. They utilize a highly stylized register of aesthetic overdetermination (Grass); the sharpness of satirical exaggeration (Elsner); or a register of traumatic recall (Forte). Authors of later generations mediate forms of a more indirect knowledge. They write from the postmemorial perspective of an inherited yet not less intense (parental) memory and use irony (Treichel) or the pared-down language of seemingly neutral description (Seiffert). Despite their generational, experiential and stylistic differences, all texts are animated by a similar concern: how to give testimony to and take responsibility for acts of historical injustice not personally committed or caused, yet nonetheless witnessed or vicariously experienced. The perpetrator perspective inevitably provokes the question of what historical innocence and its attendant projection of victimhood can or cannot mean for a perpetrator nation such as Germany. It brings into relief the myth of collective innocence, anchored and perpetuated in persistent German victimologies. These victimologies began to take shape with the initial Nazi claim that Germany was a victim of Judeo-Bolshevik aggression; they continued with 'usable war stories' (Moeller), which in the 1950s maintained that Germans were largely victims of a war started in their name; they shaped victim fantasies entertained by the 1968ers; they informed Chancellor Helmut Kohl's claim of generational innocence ('Gnade der späten Geburt'; the 'mercy of a late birth'); and most recently they find expression in claims of the alt-right that all Germans were ultimately Hitler's victims.

---

of looking. For more on the child's gaze, see Karen Lury, *The Child in Film* (New Brunswick, NJ: Rutgers University Press, 2010) and my article 'Reconfiguring the Witness of the Holocaust: The Child as a Lieu de Mémoire in Marianne Rosenbaum's Film *Peppermint Frieden*', *Seminar* 40/1 (2004): 19–34. For more on the knowing child, see Higonnet, *Pictures of Innocence*.

Assertions of German victimhood rest on a simplifying and self-serving victim–perpetrator binary, obfuscating what Debarati Sanyal has examined as complicity and Michael Rothberg has analysed as implication in larger structural and systemic injustices. Implicated subjects, Rothberg posits, are inevitably '"folded-into" (im-pli-cated in) events that at first seem beyond our agency [...]. Implicated subjects occupy positions aligned with power and privilege without being themselves direct agents of harm; they contribute to, inhabit, inherit, or benefit from regimes of domination but do not originate or control such regimes.'[22] When we pay attention to the transgenerational and transcultural effects of systemic violent legacies in both our personal and our national stories, historical agency extends into a space that is at once connected to and distinct from the original events of perpetration. Yet it remains entangled in intersections of received privilege, (unwitting) perpetuations of subjugation and gradations of enablement. I argue that the works under consideration in this book astutely trace what it means to be an implicated subject. They deploy child witnesses who challenge the reader to recognize that being subject to and a subject of history means to acknowledge legacies of historical violence both within and without. We are asked to understand that there simply is no 'outside of history' from which to claim innocence in larger structures of violence. As Bach and Nienass assert,

> innocence, especially when juxtaposed to guilt in a binary way, empowers subject positions to claim a space seemingly unencumbered and unimplicated by those complex causalities that fit uneasily into individualistic notions of responsibility. The myth of innocence thus brackets implication; yet in doing so, it implicates its subjects even more – innocence and implication are intertwined.[23]

Writing the Child examines this intimate connection between innocence and implication by focussing on fictional child witnesses who reside in fluid interspaces which expose gradations between victim and perpetrator, accomplice and onlooker.

22 Michael Rothberg, *The Implicated Subject: Beyond Victims and Perpetrators* (Stanford: Stanford University Press, 2019), 1.
23 Jonathan Bach and Benjamin Nienass, 'Introduction: Innocence and the Politics of Memory', *German Politics and Society* 39/1 (Spring 2021): 2.

The Kriegskind

The divergent voices of these imaginary 'Augenzeugen' are examined in dialogue with what I call the '*Kriegskind* narrative': autobiographical and fictional narratives that gained popularity in the context of reunification and consequent efforts to redefine German national identity. Based on a flood of autobiographical anthologies, virtual discussion groups, conferences and other acts of commemoration, *Kriegskinder* stories became popular as the last remaining traces of Nazi history. This narrative web both creates and honours a particular collective: Germans who experienced the Third Reich and its aftermath while growing up. I use the German term *Kriegskind(er)* to delineate a distinct ethnic and generational cohort: German children who were old enough to remember the Second World War but not old enough to actively participate. In contrast to its English or French equivalents, *war children*, *Besatzungskinder* [occupation children], or *enfants de la guerre*, terms which describe children born to a native German parent and a parent belonging to a military (occupying) force, the German term *Kriegskind* refers to a non-Jewish German child born just before or at the beginning of Hitler's reign. The attention given to these 'Zeitzeugen' [historical witnesses] represents the so-called 'experiential turn', a reorientation of German memory culture towards the personal. Silent about the experience of the 'other' child, the Jewish child next door, German eyewitness memories share common reference points: the deprivations of the last war years, the terror of Allied bombings, experiences of flight and expulsion, absent fathers and traumatized mothers. Uneasily juxtaposing Germans as victims with the victims of Germans, the *Kriegskind* narrative both parallels and counters institutionalized memory narratives focused on the trauma of Hitler's victims. In light of the false claim that the *Kriegskinder* voices (finally) refute a long-standing taboo to speak out about Germans traumatized under Hitler, this narrative serves as the central contextual prism guiding my analysis. In dialogue with the selected literary fictions of memory, the *Kriegskind* narrative deserves close attention as symptomatic of a larger conceptual trend in memory cultures towards a universalizing trauma discourse that knows only victims.

Critical Memory Studies

Writing the Child examines a selected body of literature as a vital contributor to the dynamic exchange that continually shapes and reshapes mnemonic narratives and practices. Like individual memory, which is anchored in retrospective constructions of an autobiographical self, fictions of memory enrich cultural memory with acts of recall that mediate personal and collective reference points of identity and belonging. Any recall of the past, whether fictional or factual, inevitably rests on a larger web of mnemonic images, tropes, narratives and practices. Offering salient points of identification for the national collective, it reflects the work of cultural memory. *Writing the Child* contributes not only to German Studies but also to cultural and memory studies. It was conceived at a time when memory studies had entered a self-critical stage and written at a moment of crisis in the ongoing tension between democracy and autocracy. In recent re-evaluations of the field, scholars from various disciplines have noted a troubling emphasis on post-catastrophe trauma and witnessing. Susannah Radstone warns that the concern with 'the continuing presence of the past – and particularly past hurts – in the present' runs the risk of de-politicizing its subject, in effect turning us all into victims of an amorphous legacy of perpetration.[24] This point of concern remains particularly valid for a perpetrator nation such as Germany, where the psycho-social legacy of the Nazi past, specifically the suffering both inflicted and endured under Hitler, remains a vanishing point of cultural memory post-1989. But ironically, the Third Reich is also the last instance of a shared history in a country not too long ago sharply divided along ideological and political lines. While questions of Nazi perpetration

---

24   Susannah Radstone, 'Memory Studies: For and Against', *Memory Studies* 1/1 (2008): 32.

became a focal point for West German memory politics, East German cultural memory was forcefully aligned with resistance against fascism and thus blind to historical accountability. Post-1990, in the Berlin Republic, the facts of the historical archive inform Germany's cultural memory and remains largely focused on the legacy of National Socialism. In contrast to the collectively curated memory, private memories about the war rarely admit knowledge of, or complicity in Nazi crimes; instead, they tend to draw on shared experiences of hardship and loss. This tension between the 'lexicon' and the 'family album' (Welzer), between institutionalized memory focused on collective accountability and personal memories focused on personal victimhood, delineates the historical focal point of the following chapters.

Writing the Child seeks to contribute to what Richard Crownshaw has called 'critical memory studies': a careful reconsideration of a trauma culture which all too readily collapses distinctions between primary events and their subsequent transmission, victims and secondary witnesses, readers and text. In the German context, this wound culture has been examined as centred on a culture of the *felt* victim; in a more global context, it has been unpacked as 'traumatic complicity' (Sanyal). Under review is a mnemonic framework that, as Sanyal writes, 'position[s] us largely as victims of history rather than potential actors who participate in history's making in myriad ways'.[25] Based in deep psychological wounds, trauma does not differentiate between (historical) cause-and-effect, as a consequence it is blind to attendant moral categories. The suffering of those targeted and murdered under Hitler is just as real as the suffering of those who experienced the brutality of the war as German soldiers, civilians or children. These uneasy juxtapositions also come to light in the selected literary fictions of memory since they parse experiences of trauma along a multitude of intersecting subject positions – including those of victims, executioners and witnesses. Rather than reinforcing victim fantasies, they move the reader through fantasies of both victimhood and perpetration. They deploy what Sanyal terms 'ironic complicity', a textual choreography of

25   Debarati Sanyal, *Memory and Complicity: Migrations of Holocaust Remembrance* (New York: Fordham University Press, 2015), 54.

self-referential mediation. Walter Benjamin has identified this stance as the narrative or dramatic 'montage', the Brechtian pause or interruption 'which always works against an illusion among the audience'.[26] In related ways, ironic complicity circumscribes 'a strategy of representation and reception that simultaneously beckons and suspends our identification [...] with the violence that we, as readers, viewers, and secondary witnesses, are called to witness'.[27] The voices of imaginary child witnesses to the Nazi past examined in this book confront the reader's systemic complicity via 'an ethical circuit in which selves and others (victim, perpetrator, and witness) circulate and make contact'.[28] Framed by differing forms of belatedness, ironic, satirical and sober registers unsettle established patterns of both memory and identification. By locating the reader in the distinctive pathway of violence and by using the lens of a (faux-)innocent, knowing or implicated child, they disrupt habitual ways of relating to both the past and the present. This memory work brings to light what Rothberg termed 'complex implication', the contours of a subject bound in multidirectional ways, by 'long-distance and non-intuitive connections [...which] position us in contradictory ways in relation to justice and injustice' beyond the rigid delineations of victimization and perpetration.[29] *Writing the Child* contends that without necessarily moving towards a progressive sense of resolution, the material under discussion offers productive and contestatory interventions in the ongoing conversation about how to recall the Nazi past and its legacy.

Finally, I have to modulate my initial assertions about the persistent presence of the Nazi past in German cultural memory in light of current populist tendencies which insist on a decisive turn away from a culture of remembrance, a turn away from memory politics centred on the legacy of the Nazi past. The political rhetoric of the AfD, Germany's alt-right party founded in 2013, blatantly draws on Nazi tropes when Björn

---

26 Walter Benjamin, 'The Author as Producer', in Anna Bostock, trans., *Understanding Brecht: Walter Benjamin* (London, New York: Verso, 1989), 99.

27 Sanyal, 54.

28 Sanyal, 55.

29 Susanne C. Knittel, Sofia Forchieri, 'Navigating Implication: An Interview with Michael Rothberg', *Journal of Perpetrator Studies* 3/1 (2020): 14.

Höcke, its prominent spokesman, evokes a 'tausendjährige Zukunft' [a thousand-year-future] for the nation and calls Berlin's holocaust memorial 'ein Denkmal der Schande', [a monument of shame], intentionally leaving open what is shameful, the monument or what it stands for. Party co-founder Alexander Gauland reframes national history along similar lines when he insists that 'Hitler und die Nazis sind nur ein Vogelschiss in über 1000 Jahren erfolgreicher deutscher Geschichte'[30] [Hitler and the Nazis are but a speck of bird shit in over thousand years of a successful German history]. A culture of remembrance based on the *felt* victim converges with demands from the right to abandon a 'Schamkultur' [culture of re-membrance based on shame] in that both appeal to affect and emotions and rest on acts of strategic forgetting. Against this backdrop, *Writing the Child*, written in a moment of danger (as I review this introduction, Russia's invasion of Ukraine to combat 'fascism', is unfolding in ever more brutal ways), seeks to contribute to memory studies as a critical tool with which to assess the stories any nation is built upon, the stories it chooses to celebrate, and the stories it chooses to forget. In light of Heinlein's ob-servation that there was 'never so much childhood of war', but also in light of the current political tensions between democracy and autocracy that draw on a new culture of forgetting, the following questions propel my analysis: how and to what extent can literature written from the perspective of those born into a perpetrator legacy serve as an incisive epistemological tool with which to understand the present in light of the Nazi past? How does a subject position framed by a legacy of perpetration find expression when focalized through a child's limited understanding and culpability? How do fictions of memory translate 'the child' – itself a culturally over-determined fiction – into a productive recall of the last years of the Second World War that lays bare complex forms of implication?

30   Vollständige Rede Dr. Alexander Gaulands vom 2. Juni 2018, <https://afdbundes tag.de/vollstaendige-rede-dr-alexander-gaulands-vom-02-juni-2018/>, accessed 1 March 2022.

The Plan of the Book

Chapter 1 focuses on the turn of the millennium as shaped by the *Kriegskind* narrative. The two decades following unification produced works of memory and commemoration that represent a historical and cultural inflection point for the unified nation. This narrative is centred predominantly on childhood deprivations during the last years of the Second World War and authorized a particular recall of the Nazi past. Moreover, based on publications that lend German war memories coherence and collective appeal, the *Kriegskind* narrative created a new generational cohort. It draws on registers of victimhood established since the end of the war and reinforces a trauma paradigm that is blind to historical context and circumstance.

Against this historical and discursive backdrop, Part I presents discussions of works written by authors of the war and *Kriegskind* generations. Informed by personal historical experiences, texts by Forte, Grass and Elsner return to the last war years from various degrees of historical remove, personal involvement and narrative verisimilitude. While Forte deploys the voice and gaze of the victimized child as a universal symbol for a failing world, Grass and Elsner reveal the extent to which the child can serve as a screen for historical obfuscation. Chapter 2 examines Dieter Forte's novel *Der Junge mit den blutigen Schuhen* (1995) as exemplary of the 'emotional' or 'experiential turn' – a refocusing on the Nazi past based on fictional and non-fictional representations of traumatic German childhood experiences. This novel serves as a point of departure for the study as a whole because it raises foundational epistemological, aesthetic and moral questions of relevance to all the case studies that follow. Using the child as a trope of knowing innocence, it not only draws attention to vulnerabilities shared by both persecutors and persecuted, but also erases incontrovertible distinctions between both. Leaning on autobiographical memories, the child witness gains gravitas as a figure of counter-memory, yet ultimately supports a persistent postwar mythology that blurs the lines between Hitler's victims and the German people.

Chapter 3 turns to one of the first postwar fictions of memories to use and complicate the figure of the historical eyewitness, Günter Grass's iconic novel *Die Blechtrommel* (1959). Written in the immediate aftermath of the war, *Die Blechtrommel* stages childlikeness as a critical epistemological tool with which to probe Adenauer's hypocritical politics of reparations and rehabilitation. It provocatively exposes core elements of West Germany's cultural memory: institutional obfuscation and collective denial of complicity and implication. Grass's novel remains one of the first literary texts to self-reflexively draw attention to the *Nachträglichkeit* [belatedness] of any aesthetic recall of history: the representational delay that negotiates fragments of the past in light of concerns rooted in the present. In light of memory as shaped by the ongoing exchange between the adult and the childhood self, this chapter examines how Grass writes the (faux-)child as a potent figure of memory. When read in critical dialogue with the author's autobiography *Beim Häuten der Zwiebel* [*Peeling the Onion*] (2006), written almost half a century later, Grass's child witness gains depth as a vehicle for screen memories that at once hide and reveal what is repressed.

Chapter 4 examines Gisela Elsner's *Fliegeralarm* (1989), a satirical novel that looks back to 1944 from the point of view of the 1980s. Elsner's text negotiates a shift in the cultural memory discourses of the 1980s and addresses issues of historical culpability. *Fliegeralarm* deftly rejects the premise of generational innocence promoted by chancellor Helmut Kohl's programmatic assertion of the 'Gnade der späten Geburt'. I argue that the novel's characters mark as absurd the possibility of an innocent historical subject position. Elsner's provocative rewriting of the *Kriegskind* stages childhood innocence as a self-serving performance, forged in the dialectic of 'knowing and not-knowing' (about Nazi atrocities) at play in both the political rhetoric of the time and the *Kriegskind* narrative.

The second part of this volume examines more prominently how issues of complicity and implication come to the fore in works by second- and third-generation authors. Treichel and Seiffert have received the history of National Socialism not only as mediated through a web of aesthetic representations but also in form of personal family stories. Chapter 5 examines Hans-Ulrich Treichel's family novel *Der Verlorene* (1998) as a text that counters the historical caesura of reunification with a story about an enduring sense of personal loss, in this case a child lost during the flight from a home in the former eastern territories. Treichel's 'writing the child' contends with living in the shadow of a received war trauma. Rather than recalling the history of the Third Reich, it exposes its subsequent transgenerational effects. The voice of this child witness exposes a collectively sanctioned apologetic stance that hinges on a purified relationship between victims and perpetrators. I argue that *Der Verlorene* critically traverses the taxonomy of post-Shoah subject positions and transposes intersections of generational remove and emotional investment into a self-reflexive and critical language of German postmemory.

Chapter 6 examines 'Lore', the middle-story of *The Dark Room* (2001), a story collection written by British-German author Rachel Seiffert. This chapter further explores postmemory work about the Nazi past from the perspective of the perpetrator. 'Lore', I argue, delineates contradictory and fluid intersections of any historical subject position, in that it not only asks who benefitted from the historical suffering of others but also what this legacy of privilege means for subsequent generations. Offering a somewhat more removed perspective, the story negotiates the relationship between a young German and the Jewish 'other'. Seiffert's text contests the harmonizing force of the family album intent on preserving a pure identity devoid of perpetration; it highlights the situational dimension of historical subject positions, shot through with differing degrees of perpetration, complicity and implication.

Finally, the epilogue offers a brief review of the insights gained from the chapters. The literature discussed in Part I engages a discursive web that rests on confessions of guilt and strategies of denial, while the literature discussed in Part II shifts attention towards the contours of the implicated subject. Although the body of work examined in this book does not progress towards a shared critique or assessment of German cultural memory, there is a notable shift from a lexis of traumatic complicity towards a lexis of ironic complicity. I close my remarks with considering how this shift towards a new lexis becomes legible in subsequent family novels written by the *Kriegsenkel* [grandchildren of war]. More recent fictions of memory echo many of the aspects central to earlier texts but deal more explicitly with questions of personal accountability, thus carving out a subject position shaped by intersecting, contradicting, imagined and received (his)stories.

PART I

The War and *Kriegskind* Generations

CHAPTER I

Kriegskinder Politics: Abiding Victimologies

As mentioned in the introduction, rather than receding, the Nazi past seems to have gained an increasing presence in the post-1989 period. Faced with having to reframe the future for the reunited nation, the birth of the Berlin Republic has also brought about a re-evaluation of the Nazi past. Despite divergent memory regimes – in the GDR, based on calculated refusals to take responsibility for Nazi crimes, in the FRG, based on strained attempts to address questions of collective accountability – the Third Reich remains one of last shared historical legacies of a once divided nation. Furthermore, the future of the past has now begun to rest on a present with fewer and fewer living witnesses to the Second World War. As a result, a collective 'anxiety of loss' has emerged, only to be countered by autobiographical accounts and literary fictions of memory concerned with the last war years, which led literary critic Ulrich Greiner to observe in 2004 that the voices of 'Zeitzeugen' [eyewitnesses] have 'gone viral'. In a polemical *Die Zeit* article titled 'Der Hund Erinnerung' ['The Dog of Memory'], he reflects on November 9 as a perennially fateful day for the German nation. Greiner compares memory to a stubborn dog refusing to follow predictable or rational rules. It is strange, he notes, how many books have recently been published about German suffering during the bombing wars. It is as if a taboo has been lifted, as if a dam has finally broken, allowing wartime memories to spread like an infectious disease. Maybe, he speculates, public commemoration has been too focused on Nazi crimes and has thus effectively silenced or displaced expressions of German suffering.[1] Greiner's use of metaphors – a dog that stubbornly refuses to obey, a broken dam, a suddenly spreading infection – indicate the

---

1   Ulrich Greiner, 'Der Hund Erinnerung', *Die Zeit*, 4 November 2004, <https://www.zeit.de/2004/46/Der_Hund_Erinnerung>, accessed 28 February 2022.

unpredictable force and seemingly unstoppable but also troubling spread of new memory narratives.

Greiner's reference to a long-standing taboo in German cultural memory has gained widespread traction through journalist Sabine Bode's book *Die vergessene Generation. Die Kriegskinder brechen ihr Schweigen* (2005) [*The Forgotten Generation: The War Children are Breaking their Silence*].[2] As the programmatic title indicates, Bode claims the *Kriegskinder* are finally ready to speak: it is time to hear the voices of those whose war trauma was never publicly acknowledged. She underscores the extent of their psychological scarring and felt compelled to write this book after she noticed how intensely the *Kriegskind* generation was affected by images of the war in Bosnia.[3] Seeing images of women and children fleeing theatres of war on the home front opened 'schlecht vernarbte seelische Kriegsverletzungen, über die in deutschen Familien kaum je gesprochen wurde und die noch weniger den Nachgeborenen vermittelt worden sind'.[4] [poorly healed psychological wounds of war that were rarely talked about in German families, wounds that have certainly not been communicated to the subsequent generations.] Supporting a new narrative framework for personal childhood experiences, publications of *Kriegskinder* memories such as Bode's represent an inflection point in German cultural memory. Particular moments in the present (in this instance, reunification and the Bosnia war) trigger memories which theretofore could not coalesce into narrative memory. Mieke Bal points out that, in contrast to traumatic memory, which is inflexible and hence resists integration into story,

> narrative memory fundamentally serves a social function: it comes about in a cultural context whose frame evokes and enables the memory. It is a context in which, precisely, the past makes sense in the present, to others who can understand it, sympathize

2   Sabine Bode, *Die vergessene Generation. Die Kriegskinder brechen ihr Schweigen* (Munich, Zurich: Piper, 2010). As of 2020, Bode's book was in its twelfth edition.

3   Bode, 16.

4   Sabine Bode, *Die deutsche Krankheit – German Angst* (Munich, Zurich: Piper, 2006), 67. In 2009, she expanded her first study of generational wounding with an examination of the mindset of the *Kriegsenkel* generation (those born between 1965 and 1975), commonly perceived to be a consumer-oriented and vacuous cohort. *Kriegsenkel. Die Erben der vergessenen Generation* (Stuttgart: Klett-Cotta, 2009).

with it, or respond with astonishment, surprise, even horror: narrative memory offers some form of feedback that ratifies the memory.[5]

In this case *Die vergessene Generation* lends authority to personal memories at odds with official memory politics. While the deprivations suffered during the last war years were deeply inscribed into the family album of both West and East Germans, they did not register in the official memory lexicon which, post-1989, remained focused on Nazi crimes. Bode's book, and others like it, not only created validation for shared and publicly unacknowledged war memories but they also made sense of traumatic war experiences in the present.

The ensuing wave of similar publications 'invented' a new memory cohort, in effect shaping a 'new memory'. The *Kriegskinder*, sociologist Michael Heinlein claims, were generating a new *Gedächtnisraum* [memory space], an imaginary site that at once called into existence and authorized the voice of a new 'historical generation'.[6] Echoing earlier victim narratives, stories of traumatized but innocent German civilians offered a new sense of national belonging for a nation that was only nominally reunited. In fact, the *Kriegskind* narrative served to stabilize a new, collective coherence based on a story of war shared by all Germans, albeit with different accents. In the following, I briefly describe different historical phases in West Germany's cultural memory and then focus more narrowly on the evolution and impact of the *Kriegskind* narrative around the turn of the millennium.

5   Mieke Bal, 'Introduction', in Mieke Bal, Jonathan Crewe and Leo Spitzer, eds, *Acts of Memory: Cultural Recall in the Present* (Hannover, London: University Press of New England, 1999), x.

6   Michael Heinlein, *Die Erfindung der Erinnerung. Deutsche Kriegskinder im Gedächtnis der Gegenwart* (Bielefeld: transcript, 2010), 30.

Remembering the Second World War

The 1940s to the 1990s

West German memory culture can be divided into two distinct phases: a first phase of mostly transactional guilt management, and a second phase based on the moral imperative 'to never forget'.[7] In the first phase, the immediate postwar period, educational and juridical strategies (initially imposed by the Allies) held high-ranking Nazi officials accountable and attempted to address a lingering fascist mindset by forcing Germans to confront their collective responsibility for Nazi war crimes. Following the establishment of the Federal Republic in 1949, Chancellor Konrad Adenauer's politics focused primarily on financial reparations, but also paved the way for reintegrating and rehabilitating former Nazi officials. Norbert Frei argues that Adenauer's 'Vergangenheitspolitik' [policy of the past] not only failed to address the moral, psychological and emotional fallout of the war, but effectively reversed the re-education efforts intro-duced by the Allies in order to bolster the fantasy of a clean break with the Nazi past.[8] This projected break with history eventually comes to rest on stories of German 'counter-victimhood', which blur distinctions be-tween Holocaust victims and German victims. Robert G. Moeller exam-ines this web of usable war stories as legitimized by and focused on the atrocities committed by the Allies against civilians and German POWs.

> By telling stories of the enormities of their losses, West Germans were able to reject charges of 'collective guilt' levelled by the victors immediately after the war, and claim status of heroic survivors. By focussing on the experiences of the expellees and POWs in the Soviet Union, they could talk about the end of the Third Reich without assuming responsibilities for its origins. In this abbreviated account of

---

7   For a more granular perspective, see Samuel Salzborn, *Kollektive Unschuld. Die Abwehr der Shoah im deutschen Erinnern* (Berlin, Leipzig: Hentrich & Hentrich, 2020), 27–44.

8   Norbert Frei, *Adenauer's Germany and the Nazi Past*, Joel Golb, trans. (New York: Columbia University Press, 2002).

National Socialism, all Germans were ultimately victims of a war Hitler had started but everyone lost.[9]

In 1951, future chancellor Helmut Schmidt, a member of the opposition party, reminded his audience to remember that

> almost all of those who survived the period are victims. But one shouldn't make this all too easy and forget that there are distinctions among them. People are beginning to forget. Indeed, things are getting to the point that even former SS [Hitler's elite guard] and SD [Nazi intelligence service] men are beginning to regard themselves as victims of National Socialism.[10]

Yet conveniently, in the decontextualized but more palatable version of the final war years, those who committed war crimes and those who suffered or died as a consequence of Hitler's politics of annihilation began often to appear in the same light.[11]

Arguably, the election of Willy Brandt as chancellor in 1969 marks the beginning of a second phase in Germany's memory culture towards taking responsibility, both collectively and individually, for Nazi crimes. Pushed by the radical interventions of a first postwar generation, the 1968ers, but also in the wake of national and international Holocaust trials, the focus of memory narratives came to rest on the moral imperative of 'Nie wieder Auschwitz' [Never again Auschwitz]. Rewritten by the sons and daughters of the war generation, who felt betrayed by the silence of their emotionally distant Nazi parents, the war story now focused on the continuation of the National Socialist mindset, manifest in hierarchical and hegemonic social and political structures. Remapping unresolved family conflicts onto the Nazi past – in particular conflicts with cruel and emotionally distant Nazi fathers – the 1968ers transposed the perpetrator–victim imaginary onto the framework of state oppression. Ironically, they saw themselves as the 'new

9　　Robert G. Moeller, *War Stories: The Search for a Usable Past in the Federal Republic of Germany* (Berkeley: University of California Press, 2001), 3.

10　Quoted in Jeffrey Herf, 'Legacies of a Divided Memory for German Debates about the Holocaust in the 1990s', *German Politics and Society* 17/3 (Fall 1999): 18.

11　As mentioned in the introduction, this rhetoric remains appealing and comes to light in the nativist agenda and Nazi rhetoric of the AfD.

Jews'; their radical social activism rested in part on a self-ascribed victim identification that obfuscates the ways in which all Germans are implicated in the history of Nazi perpetration. (I elaborate on this point in Chapter 4 in the context of Gisela Elsner's *Fliegeralarm*.)

In the 1980s, German national identity was recalibrated again, now more rigorously driven by the desire to move on from the Nazi past. Seeking to affirm a new German patriotism, Helmut Kohl's administration touted a 'geistig moralische Wende' [spiritual and moral change] and advocated a return to normality. The political vector changed direction: instead of looking backwards in order to never forget, the nation was now encouraged to look ahead, in concert with its Western allies. However, Kohl's neoconservative agenda also drew on President Richard von Weizsäcker's emphatic pledge to never forget the crimes of the Nazi past, supported by his assertion that the end of the war 'liberated all of us from the inhumanity and tyranny of the National Socialist regime'.[12] This statement evokes the earlier war stories of the 1950s: Germans are cast as victims of a leader they freely elected and largely supported. Moreover, it acknowledged very publicly the suffering of the German population, specifically of those who were too young to understand what was happening. Thus, the 'Vergangenheitspolitik' of the 1980s paved the way for a new memory space that offered acceptance for expressions of German wartime anguish.[13] The *Kriegskinder* stories hearken back to postwar discourses but gained new momentum in the 1990s and continue to reverberate today in the right-wing rhetoric of the AfD. While parallels between 'war stories' of the early postwar period and the *Kriegskinder* narrative are hard to miss – in

12   Speech by Richard von Weizsäcker, president of the Federal Republic of Germany, in the Bundestag during the Ceremony Commemorating the 40th Anniversary of the End of the War in Europe and of the National Socialist Tyranny, <http://deferred-live.net/muse/ariUploads/pdfs/speechRichardvonWeizsacker.pdf>, accessed 21 February 2021.

13   Sabine Bode was gratified that the German president finally addressed the situation of *all* Germans, including those who were traumatized by the war but had been unable to talk about it, at least not publicly. According to her, the president's speech shifted the narrative from guilt to responsibility, effectively paving the way towards a more integrated understanding of history that allows space for both Jewish and German suffering. *Die vergessene Generation*, 267.

both cases German responsibility for a war of annihilation is downplayed in light of the suffering brought upon the nation as a consequence of this war – the thrust of the argument has changed. In the 1940s and 1950s, victim narratives primarily warded off accusations of collective guilt and served a political agenda, while thirty years later, animated by the search for commonalities within disparate West and East German memory regimes in the wake of 1989, they underscored the personal and collective desire for healing unacknowledged wounds.

A New Trace of Pain

The *Kriegskind* story gained traction with the publication of three books at the beginning of the twenty-first century. W. G. Sebald's *Luftkrieg und Literatur* [*Air War and Literature*, translated as *Natural History of Destruction*] (1999), Günter Grass's *Im Krebsgang* [*Crabwalk*] (2002) and Jörg Friedrich's *Der Brand: Deutschland im Bombenkrieg: 1940–1945* [*The Fire: The Bombing of Germany, 1940–1945*] (2002) have greatly contributed to the ways the last years of the war have come to reside in the public imagination. Sebald's academic lectures about the air war speak to the legacy of wartime destruction, more specifically, they are centred around the question of why there is no notable 'Schmerzensspur' [trace of pain] about the air war in German postwar literature. Sebald, a well-known author of salient fictions of memory, who lived and worked in the UK, poses the foundational questions of whether and how memories of trauma can be translated into literature without unduly distorting the integrity of the underlying primary experiences. Germany's most celebrated postwar author, Günter Grass, also addressed the lingering effects of the war. Motivated by the desire not to leave the story of German wartime suffering to right-wing extremists, his novella *Im Krebsgang* presents the story of the *Wilhelm Gustloff*, a cruise liner which in January 1945 had taken 9,400 refugees on board before it was torpedoed and sank. This incident has become emblematic for the fate of innocent German civilians; it stands for the largely untold story of frightened and helpless subjects, abandoned by their government. *Der Brand*, Friedrich's historical

account of the last phase of the war, is a deliberately graphic account of
the Allied aerial bombing which reinforces the contrast between sober
statistical facts and harrowing personal accounts. Although divergent in
tone and format, all three texts foreground the plight of German civilians
during the last war years by highlighting their vulnerability and anguish.
Compared with Sebald's academic lectures and Grass's complex literary
novella, Friedrich's book is the most accessible and appealed to a broad
readership.[14] His offensive rhetoric deliberately appropriates Hitler's
racist and anti-Semitic propaganda to describe the devastation caused by
the air war. In fact, Friedrich's account of the war at the home front reverses the ideological thrust of Hitler's project. In the eyes of many historians, its deliberately incendiary rhetoric discredits *Der Brand* as a viable
work of historical research.[15] Due to their emphasis on the Germans as
innocent victims of Hitler's war, Sebald's and Grass's works were also criticized for rewriting history. Historian Mary Nolan pointedly asserts that
these authors wanted and found 'exemplary victims, uncompromised and
ennobled through suffering'.[16] Nonetheless, these three rather disparate
works signal the beginning of a new commemorative culture based on the
drama and the trauma of the *Kriegskind*, the new and celebrated hero of
eyewitness accounts.

In 1995, the aforementioned 'Year of Super Commemoration', the
last years of the Third Reich also became the topic of numerous feature
films and television productions. The Nazi past returned in the form of
'histotainment', intimately personal, melodramatic and faux-objective
accounts of Hitler's legacy made for general consumption. Guido Knopp,
chief history producer for the ZDF (one of Germany's public TV chan-
nels), successfully turned the Nazi period into a palatable TV event in films

---

14   Raimo Alsen notes that during the Christmas season *Der Brand* sold better than
      Harry Potter. Raimo Alsen, *Wandlungen der Erinnerungskultur. Gibt es eine "neue*
      deutsche Opfergeschichte"? (Hamburg: Diplomica Verlag, 2011), 24.

15   See for instance the contributions of Nicholas Stargardt, Horst Boog, Hans
      Mommsen and Ralph Giordano, in Lothar Kettenacker, ed., *Ein Volk von Opfern?*
      Die neue Debatte um den Bombenkrieg 1940–45 (Berlin: Rowohlt, 2003).

16   Mary Nolan, 'Germans as Victims during the Second World War: Air Wars,
      Memory Wars', *Central European History* 38/1 (2005): 32.

like *Hitler: ein Profil* [*Hitler: A Profile*] (1995), *Hitlers Holocaust* (2000), *Hitlers Frauen* [*Hitler's Women*] (2001) and *Hitlers Geld* [*Hitler's Money*] (2002), to name only a few. Other feature films, such as *Dresden* (2006), *Die Kinder der Flucht* [*The Children of Flight*] (2006) and *Die Gustloff* [*The Gustloff*] (2008) complement this media packaging of history and highlight the misery of German civilians. Devoid of context, and largely unmoored from history writ large, they propagate a universal victimology that casts Germans as innocent victims. In similar fashion, numerous print publications by and about the *Kriegskinder* de-emphasize the historical context and instead focus on harrowing experiences on the home front.[17] The message of these print publications has been further amplified on websites about war childhoods, as well as through academic and therapy-oriented projects such as the *Projekt Kriegskindheit* [Project War Childhood] at the University of Munich, initiated in 2003 by psychoanalyst Michael Ermann, a *Kriegskind* himself.[18] Two years later, renowned psychoanalysts, historians and literary scholars organized a conference on wartime childhoods in Frankfurt, 'Die Generation der Kriegskinder und ihre Botschaft für Europa' ['The Generation of War Children and their Message for Europe']. This hugely successful event engaged with questions of German childhood war experiences, which until then had not been given such explicit academic attention.[19]

17   Heinlein mentions an estimate of up to 1,000 autobiographies and autobiographical novels, as well as journalistic books per year. Heinlein, 10. For more on the wave of *Kriegskinder* publications and events, see 9–24.

18   To give but one example, as of January 2022 there were over 1,200 interviews on the WDR (local Radio Station for North-Rhine Westfalia) site about *Kriegskinder*, <https://www1.wdr.de/dossiers/kindheit-im-krieg/index.html#/?=&site=1>, accessed 10 January 2022. Extending this conversation to the following generation, so far the website 'Kriegsenkel Forum' has published over sixty memory fragments of the *Kriegsenkel*, <http://www.forumkriegsenkel.de/Lebensgeschichten.htm>, accessed 10 January 2022.

19   Two prominent web sites are still active: Kriegskindheit. Recht von Kindern, <http://www.kriegskindheit.de/>, accessed 10 January 2022, and Forschung, Lehre, und Therapie. Kriegskinderverein, <https://www.kriegskinder-verein.de/>, accessed 10 January 2022.

As noted above, although different in format and aesthetic register, the body of memory texts, films and academic events elevates a new memory hero: the eyewitness who returns history in vivid detail to those born afterward. In contrast to abstract historical research about the systemic causes and effects of National Socialism, of interest mostly to professional elites, the eyewitness offers authentic stories about the Nazi past in ways relatable to a general audience. This interest in the personal and the anecdotal could have been the result of the impending loss of the war generation, yet, as Dan Diner observes, personal testimonies are intrinsically problematic. Not only do they reproduce the bifurcation of perpetrator and victim cemented by the Nazi ideology but also fail to fully expose the monstrosity of National Socialism. The 'everyday perspective', he points out, does not know how to differentiate or how to identify similarities between 'personal banality' and 'collective atrocity' – a blind spot which Nazism knew how to exploit.[20] Around the turn of the millennium, German cultural memory came almost full circle to rest again on stories of German suffering. Contrary to the sentiment expressed in W. G. Sebald's lectures and Günter Grass's novella, stories about German suffering under Hitler were never fully suppressed. In fact, since this victimology is capacious enough to anchor otherwise divergent memory cultures, it gained ever greater currency after reunification and today remains central to the political rhetoric of the extreme right. What then contributed to the significance of the *Kriegskind* as a representative of a new generational cohort? And how do *Kriegskinder* testimonies promote Germans as innocent victims of a leader they enthusiastically supported?

20   Dan Diner, 'Zwischen Aporie und Apologie. Über Grenzen der Historisierung des Nationalsozialismus', *Gewerkschaftliche Monatshefte* 3 (2018): 153–59. Saul Friedlaender has argued along similar lines in his seminal work on *Reflections of Nazism: An Essay on Kitsch and Death*, Thomas Weyr, trans. (Bloomington: Indiana University Press, 1993).

The *Kriegskind* Imaginary

In their introduction to the 2015 special issue of the *European Review of History* on war children, Machtheld Venken and Maren Röger trace the origin of the term *Kriegskinder* diachronically. They examine its changing ideological connotations and find that the most intensive use of the term *war children* can be observed in Germany, where 'media and non-academic literature have portrayed *Kriegskinder* as an entire generation traumatized by the Second World War without differentiating between different groups of children, but ascribing a shared set of experiences solely on the basis of age'.[21] They also emphasize that the label *Kriegskinder* inevitably abbreviates complex and vastly divergent historical experiences: the *Kriegskind* simply does not exist – except as a convenient but problematic projection of generational and experiential coherence.[22]

Bode's representation of this cohort is a case in point; her book is troubling precisely because of this simplification.[23] Disregarding differences between persecutor and persecuted, she defines *Kriegskinder* primarily through shared experiences of suffering. They are introduced as passive victims defined by abstract atrocities and irreversibly marked by terrifying experiences inflicted during the last war years: 'ausgebombt, verschüttet, gefallen, vermißt. Vertreibung, Vergewaltigung, Gefangenschaft, Selbstmord'.[24] [bombed-out, buried alive, fallen, lost. Expulsion, rape, imprisonment, suicide]. As innocent victims of circumstances beyond their control, they possess no historical agency. In this story, 'the war' is likened to a force of nature and cast as an all-powerful subject that turned all involved into helpless objects. This narrow perspective is common for many *Kriegskind*

---

21   Machtheld Venken and Maren Röger, 'Growing up in the Shadow of the Second World War: European Perspectives', *European Review of History* 22/2 (2015): 202.

22   For more on this see also Gudrun Brockhaus, 'Kontroversen um die "Kriegskindheit"', *Forum Psychoanalyse* 26 (2010): 313–24.

23   Furthermore, Bode's use of both autobiographical and fictional accounts is both troubling and telling in that it reveals the extent to which the war has become a 'fiction of memory'.

24   Bode, *Die vergessene Generation*, 27.

memories which tend to skip over the earlier years, which were alive with great enthusiasm for Hitler and his project. Conveniently, they isolate the final years and the bombing wars as most representative for the German war experience. But as historian Nicholas Stargardt underscores:

> Children were neither just the mute and traumatized witnesses to this war, nor merely its innocent victims. They also lived in a war, played and fell in love during the war; the war invaded their imagination and the war raged within them.[25] [...] Children were also sharply divided by age and capacity to make sense of what they had seen. While younger children often seem to have been left with vivid but fragmentary images, older children strove to form abstract ideas about what was happening to them.[26]

Stargardt's more nuanced perspective reminds us that due to varying degrees of social and psychological maturity, childhood experiences of the Third Reich differed greatly. While *Kriegskind* memories are inscribed by differences of gender, social class, religious background, geographic location, country of origin and, above all, ethnic background, there is no homogenous generational story. In her article on child survivors of the Holocaust, Susan Suleiman argues that in times of historical disruption, Karl Mannheim's seminal definition of generation fails to be useful, since there simply were no 'common experiences' between the German and Jewish population. Instead, in Hitler's Germany arbitrary factors such as ethnicity and time or place of birth gained outsized importance and consequently shaped the life of German and Jewish children in incompatible ways. That is to say, Hitler's war of annihilation created completely divergent experiences *within* one generation. Jewish children faced dangers that were fundamentally different from those of their German counterparts. With respect to Jewish children, the degree of their vulnerability and suffering depended on their specific location, the time and, above all, on their age when anti-Semitic persecution took off. There were, Suleiman notes,

> children 'too young to remember' (infancy to around three years old); children 'old enough to remember but too young to understand' (approximately age four to

25   Stargardt, 19.
26   Stargardt, 16.

ten); and children 'old enough to understand but too young to be responsible' (approximately age eleven to fourteen). By responsible, I mean having to make choices (and to act on those choices) about their own or their family's action in response to catastrophe.[27]

Hence, variables of age and location make it impossible to claim universal or even common generational survivor experiences. In contrast to German children, Jewish children never experienced their childhoods as carefree or safe. More often than not they had to take on adult roles and were forced to make choices about their family's survival that were well beyond their level of understanding. Their childhoods were either cut short or, more likely, destroyed altogether. In other words, for a Jewish child, childhood was over before it ever began, a fact that is omitted in the German *Kriegskind* narrative.

This is not to say that German children did not also experience an abrupt end to their childhoods; they certainly suffered traumatic ruptures to their lives. In her book *Seelische Trümmer* [*Ruins of the Soul*], psychologist Bettina Alberti has documented the devastating effects of war trauma across two generations of Germans. What stands out in her account is that time and again, the interviewees (children of the *Kriegskinder*) speak of harsh and unforgiving parents who were emotionally unavailable. One woman, born in 1958, describes the extreme and, to her mind, incomprehensible rules that overshadowed her childhood. She was only able to understand her mother's behaviour, she explains, after discovering her grandmother's diary recording the family's flight from Pomerania in 1945. The grandmother recounts how her daughter's childhood had to come to an end when they were forced to endure the gruelling trek westward. For the sake of survival, the witness's mother (who was as a 12-year-old child at the time) had to abruptly become an adult: 'Die Kindheit meiner Tochter ist mit dem heutigen Tag beendet. Ich muss sie zwingen, erwachsen zu werden, jede Gefühlsduselei gefährdet unser Leben. Wenn wir durchkommen wollen, dürfen wir nicht mehr weinen.'[28] [Starting today, my daughter's childhood

---

27   Susan Rubin Suleiman, 'The 1.5. Generation: Thinking About Child Survivors and the Holocaust', *American Imago* 59/3 (Fall 2002): 283.

28   Bettina Alberti, *Seelische Trümmer. Geboren in den 50er- und 60er Jahren. Die Nachkriegsgeneration im Schatten des Kriegstraumas* (Munich: Kösel, 2012), 17.

is over. From now on, I have to force her to become an adult, sentimentality will only endanger our lives. If we want to survive, we cannot afford to cry anymore.] Although not systematically persecuted like their Jewish counterparts, German children nonetheless had to negotiate inexplicable acts of brutality and loss. Not surprisingly, as a result of the cruelties borne of war trauma, both the *Kriegskind* and Jewish child survivor fall silent. In fact, recent memory work speaks of 'Schweigekartelle' [cartels of silence] – a whole generation of Germans united in their unwillingness to speak, as well as in their efforts to split off emotions too difficult to integrate into a coherent story, let alone a sense of self.[29] This common reaction to traumatic experiences makes all too clear the extent to which psychological symptoms do not know, and thus cannot register, the difference of historical cause-and-effect. Eva Hoffman, daughter of Holocaust survivors, notes that Germans born after the war are her 'true historical counterpoint. We have had to struggle, from our antithetical positions, with the very same past.'[30]

However, while the symptoms of the psychological wounds suffered by both Jewish and German children mirror each other as experiences of unfathomable deprivations and loss, the historical context keeps them apart. While children of victims and perpetrators suffer similar psychic wounds, they face rather different responsibilities. Both have to confront the work of an unflinching acknowledgment of what happened. For children of survivors, this work honours the suffering of the previous generation and creates a sense of belonging; for German children, on the other hand, this work is animated by a sense of collective discontinuity, shot through with the moral adage of 'never again'. In other words, the divided

---

Similarly, Gabriele Schwab shows that children of perpetrator and survivor families have to contend with a family theatre that is contaminated by silences and denials. *Haunting Legacies: Violent Histories and Transgenerational Trauma* (New York: Columbia University Press, 2010), 67–91.

29   Jürgen Wiebicke, *Sieben Heringe. Meine Mutter, das Schweigen der Kriegskinder und das Sprechen vor dem Sterben* [*Seven Herrings. My Mother, the Silence of the Kriegskinder and Speaking before Death*] (Cologne: Kiepenheuer & Witsch, 2021). Susanne Fritz also uses the term 'Schweigekartelle' in *Wie kommt der Krieg ins Kind* [*How does War Enter the Child*] (Munich: btp, 2019).

30   Eva Hoffman, *After Such Knowledge: Memory, History, and the Legacy of the Holocaust* (New York: Public Affairs, 2004), 118.

memory of the Nazi past carries different responsibilities – a division that may be most adequately captured by fictions of memory which preserve, carve out, or just leave open a space for traces of the silenced other (child). (I discuss this aspect in more detail in Chapters 5 and 6 in the context of Hans-Ulrich Treichel's text *Der Verlorene* and Rachel Seiffert's 'Lore'.) Put differently, in order to avoid recreating stories that turn all Germans into victims of a war which they themselves had started and supported, fictional or autobiographical recalls of the Nazi past need to consider the interdependence of divergent and fluid historical subject positions. Michael Ermann, a psychoanalyst who specializes in the effects of wartime childhoods, underscores this point when he asserts that he simply cannot understand his own identity as a non-Jewish German without reflecting on the fate of Jewish victims:

> Ich begreife: Ich kann als Deutscher nicht Kind dieses Krieges sein, ohne Erbe der NS-Vergangenheit zu sein. Insofern werde ich als Kriegskind immer auch die jüdischen Opfer in mir lebendig halten müssen, die mir einen Teil meiner Identität spiegeln. Krieg und nationalsozialistischer Terror sind nicht voneinander zu trennen. Dieses war kein landläufiger Krieg. So werde ich mich als Kriegskind nur finden, wenn ich zugleich meine Verletzungen und die deutsche Schuld betrachte. Ein Bewusstsein dafür, ein Kriegskind zu sein, kann ich erst erlangen, wenn ich die Verstrickung von Täterschaft und Traumatisierung begreife. Ich beginne zu ahnen, dass das Jahr 1945 nicht der Endpunkt dieser Kindheit im Kriege war, sondern in gewisser Weise der Angelpunkt, an dem sich die Verletzungen aus dem Außen in einen inneren Prozess verlagerten.[31]

> [I understand: As a German, I cannot be a child of this war without also being heir to the National Socialist past. As a *Kriegskind,* I will have to keep an inner awareness of the Jewish victims since they reflect a part of my identity. War and the terror of National Socialism cannot be separated. This was no normal war. That means that I can only understand what it is to be a *Kriegskind* by simultaneously looking at my own wounds and my German guilt. I can only fully understand what it means to be a *Kriegskind* when I comprehend the interdependence of perpetration and traumatization. I am beginning to sense that the year 1945 was not the end of my

31   Michael Ermann, 'Kriegskinder in Psychoanalysen', Farewell lecture given in Munich on 20 March 2009, <https://studylibde.com/doc/2146360/abschiedsvorlesung>, accessed 10 October 2021.

childhood but rather the pivotal point at which external injuries became objects of internal reflection.]

In light of a history that was and remains divided along the lines of discrimination and persecution implemented by the Nazi regime, only works of memory that integrate the personal into a larger collective framework can most adequately provide usable (in the sense of constructive and instructive) memories moving forward. While German and Jewish memories of Nazi childhood experiences are dialectically connected, they never fully converge. But as the following chapters show, the enduring tension between them can nonetheless serve as a productive friction in subsequent aesthetic transpositions. In the remainder of this chapter, I examine how this tension is negotiated in two volumes of non-fiction, Hilke Lorenz's book *Kriegskinder: Das Schicksal einer Generation* [*Children of War: The Fate of A Generation*] (first published in 2003) and Margarete Dörr's extensive two-volume documentation *Der Krieg hat uns geprägt* [*The War Made Us*] (2007). Note that the titles of both publications make similarly broad and generalizing claims: the Second World War was an overwhelming force that fundamentally shaped a generation of Germans. In the following I examine their blind spots as representative for the contextual and discursive backdrop of the literature examined in this study.

Curating the *Kriegskind* Narrative

Although publications by and about the *Kriegskinder* are valuable as intimate portrayals of the Nazi past from the German perspective, as suggested above, they are also troubling due to their lack of contextualization. Most edited volumes fail to locate selected testimonies within the broader German war story, there is no reference to the specifics of time or location and no explanation about the socio-economic identity of the witness. Furthermore, except for the obligatory acknowledgement in the introduction, most authors and editors do not acknowledge the evolving stages of the Third Reich. These stages range widely from the early period, characterized by widespread enthusiasm for the *Führer* (as well as the establishment of the Nuremberg Laws, which stripped Jews of their basic rights); to a middle period of relative stabilization marked by a succession of military victories (as well as pogroms and the systematic murder of those deemed *Untermenschen* [sub-human]); to the later period of deprivation and suffering of German civilians during the air wars and flight and displacement (as well as the murder of millions of Jews in death camps). Since the autobiographical voices remain disconnected from the larger historical context, they generalize a German perspective focused on the last war years, marked by harrowing experiences. Thus, by showcasing the difficult experiences of German children, these publications once again erase the voices of Hitler's victims. This troubling tendency comes to light in Lorenz's book. The author, a reporter who worked for a weekly, points to the enduring psychological fallout of wartime childhoods as a way to explain the silence of so many individual eyewitnesses and, implicitly, the collective silence of the *Kriegskinder* generation. This silence, she writes is driven by survival instinct, as well as feelings of shame and guilt. According to some estimates, 74,000 German children died during the bombing war and those who survived suffered from survivor guilt and are only now, at the end of their lives, able to tell their stories – stories they never even told their own children.[32] Lorenz is careful to add that her interviewees did not share their memories with her in order to minimize their historical accountability and underscores that they are well aware of who was responsible for the Nazi genocide. They do not want to be seen as victims, let alone relativize the suffering of Holocaust victims. But, she insists in closing, now is the time to carefully survey this 'Raum, der mit "Krieg" beschriftet ist' [a space marked by war] with the help of those who still remember, in order to make sure that the past does not repeat itself. 'Die Geschichten enthalten eine so komplizierte wie einfache

---

32   This estimate seems to quote numbers provided by Jörg Friedrich in *Der Brand*. Without sourcing it, Friedrich claims that 74,000 children under the age of 14 were killed, 45,000 boys and 30,000 girls; 116,000 were injured and that, ultimately, 15 per cent of all those who died in the bombing war were children. Friedrich, 511.

Botschaft: Nie wieder!'[33] [These stories have a complicated yet simple message: Never again!] While Lorenz emphasizes in her preface that the biographical memory fragments belong to the larger story of Nazi perpetration, the remaining three hundred pages all but erase this assertion. Edited to form a cogent narrative, her book focuses exclusively on the hardships endured by German children, not their causes. Consequently, it remains a compilation of decontextualized anecdotes. In other words, the selected eyewitness memories lend disparate German war childhoods a narrative coherence that fails to register the underlying historical rupture on which this coherence is premised.[34]

Even though the title of Margarete Dörr's extensive two-volume documentation *Der Krieg hat uns geprägt* also suggests that the war was an all-powerful subject that traumatized a particular cohort, Dörr's study is a notable exception to most *Kriegskinder* testimonies. Careful not to paraphrase the voices of her witnesses, she quotes direct excerpts from their letters and diary entries, along with other realia. In contrast to many similar publications, she includes personal documents that express excitement for Hitler's war, a national project promoted in schools and reinforced at home.[35] Most importantly, Dörr charts the uneven experiential reality of National Socialism: from the enthusiastic beginnings, to the later years when destructive war experiences gradually become part of everyday life and finally culminate in the trauma of the last years. Her compilation of *Kriegskinder* voices confirms Stargardt's findings that '[c]hildren's experiences deserve to be understood across the racial and national divides, not because of their similarities but because their extreme contrasts help us

33   Hilke Lorenz, *Kriegskinder. Das Schicksal einer Generation* (Berlin: List, 2007), 23.

34   Lorenz's book is by no means the exception. Most publications of (auto)biographical wartime childhoods lack references to the larger historical context. To name only three examples: Jürgen Kleindienst, Ingrid Hanke, eds, *Kriegskinder erzählen* (Berlin: Zeitgut, 2013); the companion to the ARD TV show *Kriegskinder* edited by Yury and Sinya Winterberg, *Kriegskinder. Erinnerungen einer Generation* (Berlin: Rotbuch, 2009); and Heinrich Finkler, *Der Schrei der Kriegskinder. Eine Kindheit im Zeichen von Angst, Schwermut und Hunger* (Frankfurt a.M.: Fischer, 2014).

35   Margarete Dörr, *Der Krieg hat uns geprägt. Wie Kinder den Zweiten Weltkrieg erlebten*, I (Frankfurt: Campus, 2007), 62 ff.

see the Nazi social order as a whole'.[36] Notably, *Der Krieg hat uns geprägt* contrasts memories of deprivation and hardship with descriptions of Nazi childhoods located on a fluid range of subject positions: from victims to accomplices, bystanders, witnesses and spectators.[37]

Around the millennium, the *Kriegskind* narrative, as exemplified in the work discussed above, represents what Sara Jones has discussed as mediated remembering (in the context of memories of the East German Stasi in the Berlin Republic). In this case, it is a community of witnesses that emerges in the arena of unstable, competing and disputed historical realities of the German war experience. The *Kriegskind* narrative encodes a multitude of eyewitness testimony about the same historical period without, however, offering the recipients 'a range of conflicting accounts; rather the different voices confirm an overarching narrative about this part of the past. These are not rival testimonies mediated alongside each other, but complementary testimonies, with each supporting the "truth" of the other.'[38] Similar to what Aleida Assmann has examined as 'communicative memory', mediated remembering gains coherence and visibility through mutual recognition and reinforcement. Commonly created within the family but also generated within groups that share similar, often traumatic experiences (victim support associations, for instance), communicative memory validates a sense of coherence and community. *Kriegskind* anthologies offer what Jones describes as

> 'diachronically produced texts on the same theme [...] brought together by an editor, curator or director [...] into a single cultural product. The construction of a "remembering community", in which the narratives of the individual appear to overlap and support one another, is thus created in the process of mediation and reception, not at the point of production: these groups of testifying individuals thus form what I term a *mediated remembering community*.'[39]

36 Stargardt, 19.
37 Dörr, 104 f.
38 Sara Jones, *The Media of Testimony: Remembering the East German Stasi in the Berlin Republic* (Houndmills, Basingstoke: Macmillan Palgrave, 2014), 37. I owe thanks to the reviewer of this manuscript for this reference.
39 Jones, 38 (emphasis in original).

This kind of memory work offers what Jones calls a 'second authentication effect'. It relies on what other memory scholars have termed 'remediation', that is, a process inherent in the dynamics of cultural memory that slides across different media, incorporating, cross-borrowing and appropriating from one memorial media to another. Remediation aims to make invisible the process of remembering as a form of mnemonic encoding. It is driven by 'a desire for medial transparency as an effort towards the construction of authenticity and, in the context of testimony, of immediacy in contact with the witness – thereby mitigating the distancing effects of mediation'.[40] While the *Kriegskind* narrative offers what seems to be an unmediated, fresh, authentic and immediate access to the German war experience, it is a 'remediated' memory that raises the questions posed in the introduction: how can literary transpositions of the *Kriegskind* perspective work through historical accountability when they edit out history writ large? More specifically, how and to what extent can the *Kriegskind* perspective avoid the pitfalls of a generalizing victimology that fail to acknowledge Nazi perpetration? These questions are particularly relevant with respect to the text discussed in the next chapter, Dieter Forte's novel *Der Junge mit den blutigen Schuhen*, a trauma text that not only mirrors the limitations of the *Kriegskind* narrative but also frames the larger issues examined in this study. Can fictions of memory translate the child – itself a culturally overdetermined fiction – into a recall of the Nazi past that avoids traumatic complicity and productively navigates intersections and gradations of historical subject positions?

40   Ibid.

CHAPTER 2

The Myth of Knowing Innocence: Dieter Forte's *Der Junge mit den blutigen Schuhen*

Dieter Forte's novel *Der Junge mit den blutigen Schuhen* (1995)[1] not only aligns with, but also further validates and amplifies the *Kriegskind* narrative described in the previous chapter. Through the lens of a helpless and traumatized child witness, the contemporary reader is transported back to the last years of the Second World War and the Allied bombing attacks of a particular neighbourhood in Düsseldorf. Forte's text is representative of memory discourses that rest on the myth of collective innocence, a trend Samuel Salzborn examines in his book-length essay on the historical arc and enduring political utility of this myth. He argues the Federal Republic of Germany has changed from a society of Nazi perpetrators to a memory-resistant nation which coheres around anti-Semitic projections and fantasies of ethnic self-victimization. Ironically, he notes, in the 1990s and 2000s an increasingly refined knowledge about history corresponds to a proportionally decreasing interest in the Nazi past. Although, by this point, the legacy of the Third Reich is well understood and carefully researched, the population at large seems mostly indifferent to historical facts. As noted in the previous chapter, Germans seem to prefer media fantasies about the Nazi past made popular on national television through histotainment.[2] In the following, I consider Dieter Forte's

---

1   Dieter Forte's works are cited as follows: JBS: *Der Junge mit den blutigen Schuhen* (Frankfurt a.M.: Fischer, 2003); DM: *Das Muster* (Frankfurt a.M.: Fischer, 2003); IE: *In der Erinnerung* (Frankfurt a.M.: Fischer, 2001); and AV: "'Alles Vorherige war nur ein Umweg'", in Volker Hage, ed., *Schweigen oder Sprechen* (Frankfurt a.M.: Fischer, 2002), 45–68.
2   Samuel Salzborn, *Kollektive Unschuld. Die Abwehr der Shoah im deutschen Erinnern* (Berlin, Leipzig: Hentrich & Hentrich, 2020), 55. For more on histotainment see

novel in the context of the larger conversation about how to remember the Third Reich. My analysis builds on the work of cultural historians, psychologists and political scientists who have shown why and to what extent National Socialism and the Shoah are consistently disavowed in Germany's cultural memory while the history of German victims is increasingly foregrounded after reunifcation.[3]

Authentic Witness Account or Shoah-Kitsch?

Dieter Forte was born in Düsseldorf, two years after Hitler came to power, in 1935. He began his career writing theatre plays, as well as television and radio plays, but only found his distinct voice towards the end of his life in the late 1980s, when he began the difficult work of transposing his traumatic childhood memories into literature. *Der Junge mit den blutigen Schuhen* is part of his memory trilogy *Das Haus auf meinen Schultern* [*The House on my Shoulders*] (1999) and may be his best-known publication.[4] Forte's work has been celebrated as an 'authentic' account of a heretofore unacknowledged part of German history. Writing for the weekly *Der Spiegel*, Elke Heidenreich praised the novel as incomparable, 'thoroughly and sharply remembered, a poetic chronicle';[5] three years later

Wulf Kantsteiner, *In Pursuit of German Memory. History, Television, and Politics after Auschwitz* (Athens, OH: Ohio University Press, 2006).

3   See, for instance, Aleida Assmann and Ute Frevert, *Geschichtsvergessenheit. Geschichtsversessenheit. Vom Umgang mit der deutschen Vergangenheit nach 1945* (Stuttgart: dva, 1999); Ulrike Jureit, Ulrike and Christian Schneider, *Gefühlte Opfer. Illusionen der Vergangenheitsbewältigung* (Stuttgart: Klett-Cotta, 2010), and Wolfgang Hegener, *Schuldabwehr. Psychoanalytische und kulturwissenschaftliche Studien zum Antisemitismus* (Gießen: Psychosozial Verlag, 2019).

4   The first part, *Das Muster* [*The Pattern*], was published in 1992, the third part *In der Erinnerung* [*In Memory*] in 1998. In 2004, Forte added to the trilogy *Auf der anderen Seite der Welt* [*On the Other Side of the World*] to form a *Tetralogie der Erinnerung* [*Tetralogy of Remembrance*].

5   Elke Heidenreich, 'Farbiger Bilderbogen', *Der Spiegel*, 1 October 1995, <http://www. spiegel.de/spiegel/spiegelspecial/d-9259143.html>, accessed 12 February 2021.

Volker Hage, writing for the same magazine, described it as a 'courageous and epic march through time'.[6] Similarly, Ursula Maerz, a literary scholar and journalist, has underscored Forte's 'self-reflexive narrative style' and praised the 'beautiful hypo-tactical structure' of some passages.[7] More recently, literary scholars like Susanne Vees-Gulani appreciate Forte's prose work as 'an attempt to wrestle away his traumatic memories of the air war from [a] wordless silence and to carry them into language',[8] while Mary Cosgrove regards Forte's text to be a valid trauma narrative too easily dismissed because of its traditional narrative register.[9]

These positive readings are, however, countered by those who critique the novel for its schematic oversimplifications, a 'Hang zur Schematisierung' [tendency to generalize and simplify] and 'Überzeichnungen' [exaggerations].[10] Condemned as an unwitting contribution to what Dominick LaCapra has termed the 'pacification of the Holocaust', that is, an apologetic rewriting of a history,[11] Anne Peiter calls *Der Junge mit den blutigen Schuhen* 'Holocaust-Kitsch'. Drawing on Theodor W. Adorno's notion of 'committed art', which reconsiders the critical impetus of art as caught in the aporia between 'the sheer physical pain of people beaten to the ground

6   Volker Hage, 'Hunger und Kälte hören nie auf', *Der Spiegel*, 2 November 1998, <http://www.spiegel.de/spiegel/print/d-8029164.html>, accessed 12 February 2021.

7   Ursula Maerz, 'Die Raupenmenschen', *Die Zeit*, 22 December 1998, <https://www.zeit.de/1998/53/>, accessed 12 February 2021.

8   Susanne Vees-Guiliani, 'The Language of Trauma: Dieter Forte's Memories of Air War', in Laurel Cohen-Pfister and Dagmar Wienroeder-Skinner, eds, *Victims and Perpetrators: 1933–1945: (Re-)Presenting the Past in Post-unification Culture* (Berlin, Boston: De Gruyter, 2006), 120.

9   Mary Cosgrove, 'Narrating German Suffering in the Shadow of the Holocaust', in Stuart Taberner and Karina Berger, eds, *Germans as Victims in the Literary Fiction of the Berlin Republic* (Rochester, NY: Camden House, 2009), 162–76.

10   Walter Hink, 'Ein Schatten über Oberbilk', *Frankfurter Allgemeine Zeitung*, 9 September 1995, <http://www.faz.net/aktuell/feuilleton/buecher/rezensionen/belletristik/rezension-belletristik-ein-schatten-ueber-oberbilk-11294165-p2.html>, accessed 2 January 2021.

11   Dominick LaCapra, *History and Memory after Auschwitz* (Ithaca, NY: Cornell University Press, 1998), 18.

by rifle butts' and the aesthetic 'power to elicit enjoyment out of it',[12] Peiter critiques the novel as a well-intentioned but naïve memory text. She asserts that by highlighting acts of humanity in the face of extreme inhumanity, the novel masks the foundational moral reversals at the core of the Nazi project, and thus normalizes Nazi terror by 'making Auschwitz familiar'.[13] In a similar vein, Holocaust scholar Stefan Braese sees the novel as a narrative that uses the perspective of a child to obfuscate German culpability. German civilians, he argues, egregiously feature as 'double victims': first they were victimized by Hitler's war and later tormented by the Allies' retaliatory aerial bombing.[14]

Expanding the scope of the critiques advanced by Peiter and Braese, I examine the extent to which Forte's 'writing the child' contributes to what Anne Claire Hunter has described as the 'genrefication' of the Holocaust. Hunter refers to the web of increasingly familiar tropes, images and representational patterns established to contain an event that has come to represent a seemingly uncontainable breach of civilization. I argue the novel contributes to what might be called 'palliative aesthetics': it offers a metanarrative that facilitates engagement with the rupture of National Socialism based on what Freud termed *Deckerinnerungen*, [screen memories]. In this case, *Deckerinnerungen* mitigate the full impact of the violence committed under Hitler and thus obfuscate issues of causality and accountability.[15] Since both content and form of this text raise foundational,

---

12   Theodor W. Adorno, 'Commitment', trans. Francis McDonagh, trans., 9, <https:// unhistoricactsdotnet.files.wordpress.com/2015/01/adorno-commitment.pdf>, accessed 4 January 2021.

13   Anne D. Peiter, '"Erlebte Vorstellungen" versus "den Vorstellungen abgezogene Begriffe". Überlegungen zum Shoah-Kitsch', in Inge Stephan and Alexandra Tacke, eds, *NachBilder des Holocaust* (Cologne: Böhlau, 2007), 68.

14   Stephan Braese, 'Bombenkrieg und literarische Gegenwart. Zu W. G. Sebald und Dieter Forte', *Mittelweg* 36/1 (2002): 17. I examine the implications of this projection in more detail in the context of early postwar victimologies in the last part of this chapter.

15   Freud coined this term in his essay 'Über Kindheits- und Deckerinnerungen'(first published in *Monatshefte für Psychiatrie und Neurologie* in 1899) when he realized that difficult childhood experiences tend to return in acts of forgetting and misremembering and how strikingly they are shaped by displacements, distortions and

epistemological, aesthetic and moral questions of relevance to all the case studies that follow, *Der Junge mit den blutigen Schuhen* offers a poignant point of departure. It brings to light both the heuristic possibilities and the limitations of 'writing the child'. In the first section of this chapter, I examine the configuration of a counter-memory shaped by a child's observations from below yet blind to the larger historical context. Second, I focus on how discontinuities between life experiences and their subsequent recollection find an uneven expression in a text that simultaneously underscores and pacifies the burn of traumatic memories. I conclude this chapter with a closer look at a fiction of memory which rather than reveal, contributes to the collective silence it purports to break, evident when seen in light of early air war assessments and more recent *Kriegskinder* testimonies.

The Child as an Instrument of Memory

In a deliberate deviation from autobiographical reality, the novel opens with the birth of the protagonist on 21 March 1933, ominously described as 'ein blutiges Stück Fleisch' (JBS, 10) [a bloody piece of flesh] that is being pushed into the world. Remaining a nameless 'boy', his birth follows the wedding of his parents, Friedrich Fontana and Maria Lukacz, announced and celebrated at the end of *Das Muster* [*The Pattern*], the first volume of the trilogy. Their wedding is overshadowed by what is to come, that is, the imminent rise of National Socialism. Just as the guests are preparing for the wedding photo, they learn Dr Levi, a Jewish doctor and Maria's beloved employer, has committed suicide – news so startling the wedding photographer involuntarily releases the shutter. Thus, instead of a happy wedding party, the photo shows 'eine Gruppe von Menschen [...], die mit schreckerfüllten Augen auf ein unsichtbares Bild hinter dem Fotografen starrten, als hätten alle in dem Moment die Zukunft gesehen'

---

elisions. I discuss the relevance of screen memories in more detail the context of Grass's memory work in Chapter 3.

(DM, 319), [a group of people [...] staring at an unseen image behind the photographer with terror in their eyes, as if they had all seen the future at that very moment]. This image anticipates the events that unfold in the second volume of *Das Haus auf meinen Schultern*. The shock of the wedding party evokes the terrified gaze of Walter Benjamin's *Angelus Novus*, the hapless angel of history who, caught by the weight of constantly unfolding catastrophes, is doomed to look into the future by staring backwards at the debris of the past. Like Benjamin's angel, who sees 'one single catastrophe which keeps piling wreckage upon wreckage and hurls it in front of his feet', Friedrich and Maria are caught in a storm of catastrophic events that propels them forward.[16]

Not only does the parental wedding ceremony coincide with the death of Dr Levi, but the boy's birth also coincides with Hitler's coming to power – an implausible but effective synchronicity which identifies the text as a fiction of memory based on a reframing of personal experiences through the lens of historical hindsight. Moreover, the boy is born during an iconic moment: the transfer of power marked by the reluctant, yet fateful handshake between Hindenburg and Hitler, announced in a ceremony broadcast over the radio while Maria is giving birth. This slide between autobiographical detail and historical fact lends the accident of this particular birth a mythical significance. Born into a historical caesura, the nameless boy sees details that escape the adults. When little, he watches from below while playing on the floor; as an older child he watches from above, in a tree that overlooks the yard; and later still, when the family briefly relocates to Southern Germany and he suffers severe asthma attacks, he observes life mostly through a window while bedridden. Not hampered by the cognitive limitations of a child his age, but also not burdened by the complexities of adult introspection, he is stylized to be an exacting, yet seemingly neutral observer. In her reading of the novel Nora Maguire describes Forte's child protagonist as a *tabula rasa*, 'a "blank slate", upon which knowledge and morality may be inscribed through teaching and experience, but which comes into being with no inherent principles of

16   Walter Benjamin, 'Theses on the Philosophy of History', in Hannah Arendt, ed. and trans., *Illuminations* (New York: Schocken, 1985), 257.

knowledge or of morality [...] embodying and regenerating the moral and social codes of his family and community'.[17] I agree, insofar as the text does not describe the boy's individual character traits, but rather presents him as a medium whose perceptions are shaped by formal and informal instances of learning. In contrast to the script of a *Bildungsroman*, however, this protagonist is not a character evolving into his full humanity; instead, he is cast as a kind of instrument of memory that mimics the immutable eye of a camera which faithfully records everything it sees.

Focalized through the boy's lens, the relationship between the inhabitants of a multicultural, semi-bohemian Düsseldorf neighbourhood (conceived of as a utopian community of civic solidarity) and the country at large comes into view coloured by two distinctly different mentalities. His grandfather represents the spirit of passive resistance based on 'Bildung' [education], while his mother represents a fatalistic and deeply Catholic acceptance of life's vicissitudes. Listening to everything his grandfather says and watching intently what his mother does, he remembers everything he hears and sees as a potential story to be preserved for posterity. Not only does he understand that he is tasked with witnessing extraordinary times, but he is also aware his observations will need to be refracted through poetic imagination in order to gain gravitas. This particular charge to remember, shaped by the trauma of loss and deprivation, yet not distorted by the ideological indoctrination of the Hitler Youth, is authorized by both experiential insights and the child's precocious awareness. From this perspective, Hitler's SA [Storm Troopers] are portrayed as an enemy whose murderous power only becomes apparent when relatives disappear and are deliberately killed. Although this reference to state-sanctioned murder remains abstract – summed up in just one laconic sentence: 'Die Stadt veränderte sich.' (JBS, 83) [The city transformed.] – the boy now begins to understand that in times like these, remembering itself can become an act of resistance. 'Und der Junge wußte, dass er das alles behalten sollte.' (JBS, 79) [And the boy knew that he should remember everything.] In sync

17 Nora Maguire, *Childness and the Writing of the German Past: Tropes of Childhood in Contemporary German Literature* (Oxford: Peter Lang, 2013), 30.

with these changes his perceptions gain sharpness and gradually cohere to a counter-memory forged in resistance to the Nazi order.

When Maria and her children (her husband's whereabouts remain unclear throughout the text) flee to a village in Bavaria to escape the bombing, they have to contend with villagers whose lives have not been touched by war and who categorically refuse to believe their stories about aerial bombing: 'Hier herrschte Frieden, hier gab es keinen Krieg, hier gab es nur ein verhetztes Ausland, eine jüdisch-bolschewistische Verschwörung, die dem deutschen Mann seinen Acker und sein Haus nehmen wollte und der deutschen Frau ihre Ehre.' (JBS, 230–31) [Here, peace prevailed here, there was no war, here was nothing but despised foreign countries, a Jewish-Bolshevist conspiracy that aimed to take house and farmland from German men and honour from German women.] Hence, fearing repercussions, the family falls silent; Maria forbids her children to speak in public about the bombed-out nights, the destruction, the hunger, the dead and the concentration camp prisoners (JBS, 234). And it is this silence – the silence about the suffering of German civilians during the bombing war, enforced by a collective of strangers in a Bavarian village – which the text ultimately seeks to redress half a century later. In this rural environment, the boy is tagged as a city kid, barely tolerated by the villagers. He cannot communicate with the same ease as those around him who possess a shared vocabulary; he does not share their dialect and world view (JBS, 248). His perspective is shaped in the gap between two different writing systems and violently enforced writing conventions. When confronted with textbooks written in Latin script, he freezes, since he only knows the German *Sütterlin* script.[18] 'Er saß in der Bank, fror, rührte sich nicht vor Schreck, war erstarrt, der ganze Körper tat ihm weh, er saß da voller Entsetzen, die Welt war ihm plötzlich verschlossen.' (JBS, 247–8) [He sat at his desk, cold and too fearful to move, was paralyzed, his whole body ached, he sat there completely terrified, the world was closed to him.] At that school,

18   Commissioned by the Prussian Ministry of Science, Art and Culture, *Sütterlinschrift* was considered to be a modern German handwriting script. Designed by Ludwig Sütterlin in 1911, it was taught in German schools from 1914 until it was banned by the NSDAP (the Nazi party) in 1941 as 'chaotic' and replaced with Latin-type letters (which bear no resemblance to Sütterlin).

he endures physical punishment because he is a left-handed outsider, a hardship most vividly described in Volume Three of the trilogy, *In der Erinnerung* [*In Memory*].

> Und immer der Kampf zwischen links und rechts, immer musste er erst überlegen, in welche Hand der Bleistift gehörte, immer erst diese Sekunde des Zögerns, der Unsicherheit, bevor er schrieb, als suche man in der Dunkelheit erst den richtigen Schlüssel für ein Schloss. Er war Linkshänder, schreiben musste er mit der rechten Hand, in einer erzwungenen, für ihn ganz künstlichen Haltung, die immer bewusst eingenommen werden musste. Die Lehrer der Dorf- und Kleinstadtschulen [...] hatten sich darauf konzentriert, ihm jedes Mal, wenn er einen Griffel, Bleistift oder Federhalter in die linke Hand nahm, mit der scharfen Kante des Lineals auf die Hand zu schlagen. Die Hand war oft blutig, schmerzte. (IE, 148)

> [And there was always the battle between left and right, he always had to think first which hand the pencil belonged in, always this initial second of hesitation, of being unsure before he wrote, as if looking in the dark for the right key to the lock. He was left-handed but had to write with his right hand in a forced posture that was entirely artificial for him, that he always had to consciously assume. The village and small-town teachers were ever watchful, every time he held a slate pencil, lead pencil or fountain pen with his left hand, [...] intent on hitting him on his hand with the sharp edge of the ruler. The hand was often bloody and it hurt.]

This passage implicitly casts the boy's memory as written in a foreign script, executed with the wrong hand and in defiance to a hostile environment. But is this kind of mnemonic grammar also critical of the contemporary culture of memory? Similar to W. G. Sebald, Forte seeks to challenge what he perceives to be a collective silence within German postwar culture. 'Es wurde doch eigentlich alles verschwiegen [...] das Trauma wurde zu einem Tabu. Ein seltsamer Vorgang, über den nachzudenken es sich lohnen würde. Das Trauma verwandelte sich vor dem Hintergrund des nun kalten Krieges in ein Tabu.' (AV, 55) [Everything was kept secret [...] the trauma became taboo. A strange phenomenon worthy of reflection. Against the backdrop of the Cold War, the trauma metamorphosed into a taboo.] His reference to the ideological tenets that hamper attempts to read history against its grain is well taken; historical archives do have blind spots along hegemonic fault lines and are often less interested in the experience of marginalized groups. Yet, as I show in the next two parts of this chapter, the narrative choreography of the novel, while seeking to address a collective silence, reinforces a palliative silence that lies at the heart of the German–Jewish 'negative symbiosis'.

The Child: Crown Witness for a Society of Victims

A repetitive and non-reflective flow of anecdotes about quirky individuals portrays citizens living in a working-class neighbourhood of Düsseldorf, referred to only as 'das Quartier' [the neighbourhood]. Despite abstract meta-historical passages that introduce the bombing war through the voice of an omniscient narrator, who is aware of the gravitas of his mission to preserve the story of the past for posterity, the broader historical context of the 1930s and 1940s remains obscured. Forte's text does not make explicit the tension between an ostensibly objective narrator and the immediacy of an experiencing and vulnerable 'I'. Instead, it relies on what Birgit Neumann has described as the 'experiential mode', a mode of focalization which presents lived-through experience and thus simulates the authenticity of living memory. As one of the most intimate forms of literary recall, this register largely obscures the interdependence of the two temporal plains: 'The present context of remembering is scarcely fleshed out and the temporal interval between the remembering and re-membered "I" is primarily indicated by the use of the past tense.'[19] There are, however, passages which complement the approximations of the re-membering child eyewitness with abstract speculations of a philosophical narrator. These passages project what Neumann terms the 'monumental mode'. Distanced and deliberate, the reflections of the narrator evoke the *longue durée* and lend the chronicle mythical gravitas. In fact, the text conveys a sense of transgenerational continuity manifest as a generalized story of persecution: when the boy stands in front of his burning house

19   Birgit Neumann, 'The Literary Representation of Memory', in Astrid Erll and Ansgar Nünning, eds, *A Companion to Cultural Memory Studies* (Berlin, New York: de Gruyter, 2010), 337.

in Düsseldorf, he knows that he is simultaneously looking at the burning houses of his family in Poland and his family in Lyon (JBS, 134).

Forte's novel focalizes the events through the limited lens of a child, a witness, who sees from below and from above, who is caught in the terror of the moment and who becomes an increasingly silent onlooker. However, this focalization gains universal meaning through the voice of a narrator, who at times gains an explicit presence, but more often remains implicit. Gérard Genette has argued that the heuristic power of literature rests on negotiations between a focalizer and a narrator, between what he terms 'story', or the narrative content (in this case the boy's experiences) and 'acts of narrating', of 'raconter' or 'erzählen' (in this case an auctorial voice). Genette directs attention to the relationship between 'a discourse and the events that it recounts [... and] between the same discourse and what produces it.'[20] He posits that the meaning of 'narrative' or 'text', that is, literature, rests on the interaction of different temporal choreographies (of *when* the story is told in relation to the events it relates), choreographies of distance (to what is told) and choreographies of speed (of how time is contracted or expanded), all of which extend to choreographies of narrative awareness attributed to the particular voice of a focalizer. The fictions of memory examined in this study all focalize the *story* through a child's consciousness, that is, a specific perceptual range relayed by a narrating voice, which in some instances overlaps with, and in others differs from the child's 'strange' consciousness. What is under examination, then, is how 'writing the child' makes productive the implicit or explicit dialogue (and in some cases the tension) between an instance that *sees* and an instance that *speaks*. (This is of particular importance in *Die Blechtrommel* examined in the following chapter.)

Der Junge mit den blutigen Schuhen focalizes the last years of the war through a lens of 'knowing innocence'. As such, the boy belongs to a group of eyewitnesses whom Sigrid Weigel has referred to as the 'secret first generation': he is 'lucky enough to *not yet* or only marginally have been dragged into politics and responsibility, but [...] *old enough* to be affected

---

20   Gérard Genette, *Narrative Discourse: An Essay in Method*, Jane E. Lewin, trans. (Ithaca, NY: Cornell University Press, 1980), 27.

emotionally and mentally by the morally confusing suggestive power that the NS-Regime had, at least in the area of youth educating'.[21] This generational cohort, Weigel contends,

> secretly bear(s) the title 'first generation', although not in the sense of numerical time but in terms of hierarchy of memories. Still, even the origin is not whole, homogeneous, or uniform. Instead, a trace of *divided knowledge* that goes back to the *diversity and incompatibility of historical experiences* and that is propagated in the memory of the descendants arises from the past events in which individuals were involved as perpetrators of crimes, as victims, as collaborators, witnesses, or merely spectators.[22]

What Weigel calls the 'trace of a divided knowledge' which 'goes back to the diversity and incompatibility of historical experiences' – in this case, the difference between a German child and a child deemed of inferior race and marked for annihilation – escapes the boy's awareness.

Forte's text brings to the fore a question central to all efforts to recollect traumatic historical experiences: the question of *Mitwisserschaft*. While this term narrowly translates to having been an 'accomplice', I am using it here to refer to the nuance implied in the German term, as a kind of *tacit knowing*. When it comes to histories of violence and their legacies, the disparity between those who knew, those who did not know and those who pretended not to have known becomes a central concern. It brings up the question of trust raised by any form of historical testimony that lies at the tenuous juncture between lived experience and subsequent renderings remediated by the passing of time. In his reflections on everyday experiences and historical knowledge, Reinhart Koselleck asks how Hitler could have carried out an unprecedented genocide without the German people knowing about its goals, scope and execution, or even only parts of it. How could those who survived the war not have known about the death camps? Based not only on his own life experiences but also filtered through his expertise as a historian, he answers with two scenarios: first, there were those who could not have known about the death camps due to fairly strict censorship practices and the fact that the sites of mass killings

---

21   Sigrid Weigel, '"Generation" as a Symbolic Form. On the Genealogical Discourse of Memory since 1945', *Germanic Review* 77/4 (Fall 2002): 271.

22   Weigel, 271 (my emphases).

were carefully hidden. But second, there were those who simply did not want to know or who pretended not to know.[23] By writing from the position of knowing innocence, which balances anti-Semitic violence with acts of solidarity with Jewish victims, Forte's novel circumvents these questions altogether. If the text had been conceived as an autobiography, this kind of elision might be acceptable, but since it is an ambitious and explicit fiction of memory we need to ask: how are we to understand the contradictions between a writing of verisimilitude that claims experiential accuracy and a focalizer who cannot grasp the historical context of what he sees?

As the war goes on, the boy becomes increasingly traumatized; he cannot get enough air. His asthma cripples him to the point of constant panic attacks (the text mentions his asthma repeatedly) until he finally loses his speech altogether and starts to stutter (JBS, 144). Marked by relentless bombing attacks, the sudden death of his brother and an absent father, his childhood mirrors those of many *Kriegskinder*. However, in contrast to other German children who lived through the war, let alone Jewish children who were systematically persecuted and murdered, Forte's protagonist ultimately emerges as a heroic German child. This becomes particularly apparent in a passage which concludes the first part of the novel and describes the St. Martin's Day parade on 9 November 1938, known as *Kristallnacht* [Night of Broken Glass, a convenient euphemism for the November pogrom carried out against Jewish businesses]. The parade comes into view less as a coherent sequence of events than as a cacophony of auditory and visual sensations. The children sing 'Laterne, Laterne, Sonne, Mond und Sterne', a well-known song reserved for this parade, and the boy is equally mesmerized and confused by his wildly flickering paper lantern. Caught in the indeterminate space of a celebratory march, semi-darkness and broken glass, he stumbles along. '[D]er Junge stolperte über Steine, rutschte auf Glasscherben aus, Maria zog ihn an der Hand, in der anderen Hand trug er eine Papierlaterne mit dem Clownsgesicht, Mondgesicht, Sonnengesicht, das er nicht auseinanderhalte konnte.' (JBS, 97) [The boy stumbled over cobble stones, slipped on shards of glass, Maria pulled him along holding his hand, in the other hand he carried a paper lantern with

23   Koselleck, 217.

the face of a clown, the face of a moon and the face of a sun, which he could not distinguish from one another]. When he gets hurt by a glass splinter on the ground – a rather oblique reference to the violence against the Jewish population unleashed that day – he hears the admonishing voice of a stranger uttering a Hitler Youth directive, 'Ein deutscher Junge weint nicht' (JBS, 100) [A German boy does not cry]. Outraged and distraught, he tries to kick the man and spits at him. While those who were the true victims of *Kristallnacht* remain unnamed and invisible, the boy's steadfast resistance to Nazi indoctrination makes him stand out as the insulted and injured victim.

In this passage, the historical relevance of an event that foreshadows programmatic mass murder is first displaced by the outrage of a random bystander about a crying German boy, and secondly a German boy who is outraged because he feels he has been treated unfairly. In other words, the text slides seamlessly from a reference to Hitler Youth ideals to the Nazi strategy of blaming the victim, thus keeping the violent core of National Socialism hidden behind contiguous German and Jewish injuries. Forte's boy, then, emerges as the poster child of a new victimology: a German boy resisting Hitler Youth ideals. He belongs to a new cohort of witnesses whom Klaus Naumann calls 'Kronzeugen der Opfergesellschaft'[24] [crown witnesses for a society of victims], a provocative turn of phrase which sums up collective strategies of 'Schuldabwehr' [displacement of guilt], which I examine below in more detail.

Deepening the Silence: A Negative Symbiosis

As mentioned in the introduction, Ulrike Jureit and Christian Schneider argue that Germany's cultural memory has become a victim-centred

---

24   Klaus Naumann, 'Aus Anklage ist Klage geworden. Kronzeugen der Opfergesellschaft? In zahlreichen Buchveröffentlichungen melden sich die "Kriegskinder" als eine neue Erinnerungsgemeinschaft zu Wort', *Frankfurter Rundschau*, 17 April 2004.

culture of commemoration. Resting on empathic identification with the victims, but unwilling to address questions of complicity, the nation's memory politics are focused on 'die Figur des *gefühlten* Opfers' [figure of the *felt* victim]. Not unlike literary and cultural scholars Debarati Sanyal, Michael Rothberg and Anna Claire Hunter, social historians like Jureit and Schneider are critical of narratives that blur historical differences and obscure or even erase that which they proclaim to remember. Jureit notes that 'Diese deutsche Erinnerungskultur tendiert dazu, eine Vergessenskultur zu werden, die sich paradoxerweise gerade dadurch auszeichnet, dass sie zwanghaft erinnert.'[25] [German memory culture is becoming a culture of forgetting which, paradoxically, is marked by compulsive acts of remembrance.] Forte's novel is a case in point, since it displaces the story of those targeted by Hitler's policies of annihilation and thus spares the reader uncomfortable questions of accountability. In the sense laid out by Omer Bartov, the text illustrates a central tenet of Germany's memory politics evident in 'the manner in which postwar German representations of Jewish absence serve an apparently crucial need in German society and culture to identify, or empathize, with its own immediate predecessors and to perceive itself as the inheritor of a tragic history of [its own] victimhood and suffering.'[26]

As noted above, there is a fundamental discontinuity between life experiences and their retrospective recollection, particularly when shaped by traumatic events. Inevitably, individual experiences are moulded by contingent circumstances that at the moment of their unfolding occlude the broader historical context; awareness of the historical import of any experience can only emerge in retrospect.[27] But when it comes to perpetrator

25 Ulrike Jureit and Christian Schneider. *Gefühlte Opfer. Illusionen der Vergangenheitsbewältigung* (Stuttgart: Klett-Cotta, 2010), 36.

26 Omer Bartov, '"Seit die Juden weg sind …". Germany, History, and Representations of Absence', in Scott Denham et al., eds, *A User's Guide to German Cultural Studies* (Ann Arbor: University of Michigan Press, 1997), 213.

27 This discrepancy is central to Martin Walser's novel *Ein springender Brunnen*. Premised on the observation that past experiences remain forever closed upon themselves, the text presents memories of a childhood under the Third Reich as 'innocent' experiences, that is, as 'untainted' by subsequent insights: 'Solange etwas ist, ist es nicht das, was es gewesen sein wird. Wenn etwas vorbei ist, ist man nicht

legacies such as National Socialism, the question of tacit knowledge – of who could have known what and when, of who chose to look away and who genuinely did not know about the mass killings – gains heightened relevance. Koselleck introduces his reflections on these questions in a seminal article published in 1999 with a poignant autobiographical anecdote.

At the end of the war, in May 1945, when he was a Russian POW and imprisoned at Auschwitz, one of his guards, a Jewish survivor, confronted him with what the Germans had done there to the Jews. At that point in time, Koselleck was unaware of what had happened in Auschwitz and did not believe rumours about the Holocaust. Urging all prisoners to work faster, his guard eventually lifts a wooden stool to bash in Koselleck's head, only to stop abruptly and proclaim in broken German 'Was soll ich dir schlaggen Schädel ein, ihr habt ja vergasst Millionen.'[28] [Why should I bash your head in, you have gassed millions.] In a flash, Koselleck understood that this man had spoken the truth. To him, the all-consuming anger of his captor followed by an exclamation of bitter resignation made instantly clear, without historical evidence or proof, that claims about the gas chambers were true. What is the point of revenging the murder of millions, this guard seems to say, by killing just one German? Although self-evident to him, the experiencing subject, the author is acutely aware that moments like these remain categorically untransferable. There is what may be called the veracity gap: the discrepancy between categorically untransferable personal experiences. John Durham Peters points out that '[w]itnessing presupposes a discrepancy between the ignorance of person and the knowledge of another: it is an intensification of the problem of communication more generally. It always involves an epistemological gap whose bridging is always fraught with difficulty. No transfusion of consciousness is possible. Words can be exchanged, experiences cannot.'[29] As Koselleck notes, 'Es gibt keine

---

mehr der, dem es passierte.' Martin Walser, *Ein springender Brunnen* (Frankfurt a.M.: Suhrkamp, 2008), 9. [As long as something is, it isn't what it will have been. When something is past, you are no longer the person it happened to, but you're closer to him than to others.] Martin Walser, *A Gushing Fountain*, David Dollenmayer, trans. (New York: Arcade, 2015), 8.

28   Reinhardt Koselleck. 'Die Diskontinuität der Erinnerung', *Deutsche Zeitschrift für Philosophie* 47/2 (1999): 214.

29   John Durham Peters, *Witnessing, Media, Culture, Society* 23/6 (2001): 710.

Primärerfahrung, die man macht oder sammelt, die überhaupt übertragbar wäre, denn es zeichnet Erfahrungen aus, dass sie eben nicht übertragbar sind – darin besteht die Erfahrung.'[30] [There is no primary experience one has or collects which is transferable, since it is the fundamental hallmark of experiences that they are not transferable – that is, in fact, the core of every experience.] Continuing his reflections on the transposition of personal experiences, he notes that, at that time, knowledge about the scale and extent of Hitler's extermination policies was uneven at best.

> Jeder wusste von etwas, aber niemand wusste alles über alles. Jeder wusste etwas von etwas, aber niemand wusste alles. Und die Folge ist, dass die damalige Erfahrungsstruktur der Generation, die um 1945 lebte, ganz segmentäre Erinnerungsweisen voraussetzte, die fragmentierte oder prismatisch gebrochene Räume herstellten, in denen sich völlig verschiedene Erfahrungen so oder so bündelten oder brachen, die mit dem Gesamtgeschehen, so wie wir es heute kennen, relativ wenig zu tun hatten.[31]

> [Everybody knew about something, but nobody knew everything about everything. Everybody knew something about something, but nobody knew everything. And as a result, the historical experience of the generation who lived around 1945 produced very segmented ways of remembering, resulting in fragmented or prismatically broken spaces in which completely disparate experiences were bundled or refracted in different ways that had relatively little to do with the totality of the historical event as we know it today.]

In *Der Junge mit den blutigen Schuhen*, this grey zone between knowing and not-knowing, the fact that 'everybody knew about something, but nobody knew everything about everything', is articulated as an increasing anxiety attributed to a diffuse collective subject: 'die Menschen' [people] or simply 'man' [one]. 'Menschen' are seeing things without, however, witnessing anything. 'Man war Parteigenosse, Wehrmachtsangehöriger, Dienstverpflichteter, kriegswichtig, kriegsverwendungsfähig, stand zur besonderen Verfügung, und in dieser Eigenschaft hatte man zu funktionieren. [...] Die Menschen verloren ihr Gedächtnis und warteten ergeben auf den Befehl des Führers'. (JBS, 86–87) [One was a member of the party, member of the *Wehrmacht*, conscript, important for the war, fit

30   Koselleck, 214.
31   Ibid.

for active service, ready for special deployment, and in this capacity had to function as such. [...] People lost their memory and waited devotedly for the command of the *Führer*]. The disappearance of Jewish citizens comes to light in an equally abstract manner; they belong to an unspecific collective of victims: 'people' disappear; it is not Jewish apartments that are suddenly vacated but simply apartments. While these observations, presented in a repetitive rhetoric that mimics the relentlessness of the events it recounts, indicate a vague awareness of anti-Semitic persecution, the text insists this knowledge did not lead to acts of overt resistance. Rather, in sync with the author's personal recollections, the disappearance of fellow citizens created a kind of covert solidarity between Germans and those targeted under Hitler.

In his lengthy interview with Volker Hage in 2000, Forte speaks about the primary experiences that shaped his novel and asserts that German citizens knew what was going on around them:

> Also zu sagen, wir haben es nicht gewußt, ist albern. Alle haben es gewußt, die ganze Stadt war voll mit diesen KZ-Gefangenen. Und in der Not, wenn die Bomben fielen, duckten wir uns in das gleiche Erdloch. Und wenn jemand was zu essen hatte, gab er dem anderen auch davon. Das habe ich erlebt. (AV, 52)

> [So to say that we didn't know it is ridiculous. Everybody knew, the whole city was full of concentration camp prisoners. And in cases of emergency, when the bombs dropped, we ducked into the same hole in the ground. And when somebody had something to eat, he also shared. I have experienced that.]

Thus, in the novel, the coexistence of regular citizens and concentration camp prisoners in one city indicates personal experiences not yet reframed by historical hindsight. The text briefly lingers on the fate of Düsseldorf's Jewish population and those mistreated as POWs; there is mention of concentration camps in the middle of the city and the boy describes the work performed by concentration camp inmates (JBS, 91, 165, 169, 173). However, these passages only serve to describe acts of solidarity between KZ [concentration camp] prisoners and the heroic local population. United in their suffering and deprivation, Germans and Jews are part of a community of victims: 'Keiner von ihnen [war] frei [...], weder die Fremden noch die Einheimischen, weder die Gefangenen noch die

Einwohner' (JBS, 130) [None of them was free [...], neither the strangers nor the locals, neither the prisoners nor the inhabitants]. Thus, while appearing to facilitate engagement with the Nazi past, both the emphasis of solidarity between Germans and Jewish concentration camp inmates, and the use of Holocaust tropes – the neighbourhood becomes a 'ghetto within the city' (JBS, 164) – provide a palliative screen for the damaging effects at the core of the Nazi project.

The novel's depictions of civic solidarity rests on the foundational contradiction central to 'Shoah-Kitsch': the use of phantasms that mitigate the impact of collective violence. Adorno has pointed out that in literature navigating the legacy of genocide, 'it becomes easier to continue to play along with the culture which gave birth to murder. There is one nearly invariable characteristic of such literature. It is that it implies, purposely or not, that even in the so-called extreme situations, indeed in them most of all, humanity flourishes.'[32] In the boy's 'Quartier', humanity continues to flourish, even under extreme duress, a narrative choreography which Eric Santner describes as 'narrative fetishism'. It is 'designed to expunge the traces of the trauma or loss that had called that narrative into being in the first place. [...] it is a strategy of undoing, in fantasy, the need for mourning by simulating a condition of intactness, typically by situating the site and origin of loss elsewhere.'[33] The boy's family and most citizens seem to retain their moral integrity, while Nazi perpetration – the original loss that called this narrative into being – remains obscured. Not surprisingly, this aspect appeals to readers who are eager to connect with their own or their family's wartime trauma but less interested in the reminder that German wartime suffering was self-inflicted.

Forte's representation of civility in times of unprecedented collective violence mirrors the exculpatory dynamics which reconfigure memories in the family album. As the work of social historians and psychologists has shown, when faced with violent chapters of history, family memory tends to 'correct' the record, in some cases hiding, and in some cases denying

---

32 Adorno, 9.

33 Eric Santner, 'History beyond the Pleasure Principle', in Saul Friedlaender, ed., *Probing the Limits of Representation* (Cambridge, MA: Harvard University Press, 1992), 144.

participation in or complicity with the regime. Based on interviews with 'Children of Nazi Germany', psychiatrist Michael Ermann observed that 'most families avoided openly dealing with anti-Semitism and persecution. But when describing what had really happened and what they remembered, there appeared contradictions which show deeper involvement and sometimes even collaboration.'[34] Similarly, in his work on transgenerational family communication, social historian Harald Welzer asserts that, although stories about Nazi perpetration within families were not necessarily supressed, they remain marginal and do not shape family lore across generations. His socio-psychological study *Opa war kein Nazi* [*Grandpa Wasn't a Nazi*] examines this tension and describes why, how and to what extent personal/familial memories and historical reality differ. Based on interviews with *Kriegskinder* and their descendants, the *Kriegsenkel*, his team surveyed the disconnect between the lexicon (historical facts) and the family album (personal memories).[35] In a 2004 interview, Welzer notes that the family album has great emotional depth but disregards factual reality. In other words, the desire to belong to a good (i.e. non-perpetrator) family easily outstrips the wish to see the objective horrors of their grandparents' participation in Nazi crimes captured in the lexicon. This comes to light in a telling survey from 2002: when asked about their family's involvement in National Socialism, 65 per cent of those who belonged to the upper classes thought highly of their parents, convinced that their family had suffered a lot during the war; 63 per cent remembered the Nazi period fondly as a time of 'tight community'; 26 per cent believed that their family had helped those persecuted during the Third Reich; 17 per cent were convinced that family members had consistently protested against injustice; 13 per cent believed that their family had been active in the resistance. By contrast, only 3 per cent of those interviewed believed that their family had held anti-Semitic views; 2 per cent were aware that their family had a positive view of National Socialism; and just 1 per cent acknowledged that their family

---

34   Ibid.
35   Harald Welzer, Sabine Moller and Karoline Tschugnall, eds, *Opa war kein Nazi. Nationalsozialismus und Holocaust im Familiengedächtnis* (Frankfurt a.M.: Fischer, 2015).

had participated in Nazi crimes.[36] Since 'acquisitions and applications of the past always follow the needs and demands of the present', stories about the family's involvement in acts of perpetration are not only ignored but corrected, in effect turning these family members into 'good Germans'.[37] Echoed in earlier wartime accounts, as well as in the more recent autobiographical *Kriegskinder* memories, such findings explain the enthusiastic reception of Forte's text and its appreciation as an authentic eyewitness document, which I noted at the beginning of this chapter. Based on the author's own supressed memories, what he calls 'das Verschwiegene' [the suppressed, the secrets within], the novel at once conceals and reveals what it represses, a cognitive disconnect that ironically contributes to the very silence about the Nazi past it purports to break.

Displacing Silence: A New Fiction of Memory

In a lengthy interview from 2000 about *Der Junge mit den blutigen Schuhen*, Forte underscores that the lines between reality and fiction are fluid. He leaves no doubt that he is 'the boy' who hears, sees and feels his way through cataclysmic experiences. At the same time he insists that this

---

36 Harald Welzer, 'Die Nachhaltigkeit historischer Erfahrungen. Eine sozial-psychologische Perspektive', in Hartmut Radebold, Werner Bohleber and Jürgen Zinnecker, eds, *Transgenerationale Weitergabe kriegsbelasteter Kindheiten. Interdisziplinäre Studien zur Nachhaltigkeit historischer Erfahrungen über vier Generationen* (Weinheim, Munich: Juventa 2002), 76. Samuel Salzborn quotes a more recent MEMO study from 2019 stating that 69.8 per cent of Germans who were asked about their family history did not believe that their ancestors were Nazi perpetrators; 35.9 per cent believed that family members had been victims during the Third Reich; and 28.7 per cent asserted that family members helped potential Nazi victims. *Kollektive Unschuld. Die Abwehr der Shoah im deutschen Erinnern* (Berlin: Hentrich & Hentrich, 2020), 20.

37 Harald Welzer, 'Re-narrations: How Pasts Change in Conversational Remembering', *Memory Studies* 3/1 (2010): 6–7.

autobiographical perspective, coloured by childhood trauma, is tempered
by the objectifying and objective distance of fifty years.

> Dadurch, dass ich 'der Junge' geschrieben habe, hatte ich den Jungen in seinen Ängsten
> in mir, sah durch seine Augen, was er sieht, und gleichzeitig war ich der zurückgesetzte,
> objektive Erzähler, der aus der heutigen Perspektive schreiben konnte, das ergibt
> einen Schwebezustand, man ist in der Person und erzählt doch von außen. [...]
> Es war wichtig für mich, dass ich das in eine Distanz rücken konnte. Das ist das
> Entscheidende. [...] Er ist es, der sich in seinen endlosen Tagen und Nächten die
> Welt ordnet. Ich bin nur das Kameraauge, das alles beobachtet. (AV, 45–46, 65)

> [By writing 'the boy', I had the boy with all his fears in me, saw what he sees through
> his eyes and at the same time I was the detached, objective narrator who could write
> from a present-day perspective; this amounts to a state of suspension – one is in the
> character and yet narrates from outside. [...] It was important for me to be able to
> distance myself. That is what is decisive. [...] It is the boy who, in his endless days
> and nights, sorts out the world. I am but the camera's eye that observes everything.]

In other words, 'the boy' is at once subject and object, focalizer and narrator of a story which, fifty years later, mediates traumatic memories.
As Mary Cosgrove notes, the author explains the belated creation of
his trilogy 'by invoking the model of traumatic repression to explain
the fifty-year incubation period between his childhood experiences and
their belated transformation into literary prose. [...] Forte emphasises
the moment of epiphany that accompanied the magical emergence of
crystal-clear memories'.[38] While this claim describes how the author may
have experienced the process of writing down his most painful childhood
memories, the idea of an 'objective' narrator who allegedly functions as a
mere 'camera eye' obfuscates the subjective nature of this intimately personal narrative by laying claim to both truth and impartiality. This stance
is in fact the blind spot of every aesthetic programme that invokes representational objectivity without questioning its own premises. Unable
to register aspects of history that escape personal experience yet are still
foundational to them – in this case the 'privilege' of being German and
not Jewish – Forte's narrative rests on equivocations and simplifications

---

38   Cosgrove, 171.

that inevitably structure personal memory.[39] *Der Junge mit den blutigen Schuhen* simulates what Paul Frosh calls a 'witnessing text', that is, a text that is the residue of the outcome of the act of speaking or writing about personal experiences and claims indexicality to the past based on the moral authority of the victim's voice, albeit transposed into fiction in this case.[40]

As the above quote makes clear, Forte's auctorial position is coloured by his childhood trauma; he is a silenced victim: 'Also schweigen. Das Schweigen der Opfer. Erdulden und ertragen' (AV, 71) [To remain silent. The silence of the victims. To suffer and endure]. Well aware that he is struggling with collectively suppressed memories, the author fails to see how they manifest as a text which reinforces the very gap it seeks to close. When reminded by the interviewer that in this case the silence of German civilians about their own suffering was well justified, not only in light of state-sanctioned genocide supported by many, but also in light of other acts of sustained aggression that resulted in the air war, Forte deflects:

> Und nun zur Schuld dieses Volkes: Das eine ist ja ohne das andere nicht zu denken. Wir haben ein großes Unrecht getan, und es brach darüber ein Krieg aus. [...] Wenn ich Vergeltung beschreibe, dann ist die Ursache ja gegeben. Man muss nicht auch noch sagen: 'Es gab da Auschwitz.' Das setze ich doch voraus, das ist doch selbstverständlich. Die Bomben fielen ja, weil es Auschwitz gab. (AV, 67)

> [Turning now to the guilt of this nation: The one thing simply cannot exist without the other. We committed a great injustice, and a war broke out because of it. [...] When I describe retribution, then the cause is, of course, obvious. It is unnecessary

---

39 Not surprisingly, Sabine Bode appreciates the novel as an apt expression for re-pressed war experiences. She fails to differentiate between representational regis-ters of literature and raw eyewitness interviews when she refers to *Der Junge mit den blutigen Schuhen* as an exemplary autobiographical trauma narrative. *Die vergessene Generation* (Munich, Zurich: Piper, 2010), 209–10. This is no accidental confusion but indicates that Forte's fiction of memory can easily be mistaken for an autobio-graphical *Kriegskind* testimony.

40 Paul Frosh, 'Telling Presences: Witnesses, Mass Media, and the Imagined Lives of Strangers', in Paul Frosh and Amit Pinchevski, eds, *Media Witnessing: Testimony in the Age of Mass Communication* (Houndmills, Basingstoke: Palgrave Macmillan, 2009), 60.

to add: 'Don't forget Auschwitz.' I take that for granted, that is self-evident. Bombs
fell, of course, because Auschwitz existed.]

The author's claim that his text is intrinsically premised on 'Auschwitz'
rings hollow. By 2000, Forte would have been aware that the cause of
Auschwitz was no longer of interest to the younger generations of
Germans. His curt acknowledgement of Germany's foundational accountability for the (air) war belies the reality of a histotainment culture
centred on mythologies that proclaim the opposite, that is, German victimhood and innocence. Unwittingly, then, Forte's novel reveals a different kind of taboo, a 'second guilt', to use Ralph Giordano's term. Based
on the tension between a forgetting of and an obsession with, the novel
reveals that at its core the 'Geschichtsversessenheit' [historical obsession]
of the 1990s rests on a tenacious 'Geschichtsvergessenheit' [historical for-
getting].[41] This tension continues to animate what Dan Diner and Omar
Bartov have described as the 'negative symbiosis' between Germans and
Jews, discussed above: a latent presence of the Nazi past that edits out
the core of Auschwitz and effectively silences Hitler's victims once again.

> Die bedrohliche Präsenz der Juden im kollektiven Bewusstsein in Deutschland nach
> Auschwitz treibt paradoxe Formen des Umgangs mit 'der Vergangenheit' heraus,
> etwa das Phänomen der Deckerinnerung. Mit Deckerinnerungen ist jene Art des
> Umgangs mit der Vergangenheit gemeint, eine neue Geschichtsbeflissenheit, die
> sich den Ereignissen von 1933–1945 zwar nähert, dabei aber gleichsam den Kern
> des eigenen Unbehagens ausspart, d.h. weitere Opfer des NS in den Vordergrund
> rückt, um die dennoch empfundene Besonderheit des Judenmordes zu umgehen.[42]

> [The threatening presence of the Jews in Germany's collective consciousness after
> Auschwitz results in paradoxical ways of dealing with 'the past', for example the
> phenomenon of screen memory. By screen memories, we mean a way of dealing

---

41   This tension within German cultural memory is examined in great detail by Aleida
     Assmann and Ute Frevert in their study with the same title, *Geschichtsvergessenheit.*
     Geschichtsversessenheit: Vom Umgang mit deutschen Vergangenheiten nach 1945
     (Stuttgart: DVA, 1999).
42   Dan Diner, 'Negative Symbiose, Deutsche und Juden nach Auschwitz', in *Ist der*
     Nationalsozialismus Geschichte? Zu Historisierung und Historikerstreit (Frankfurt
     a.M.: Fischer, 1987), 191–92.

with the past whereby a renewed and pointed consideration of history examines the events of 1933–1945 more closely, but in doing so omits the cornerstone of one's own unease. That is, it edges other victims of the NS [National Socialism] into the foreground in order to circumvent the singularity of the Jewish genocide, which is nevertheless sensed.]

As my reading has shown, the novel's child focalizer provides an ideal foil for giving voice to screen memories: while registering history in seemingly authentic detail, this witness persistently omits 'den Kern des eigenen Unbehagens' [the cornerstone of one's own unease] that plagues the adult looking back on his childhood.

Usable War Stories Redux

In conclusion, in order to delineate the novel's heuristic significance for the case studies that follow, I want to return to the insights gained in the previous chapter about abiding victimologies which similarly bracket that which they purport to describe. Early historical accounts of the air war, while straining to be objective representations of historical facts, also cast Germans as double victims under attack by both their government and the Allied Forces. Take, for instance, the account of civil-defence specialist Hans Rumpf from 1961, *Das war der Bombenkrieg* [*The Bombing of Germany*]. The author carefully parses details of the bombing war, yet egregiously fails to even once mention its historical cause. Instead, German civilians feature as 'survivors' whose 'profound physical and moral exhaustion left behind by three and a half terrible years of mass bombing' makes it impossible to discuss 'this most tremendous of all mass acts of destruction [...] without anger and indignation.'[43] His account culminates in the assertion that the German people were indeed 'double victims': 'The blind savagery of the last few months of the war could mean nothing but a systematic attempt to wipe them [the Germans, S.B.] out altogether. *Both the enemy leadership and their own* had condemned them

---

43   Hans Rumpf, *The Bombing of Germany*, Edward Fitzgerald, trans. (New York, Holt, Rinehardt and Winston, 1962), 12.

to the same fate.'[44] As victims of Nazi propaganda, at the end of the war, they are finally beginning to realize 'how brutally they had been deceived, and how [...] their ideals and their virtues were still cynically exploited by clever propaganda'.[45] According to the translator, this book 'deplores unnecessary destruction of life and property [...] as dispassionately as his experience and training will allow'.[46] Ostensibly written 'neither in anger nor indignation', Rumpf does not consider the larger context of the bombing war because he considers this to be 'an old story without interest for people today'.[47] What we get, however, is what Salzborn and others have identified as 'Schuldumkehr', the reversal of victims and perpetrators, that is, a palatable distortion of historical causality.

As discussed in the previous chapter, four decades later, the *Kriegskind* narrative builds on such projections of innocent suffering, albeit in a more nuanced way that begins to take into account the initial enthusiasm for Hitler's project. In her evaluation of letters written by children to their fathers at the Russian Front, Gudrun Brockhaus notes that German children celebrated the war as a patriotic adventure and remained enthusiastic even in later years, despite experiences of bombing, death and evacuations.[48] Similarly, Margarete Dörr documents that German children enjoyed the war as an adventure to be traced on maps or to be followed by listening to the radio.[49] Only when the bombing of German cities became an omnipresent threat, totally overshadowing the lifespan of children born after 1933, did this enthusiasm turn to desperation. Eyewitnesses expressed intense feelings of fear and traumatization – sentiments mirrored in Forte's fictional account. Time and again, members of the *Kriegskinder* cohort assert they will never forget the sound of the sirens and remain traumatized by this sound to this day. One witness writes, 'Beim ersten Sirenenton bekam

---

44   Rumpf, 205–6 (my emphasis).
45   Rumpf, 199.
46   Rumpf, unpaginated 'Publisher's Note'.
47   Rumpf, 9.
48   Gudrun Brockhaus, 'Kontroversen um die "Kriegskindheit"', *Forum Psychoanalyse* 26 (2010): 318.
49   Margarete Dörr, *Der Krieg hat uns geprägt. Wie Kinder den Zweiten Weltkrieg erlebten,* I (Frankfurt a.M.: Campus, 2007), 26–46.

ich schon Magenschmerzen, so dass ich oft am nächsten Tag nicht zur Schule gehen konnte. Die Magenschmerzen begleiten mich noch heute.'[50] [When the sirens started up, my stomach became upset so that I could not go to school the next day. To this day I suffer from a stomach disorder.] Another witness notes, 'Nie war man sicher, ob man nicht durch eine Sprengbombe zerfetzt werden würde oder im Keller verschüttet und nicht gefunden würde. Ich saß dann grundsätzlich zähneklappernd im Keller, dem Geschehen hilflos ausgeliefert.'[51] [You were never sure if a bomb would tear you to pieces, or if you would be buried in the cellar, never to be found. I always sat in the cellar, teeth chattering, feeling helplessly exposed.]

While both Brockhaus and Dörr document the *Kriegskinder*'s evolving attitudes from enthusiasm to anxiety and terror, most publications about war childhoods are focused on the last phase of the war. In popular eyewitness accounts (such as Bode's and Lorenz's), historical gradations are lost, transposed into one coherent story of suffering – a hallmark of mediated remembering. As Jones has argued, mediated remembering communities address questions of veracity and trustworthiness by creating a sense of intrinsic authenticity through staging and performing a seemingly intimate dialogue and uncontested consensus about a particular historical moment. In contrast to any individual witness whose testimony may or may not be considered to be significant for a broader understanding of history, 'the mediation of witness voices alongside each other and as if they were in communication with one another, each confirming the account of the other, thus lends authority to the broader relevance of their account of the past'.[52] In this case, *Kriegskind* anthologies present German children as a collective subject, traumatized victims of a war they did not understand – all but dissolving distinctions between the psychological, the political and the ethical dimensions of memory. Klaus Latzel summarizes the troubling core of such accounts.

> Die Psychologisierung über den Traumabegriff ermöglicht zugleich, was lange bei der ehedem beliebten Pathosformel 'Den Opfern von Krieg und Gewaltherrschaft'

---

50   Dörr, 108.
51   Dörr, 114.
52   Jones, 39.

unterlegt war: die deutsche Teilhabe an einem nivellierenden Opferbegriff, der
auf psychologischer Ebene oder hinsichtlich der je eigenen, unhintergehbaren
'Primärerfahrung' des Leidens kaum kritisierbar, in gedenkpolitischer Hinsicht
aber schlichtweg verlogen ist.[53]

[The use of psychological paradigms, in particular the notion of trauma, integrates
what was heretofore expressed in commemorative adages such as 'In Memoriam of
the Victims of War and Terror': German participation in a general victimology. This
can hardly be criticized on the level of psychology or 'primary experience', but it is
simply false with respect to the politics of collective memory.]

In short, Forte's fiction of memory not only draws on the earlier 'war
story', which in the 1950s and 1960s was focused on German victimhood
at the expense of those victimized by Hitler, but also amplifies popular
Kriegskinder accounts of unresolved trauma.

In sum, although dissimilar with respect to their representational
registers, Forte's novel, Rumpf's historical account, as well as *Kriegskind*
testimonies converge in their focus on the last war years, omitting the
collective excitement which Hitler's war project generated, underscoring
instead the suffering of German civilians, once again displacing Jewish
victims.[54] What, then, are the possibilities and limitations of 'writing the
child' as evident in this particular case? *Der Junge mit den blutigen Schuhen*
is what I would call an 'open text'. It allows readers to immerse themselves
in moments of everyday history, contingent but nonetheless consequential
moments not captured in history books. Forte's unflinching, insightful

---

53   Klaus Latzel, 'Kriegskinder, Kriegsopfer und kriegskompetente Mädchen', in
     Hans-Heino Ewers, ed., *Erinnerungen an Kriegskindheiten. Erfahrungsräume,
     Erinnerungskultur und Geschichtspolitik unter sozial- und kulturwissenschaftlicher
     Perspektive* (Weinheim: Juventa, 2006), 208.
54   More current publications on local histories under the Third Reich continue to
     tell the story of German suffering. Bill Niven mentions the Wartberg series which
     focuses 'centrally on the terrible impact of the bombing of German urban commu-
     nities. Again, these communities are portrayed as innocent collectives untouched
     by Nazism – composed not of Nazis or fellow-travellers, but simply of "ordinary
     citizens". Such portrayals denazify the Nazi people's community.' Bill Niven,
     'Introduction: German Victimhood at the Turn of the Millennium', in *Germans as
     Victims* (Basingstoke, New York: Palgrave Macmillan, 2006), 13.

and, most importantly, innocent eyewitness offers exculpatory reading pleasures: identification with 'the felt victim' through the seduction of traumatic complicity. On the other hand, the novel is also what I would describe as a 'closed text'. It relies on a child focalizer to recall a perpetrator legacy without regard for the ethical imperatives firmly in place half a century later. Although the novel acknowledges Hitler's designated victims, it does so through troubling equivocations; it cannot recognize what Arendt calls 'this vicarious responsibility for things we have not done, this taking upon ourselves the consequences for things we are entirely innocent of'.[55] Mirroring the 'negative symbiosis' between Germans and Jews, it relies on a traumatized child eyewitness to tell the story of National Socialism and thus contributes to the pacification of the Holocaust in German cultural memory. It is in this sense, then, that the Shoah remains 'das Verschwiegene, vor sich selbst Verheimlichte' [the unsaid, the secrets kept within]. Hence, to go back to the telescoping of time that shapes this cultural moment, instead of becoming closer, the fate of Hitler's victims is receding further into the past, even or precisely because German wartime suffering has become ever more present. The psychological and political dynamics behind this displacement come into sharp view in Günter Grass's novel *Die Blechtrommel*, examined in the next chapter. In contrast to Forte's novel, *Die Blechtrommel* not only delineates but also makes productive the gap between postwar strategies of collective obfuscation and personal denial, claims of knowing and not-knowing, the theatre of disavowal and confession. Like Forte, Grass draws on autobiographical experiences but, in striking contrast to Forte, his fictional recall of the Nazi past provocatively asserts, exhibits and examines the naturalizing manipulations of any memory text, probing the power of 'writing the child'.

---

55   Hannah Arendt, 'Collective Responsibility', in Jerome Kohn, ed., *Responsibility and Judgment* (New York: Schoken, 2003), 157–58.

CHAPTER 3

Performing Childhood: Günter Grass's *Die Blechtrommel*

Published three decades apart and written by authors who experienced the Second World War as children or adolescents, *Die Blechtrommel*[1] and *Der Junge mit den blutigen Schuhen* both belong to memory trilogies[2] which reckon with its lasting effects. Although written from similar generational vantage points, they differ sharply with respect to how they 'write the child'. While the experiential mode of Forte's novel relies on the naturalized perspective of a child witness who claims historical veracity, the auctorial reflexivity of the childlike witness in *Die Blechtrommel* is premised on the untrustworthiness of its narrator and thus implicitly contests the veracity of any literary recall of the past. While Forte's text elides the gap between an experiencing 'I' and a narrating 'I', *Die Blechtrommel* foregrounds this gap time and again, drawing attention to the difference between narrated time and narrating time. While Forte's text is centred on a child witness who invites identification with a community of suffering, Grass's text critiques a self-serving performance of remorse. While

---

[1] The works of Günter Grass are cited from the *Werkausgabe in zehn Bänden* edited by Volker Neuhaus (Darmstadt und Neuwied: Luchterhand, 1987). BT: *Die Blechtrommel*, 2; JB: 'Jungbürgerrede. Über Erwachsene und Verwachsene', in *Günter Grass Essays*, 9, 429–39; RB: 'Rückblick auf die Blechtrommel – oder Der Autor als fragwürdiger Zeuge – Ein Versuch in eigener Sache', ibid, 624–33; STG: 'Sisyphos und der Traum vom Gelingen', ibid, 323–41; HZ: *Beim Häuten der Zwiebel* (Göttingen: Steidel, 2006); TD: *The Tin Drum*, Ralph Mannheim, trans. (London: Vintage Books, 1998); and PO: *Peeling the Onion*, Michael Henry Heim, trans. (Orlando, Austin: Harcourt, 2007).

[2] *Die Blechtrommel* is the first part of the *Danzig Trilogy*, the novella *Katz und Maus* [*Cat and Mouse*] followed in 1961, and *Hundejahre* [*Dog Years*] was published in 1963.

Forte's text testifies to a continuing sense of trauma, Grass's text contends first and foremost with a collective culture of denial and obfuscation. While Forte's text is centred on a stance of knowing innocence, Grass's text is centred on a stance of faux-innocence.

In the following, I examine *Die Blechtrommel* as one of the first and possibly most influential examples of German postwar literature to address and complicate the figure of the historical eyewitness to National Socialism and its legacy. Oskar Matzerath, the protagonist and focalizer of *Die Blechtrommel* (1959) may be one of the most provocative protagonists of postwar West German literature. Equipped with a drum and a glass-shattering voice, he critiques the denials and hypocrisies of the postwar years through a performance of childhood exceptionalism. Having decided to stop growing at the age of three – to remain a 'Gnom', 'Däumling', and 'nichtaufzustockende[r] Dreikäsehoch' (BT, 64) ['a pigmy', 'Lilliputian', and 'midget' (TD, 46)] – he drums, lies, argues and screams his way through the recounting of his life, framed by Hitler's rise and demise. The novel stages 'childlikeness' as an epistemological tool with which to expose Adenauer's politics of rehabilitation which, as I have described in Chapter 1, rested on usable war stories that focused on German suffering yet remained largely silent about acts of German perpetration. Grass's novel represents one of the early postwar fictions of memory to explicitly draw attention to the mnemonic dynamics of *Nachträglichkeit* [afterwardsness] characteristic of any aesthetic recall of history. Drawing on a witness who poses as a child and skilfully mimics the innocence of an impassive bystander (to the rise and fall of the Third Reich), the text speaks from the perspective of the 1950s. It unfolds across the span of five decades, from 1899 to 1954, and deftly comments on the postwar climate of the Federal Republic of Germany, described in the author's autobiography *Beim Häuten der Zwiebel* (2006) as 'die sich christlich gebende Heuchelei, die Kehrreime lügenhafter Unschuldsbeteuerungen und der zur Schau getragene Biedersinn einer verkappten Verbrecherbande' (HZ, 341) [hypocrisy disguised as Christianity, the mendacious claims of innocence, the effusive philistinism of a band of wolves in sheep's clothing (PO, 303)].

Grass may be the most internationally known German author. Born in 1927 in the Free City of Danzig (now the Polish city of Gdansk), he was a novelist, playwright, illustrator, graphic artist and stone mason. A lifelong member of the Social Democrats, Germany's liberal party, he became a critical and engaged observer and commentator of politics and society. Like most German males of his generation, he was drafted into Hitler's army in 1944 as a *Flakhelfer* (adolescents, born between 1926 and 1929, conscripted as Air Force youth auxiliary during the last years of the war). But unlike many, out of juvenile veneration for the Waffen-SS, Grass signed up for Hitler's elite troop, notorious for its ruthlessness. In his autobiography he explains his 17-year-old self with a rhetoric of deflection that shapes the author's late text as a whole: 'Eher werde ich die Waffen-SS als Eliteeinheit gesehen haben [...]. Dem Jungen, der sich als Mann sah, wird vor allem die Waffengattung wichtig gewesen sein' (HZ, 126) [I more likely viewed the Waffen-SS as an elite unit [...]. The boy, who saw himself as a man, was probably more concerned with the branch of service (PO, 110)]. Yet, his belated confession about his SS membership in 2006 was met with public outrage and damaged the author's reputation significantly, his 1999 Nobel Prize in Literature notwithstanding. Nonetheless, *Die Blechtrommel* remains one of his best-known works, centred like many subsequent texts on memories about the author's childhood in Danzig that was coloured by the rise and fall of National Socialism. Like other German postwar texts, this novel rehearses the aesthetic codes of retrospection, the gap between primary experiences and their subsequent recall (discussed in the previous chapter and expanded below). Harnessing the full force of poetic recall, the text reveals how the cultural memory of the FRG, not unlike the memory of an individual, rests on omissions, revisions and displacements of unpalatable parts.

In this chapter I show what underlines the productive force of memory inscribed by the kind of autobiographical grammar first examined by Sigmund Freud as displacement. In *Studies in Hysteria*, one of his first case studies from 1885, Freud explored how early childhood experiences readily find expression as neurotic symptoms in the adult. His poignant phrasing that 'hysterics suffer for the most part from reminiscences' posits that the adult self maintains a constant if uneven dialogue with his or her childhood self, a dialogue that continues to unfold in unpredictable ways during the course of our lives.[3] If primary experiences were unable to find a way into language because they were too problematic or traumatic, they express belatedly in the form of verbal slips or become displaced onto the language of bodily symptoms. Freud goes even further to claim that the adult retrospectively creates a childhood self by relying on screen memories put in place to guard memories deemed too 'objectionable' to be expressed as primary experiences. He termed this complex tension between past and present *Nachträglichkeit* (originally translated as 'deferred action', later revised to 'après-coup' or 'afterwardsness') in order to mark the dynamic and bilateral interchange between the adult and his childhood self. His central question is whether we even have childhood memories or only just memories *about* our childhood that find articulation in self-referential narratives based on displacements which, driven by unresolved questions that concern the present, reach back in time for answers. In Grass's novel, the tension between a childlike focalizer and the multitude of narrative voices that frame him makes legible intersections and continuities, as well as discontinuities between different temporal layers, in this case the present of the 1950s (*Erzählzeit*, what Genette terms 'narration') and the rise and fall of the Third Reich (*erzählte Zeit*, what Genette terms 'story'). Oskar Matzerath's protestations, denials and admissions reveal the haunting of the present by a past that emerges in seemingly disconnected memory fragments in the way of a palimpsest.[4] Originally, the palimpsest referred to an ancient writing surface that was repeatedly scraped clean to be used again. While devised to use limited resources efficiently, this process of 'overwriting' produced insights into the script of a present unwittingly complemented by past inscriptions. As this chapter shows, the voice of Grass's childlike witness recalls the Nazi past from the vantage point of the Adenauer era in the seamless sense described by Max Silverman.

3   Quoted in Rachel Bowlby, 'Introduction: Never Done, Never to Return', *Studies in Hysteria* by Sigmund Freud, Nicola Luckhurst, trans. (London: Penguin Classic, 2004), vii.

4   Freud first described memory along these lines in 'Notes on the Mystic Writing Pad' (1925).

First, the present is shadowed or haunted by a past which is not immediately visible but is progressively brought into view. The relationship between present and past therefore takes the form of superimposition and interaction of different temporal traces to constitute a sort of composite structure, like a palimpsest, so that one layer of traces can be seen through, and is transformed by, another. Second, the composite structure [...] is a combination of not simply two moments in time (past and present) but a number of different moments, hence producing a chain of signification which draws together disparate spaces and times. [...] the two are shown to be profoundly connected, so that one might have thought two distinct moments in time and space are recomposed to create a different spatio-temporal configuration.[5]

Grass's fiction of memory draws together different moments in time and space to form what Silverman calls 'unstable correspondences by means of similarity and difference', in this case of a particular mentality that provided an opening for National Socialism and lingers on.[6] Due to the limited focus of this book, I cannot address the novel as a whole, nor the prolific scholarship it produced. Given my focus on 'writing the child' as a historical witness in the wake of National Socialism, I focus predominantly on the first part of the novel, that is, the narrative staging of Oskar Matzerath as a complex yet flawed *Kunstfigur* of memory. The second part of this chapter complements this analysis in dialogue with the author's autobiography *Beim Häuten der Zwiebel* in order to show how this *Kunstfigur* propagates screen memories that cloud a personal sense of complicity, both on the character as well as on the autobiographical level.[7] In conclusion, I further explore this mnemonic blind spot in light of Grass's neologism 'Verwachsnige' [stunted adults], a term the

---

5   Maxim Silverman, *Palimpsestic Memory: The Holocaust and Colonialism in French and Francophone Fiction and Film* (New York, Oxford: Berghahn Books, 2013), 3.

6   Silverman, 24.

7   In his book-length study, *Günter Grass and the Gender of German Memory: From the Tin Drum to Peeling the Onion* (Rochester, NY: Camden House, 2021) Timothy B. Malchow examines adjacent, if not similar questions through the lens of gender. In Chapters 2 and 3, he parses the memory work of *The Tin Drum* in intimate dialogue with the authors' biography and in light of contemporary mnemonic frameworks as inflected by the masculinity of the authorial perspective. Since it was published after completion of this manuscript, I could not engage in more depth with this incisive study.

author used in a speech from 1970 to critique an exculpatory attitude of infantilism in both the war and the first postwar generation.

Framing Oskar, Reframing the Witness

Premised on the strategy of 'plausible deniability', *Die Blechtrommel* is a fiction of memory that questions simplifying binaries by way of a muscular and overdetermined prose; it fuses facts and fiction, truths and lies, authenticity and falsehoods, innocence and guilt and gleefully obfuscates differences between perpetrators and victims, witnesses and bystanders.[8] Famously, the first sentence of the lengthy text addresses the reader with a confession of unreliability. Oskar admits that he resides in a mental hospital and is under constant surveillance by the institutional authorities: 'Zugegeben, ich bin Insasse einer Heil- und Pflegeanstalt, mein Pfleger beobachtet mich, lässt mich kaum aus dem Auge.' (BT, 1) [Granted: I am the inmate of a mental hospital, my keeper is watching me, he scarcely lets me out of his sight. (TD, 1)] This opening sentence is programmatic. It underscores how the narrative unfolds as a dialogue between a focalizer (Oskar), who fluidly fuses or contrasts with various narrating instances, and an imagined audience (represented by his keeper). The mute presence of the listeners, that is, the reading public, covertly structures Oskar's story. Mediated by a focalizer who revels in self-incriminations, the text accentuates the interdependence of different temporal layers, expressed as a choreography of confessional hypocrisy performed by Oskar and his imagined audience alike.

---

8   In many ways, *Die Blechtrommel* anticipates the increasingly complex navigation of Germany's past in literature written by the 'third generation'. For more on this see Friedericke Eigler, *Gedächtnis und Geschichte in Generationenromanen seit der Wende* (Berlin: Erich Schmidt, 2005), as well as Anne Fuchs, *Phantoms of War in Contemporary German Literature, Films, and Discourse: The Politics of Memory* (Houndmills, Basingstoke: Palgrave Macmillan, 2008).

Oskar presents improbable stories. The novel is centred on a homodiegetic staging which repeatedly draws attention to tensions and continuities between the Nazi past and the postwar present. In that sense it presents the opposite of Forte's fiction of memory that naturalizes the process of remembering. According to Neumann's mnemonic taxonomy, self-reflexive memory texts of this kind offer a narrative in which

> the context and the motivation underlying the present act of autobiographical re-telling are highly salient and distinct. In this instance of homodiegetic narration, the focus is shifted from the diegetic to the extradiegetic level of the retelling. Accordingly, the narrative focus often alternates between simple chronological succession of the frame narrative and the multi-temporal levels of embedded memory streams [...] self-reflexively depicting memories as intertwined with the context in which they are recalled.[9]

Conceived as both a perceptive eyewitness and a dislocated critic of postwar discourses, Oskar is a *Kunstfigur* of memory who navigates both the diegetic and extradiegetic – the narrating time of the 1950s and the narrated time of the Third Reich. His confinement in a mental institution, that is, a space of social remove, indicates that this memorial perspective is shaped by rupture and social isolation. Oskar does not recall or recover the past as a coherent story; rather he presents discontinuous, episodic memories that, as noted above, do not progress in linear fashion. His narration seems to be guided by an insight which Grass articulates in his autobiography, 'Danach ist immer davor. Was wir Gegenwart nennen, dieses flüchtige Jetztjetztjetzt, wird stets von einem vergangen Jetzt beschattet, so dass auch der Fluchtweg nach vorn, nur auf Bleisohlen zu erlaufen ist.' (HZ, 164) [After is always before. What we call the present, this fleeting nownownow, is constantly overshadowed by a past now so that the escape route known as the future can only be marched toward in lead-soled shoes. (PO, 144)] Inevitably, every present moment is surrepti-tiously inscribed by a past and weighs down any path into the future. The text portrays the miraculous conception of Oskar's mother at the turn of

9 Birgit Neumann, 'The Literary Representation of Memory', in Astrid Erll and Ansgar Nünning, eds, *A Companion to Cultural Memory Studies* (Berlin, New York: De Gruyter, 2010), 337.

the twentieth century, followed by Oskar's birth in 1924, his improbable resolution to stop growing past the age of three, his youth and adolescence, and finally his incarceration as a young man. Although not obvious to those around him, his adulthood begins with the death of his parents and, most importantly, the historical 'before', that is, the rise and fall of the Third Reich. The 'after' begins after the end of the war, culminating in the narrative present of 1952–54. Who, then, is this unreliable focalizer and what kind of truths does he have to offer? What animates the self-reflexive dialogue with his various 'keepers', who are at once narrative instances and figures of reception standing in for the contemporary public at large, as well as all readers?

As mentioned above, Oskar Matzerath is not a child but a childlike *Kunstfigur*, a fantastical and improbable witness who occupies a liminal and unstable space between child and adult. While he looks like a 3-year-old, he is an adult from birth, equipped with the intellectual faculties and sexual desires of an adult. With satirical reference to two foundational texts, the *Book of Genesis* and Goethe's *Dichtung und Wahrheit* [*From my Life: Poetry and Truth*] (1833),[10] the third chapter explains the inexplicable, a baby born as an adult: 'Damit es sogleich gesagt sei: Ich gehöre zu den hellhörigen Säuglingen, deren geistige Entwicklung schon bei der Geburt abgeschlossen ist und sich fortan nur noch bestätigen muß.' (BT, 46) [I might as well come right out with it, I was one of those clair-audient infants whose mental development is completed and after that merely needs a certain amount of filling in. (TD, 33)] Oskar refutes the teleological and totalizing gesture of the *Bildungsroman*. Instead, he claims an autonomous space carved out of a defiant 'refusal to be identified, appropriated and socialized'.[11]

10   This is a satirical reference to Genesis 1–3: 'the words of the bible, "Let there be light and there was light", still strike [Oskar] as an excellent publicity slogan for Osram light bulbs' (TD, 32). Evoking Goethe's autobiographical text *From My Life: Poetry and Truth*, which opens with a description of the astrological constellation of the author's birth, Oskar's birth is described as determined by a particular astrological constellation (TD, 34).

11   Robert Craig, '"Ist die Schwarze Köchin da? Jajaja...". Mimesis and Günter Grass's *Die Blechtrommel*', *Monatshefte* 108/1 (Spring 2016): 104.

[I]ch blieb der Dreijährige, der Gnom, der Däumling, der nicht aufzustockende Dreikäsehoch blieb ich, um Unterscheidungen wie kleiner und großer Katechismus enthoben zu sein [...] Um nicht mit einer Kasse klappern zu müssen, hielt ich mich an die Trommel und wuchs seit meinem dritten Geburtstag keinen Fingerbreit mehr, blieb der Dreijährige, aber auch der Dreimalkluge, den die Erwachsenen alle überragten, der den Erwachsenen so überlegen sein sollte, der seinen Schatten nicht mit ihrem Schatten messen wollte. (BT, 64)

[I remained the three-year-old, the gnome, the Tom Thumb, the pigmy, the Lilliputian, the midget, whom no one could persuade to grow. I did so in order to be exempted from the big and little catechism. To avoid playing the cash register I clung to my drum and from my third birthday on, refused to grow by so much as a finger's breadth. I remained the three-year-old, towered over by grownups but superior to all grownups, who refused to measure his shadow with theirs. (TD, 46)]

Based on resistance to the status quo, Oskar's subject position is paradoxical. The limitations of his stature confine him to the realm of bystander – he is easily overlooked. Although neither an innocent, let alone a guileless child, but to the contrary a cruel, opportunistic and cunning adult, he is often the target of cruelty by other children. Both victim and victimizer, Oskar flaunts the picaresque position of marginality wedded to a fantastic intellectual superiority that affords him an elevated position of insight from which to refute the social contract, in particular, the petit-bourgeois conventions he is born into.

He uses his drum and the unusual force of his voice in protest against social conventions and shortcomings: 'Ich spielte nie, ich arbeitete auf meiner Trommel.' (BT, 69) [I never played, I worked on my drum. (TD, 50)]. The use of the drum is never child's play, nor is it triggered simply by 'kindliche Zerstörungswut' (BT, 69) [a childlike passion for destruction (TD, 50)]. Rather, his drumming performs a counter-narrative, a social critique that disavows all ideologies yet ultimately, like Forte's boy, cannot acknowledge its own implication (a position I expand upon in the last part of this chapter).

Ich trommelte nicht nur gegen braune Versammlungen. Oskar saß den Roten und den Schwarzen, den Pfadfindern und Spinathemden von der PX, den Zeugen Jehowas und dem Kyffhäuserbund, den Vegetariern und den Jungpolen von der

Ozonbewegung unter der Tribüne. Was sie auch zu singen und zu blasen hatten, meine Trommel wusste es besser. Mein Werk war also ein zerstörerisches. (BT, 146)

[For it was not only demonstrations of a brown hue that I attacked with my drumming. Oskar huddled under the rostrum for Reds and Blacks, for Boy Scouts and Spinach Shirts, for Jehovah's Witnesses, the Kyffhäuser Bund, the Vegetarians, and the Young Polish Fresh Air Movement. Whatever they might have to sing, trumpet or proclaim, my drum knew better. Yes, my work was destructive. (TD, 110)]

While Oskar's drumming seeks to expose the blind spots of all ideologies, here it explicitly targets a myth popular in the 1950s: the figure of the resistance fighter. Satirizing the stance of overt political and covert aesthetic opposition to the Nazi regime, Oskar uses the term *resistance* only sarcastically: 'Das Wort ist reichlich in Mode gekommen. Vom Geist des Widerstands spricht man. Man soll den Widerstand sogar verinnerlichen können. Das nennt man dann: Innere Emigration.' (BT, 145) [That word resistance has become very fashionable. We hear of the spirit of resistance, of resistance circles. There is even talk of an inward resistance. (TD, 109)] Yet, although he critiques the German intelligentsia who silently resisted National Socialism, Oskar himself belongs to this cohort. In 1943, he joins Bebra's 'Fronttheater' [Theatre at the Front], a group of artists covertly dedicated to resistance but making their living by entertaining Hitler's soldiers.[12]

Both the work of Oskar's drum and his glass-shattering voice create a non-linear narrative that refers to key historical events only obliquely from the vantage point of an aesthetic space in which chronology and sequential causality are suspended and, as suggested earlier, lines between perpetrators, bystanders, victims and resistance fighters are blurred. The novel's narrative framework and its story are at once shaped, destabilized and undermined by questions of devious spectatorship, passive complicity, active subversion and enduring victimhood. Thus, the text provocatively exposes postwar narratives about historical innocence, exoneration, accountability and victimhood, which Grass later describes as the political

12   Oskar's implication as knowing witness and bystander is made explicit in the chapter 'Beton besichtigen – oder mystisch barbarisch gelangweilt' ['Inspections of Concrete or Barbaric, Mystical, Bored'].

hypocrisy of the Adenauer era: the disguise of piousness framed by end-lessly repetitive and mendacious claims of innocence (HZ, 341; PO, 303). More specifically, *Die Blechtrommel* exposes the insincerity of self-styled 'survivors of the Third Reich' who, as historian Wulf Kantsteiner notes, saw their experiences in a very different conceptual framework than the one we use today.

> The former Nazis and bystanders might have had a general understanding of the crimes of the regime, but they focused primarily on their own suffering. All victims with whom they did not identify, including the six million European Jews, disappeared behind a mountain of fallen German soldiers and civilians. For these 'survivors', the task of finding acceptable ways of expressing and alleviating their misery became the basis of their new identity.[13]

Kantsteiner's observations echo Robert G. Moeller's findings about West German victimologies, which in the 1950s served to build up a new sense of national identity and refute international accusation of collective guilt by projecting a story in which all Germans feature as victims of a war their tyr-annical leader had started but everyone lost.[14] Oskar's 'work' on the drum both mimics and confronts the defensive and evasive politics advanced under Adenauer, in particular his strategies of *Wiedergutmachung* [restitu-tion] which were accompanied by the rehabilitation of Nazi perpetrators and rested on a widespread silence about personal and collective responsi-bility for Nazi crimes.

How, then, does the novel's narrative framework stage the heuristic force of a character who is born as an adult but masquerades as a child and looks back to the Nazi past from the vantage point of the 1950s? Oskar figures at once as hero and extravagant focalizer of his story; yet he is also held up to relentless scrutiny by auctorial instances that express concerns about his truthfulness. In other words, as Elizabeth Krimmer observes, '[a]lternating between the first and third person singular, the novel casts

13   Wulf Kantsteiner, *In Pursuit of German Memory: History, Television, and Politics after Auschwitz* (Athens, OH: Ohio University Press, 2006), 187.

14   Robert G. Moeller, *War Stories: The Search for a Usable Past in the Federal Republic of Germany* (Berkeley: University of California Press, 2001).

Oskar as both the subject and the object of his story'.[15] While this narrative configuration does not invite a seamless identification with the innocent child protagonist (as was the case for Forte's text), it nonetheless reveals how 'writing the child' in postwar German literature can serve as an effective epistemological lens for critically assessing divergences between primary historical experiences and their subsequent recall.

As pointed out earlier, the novel's first sentence frames Oskar's voice as insane and untrustworthy.[16] He is under constant surveillance by his 'Pfleger' [keeper],[17] a representative of a state institution who watches him through a peephole in the door. Yet this obvious imbalance of power between insane patient and sane keeper is counterbalanced by an intellectual asymmetry that grants the patient the upper hand. Oskar slyly declares, 'Meines Pflegers Auge ist von jenem Braun, welches mich, den Blauäugigen, nicht durchschauen kann.' (BT, 6) [My keeper's eye is the shade of brown that can never see through a blue-eyed type like me. (TD, 1)] Oskar maintains that he feels compelled to tell the stories of his life to his keeper. Yet the narrative present, framed by spatial intimacy and verbal 'confessions' between patient and keeper/caretaker, is bounded by the patient's wish to have the bars of his metal bed built up higher 'damit mir niemand zu nahe tritt' (BT, 6) [to prevent anyone from coming too close to me (TD, 2)]. While the text at once resolutely minimizes Oskar's authority and underscores his sly powers of observation and manipulation, this introductory

---

15   Elisabeth Krimmer, '"Ein Volk von Opfern?" Germans as Victims in Günter Grass's *Die Blechtrommel* and *Im Krebsgang*', *Seminar: A Journal of Germanic Studies* 44/2 (May 2008): 277.

16   The *topos* of the unreliable narrator in *The Tin Drum* has been discussed extensively. See more recent contributions by Patrick O'Neill, 'The Tin Drum: Implications of Unreliability in Günter Grass's *Die Blechtrommel*', in *Acts of Narrative: Textual Strategies in Modern German Fiction* (Toronto: University of Toronto Press, 1996), 97–116, as well as Craig and Krimmer. Oskar's resistance to the status quo is poetically circumscribed as a kind of self-reflexive *Blauäugigkeit* [blue-eyedness], simultaneously evoking the trope of childlike naiveté and Hitler's racial ideal.

17   The German term *Pfleger* implies therapeutic attention and care and is less harsh than its English translation 'keeper', which implies a kind of forced guardianship; caretaker comes closer to the meaning of 'Pfleger' but does not evoke the aspect of institutionalized restriction.

set-up describes not only the relationship between focalizer/protagonist and his limited audience of one, but also the connections among observer/ reader, text and public sphere. Although Oskar tells his stories within the confines of constant observation and institutional control, he relies on his keeper, Bruno Münsterberg, to help him. As a stand-in for the public at large, Bruno is just as important as Oskar: 'Für mich, Oskar, und meinen Pfleger Bruno möchte ich jedoch feststellen: Wir sind beide Helden, ganz verschiedene Helden, er hinter dem Guckloch, ich vor dem Guckloch' (BT 9) [But as far as I and my keeper Bruno are concerned, I dare say that we are both heroes, very different heroes, he on his side of the peephole, and I on my side (TD, 3)]. The relationship between Oskar, a member of the war generation, and Bruno, his audience and helper, is staged as a theatre of intimate but dishonest confessions. This complicated drama of storytelling warns the reader that the stories to follow are provisional at best, unreliable recalls in need of constant examination, correction and authorization.

There is also the 'voice' of the drum itself, a voice which represents the work of irreverent and critical recollections of the Nazi past: 'die Kunst des Zurücktrommelns' (BT, 584) [the art of drumming back the past (TD, 452)]. This voice is conceived as the most important corrective to the episodic memory fragments presented by Oskar. The sound of the toy drum exposes various forms of fascist collaboration during the Third Reich except, however, those of its owner. Oskar's drums come from a toy store owned by Sigismund Marcus, who represents the only significant Jewish figure and decides to kill himself during *Kristallnacht* rather than to face Hitler's henchmen. Hence, the memory work performed by the drum obliquely rests on the silenced voices of Hitler's victims. And finally, there is the elusive voice of a narrator who frames the narrative as a whole yet is only discernible in a brief turn of phrase or a change of pronoun and thus requires an attentive and careful reader. Robert Craig underscores this aspect when he discusses *Die Blechtrommel* as a text that modulates the aesthetic concept of mimesis put forth by Adorno and Horkheimer. He observes that this narrative configuration is part 'of the countless self-exonerating and self-protective slippages between Oskar's deictic presence *in* narrative and his third-person reinscription of himself *as* narrative'.[18] We see this in his reflection on the significance of Oskar's signature powers in a moment of danger when he uses his drum and his glass-shattering voice: 'Oskar möchte nicht undankbar sein. Meine Trommel blieb mir noch. Auch blieb mir *meine* Stimme [...] *mir war jedoch Oskars Stimme über der Trommel ein ewig frischer Beweis meiner Existenz.'* (BT, 445, my emphasis) [Oskar would not like to seem ungrateful. I still had my drum. I still had *my* voice [...] *but to me Oskar's voice, even more than his drum, was proof of my existence.* (TD, 343–44, my emphasis)] The narrator's *raison d'être*, the 'proof of his existence' is Oskar's voice, the focalization of picaresque exceptionalism which, as I show in the next segment, suspends the laws of causality and holds together discontinuous episodic memories. Moreover, it seeks to expose the hypocrisy of German citizens who rigorously deny their complicity in Hitler's project and indulge in self-pity masked as contrition and remorse (BT, 642–61; TD, 496–512). As described earlier, this slippage between the homodiegetic and the heterodiegetic choreographs the mnemonic power of literature that offers a remapping of the past in light of its aftermath.

Plausible Deniability

Oskar's sly unreliability represents a direct, if symbolic challenge to Chancellor Adenauer's well-known motto, 'Keine Experimente' [No experiments]; from the vantage point of 1954, Oskar's drum mocks West Germany's relentless future building. As noted in Chapter 1, Adenauer's restorative politics rested on carefully calibrated and predictable measures meant to reassure a physically and psychologically shattered nation. While the conservative agenda of Germany's first and long-serving chancellor addressed the Nazi past mostly in transactional ways, more liberal-leaning members of the intelligentsia, like Günter Grass, Martin Walser and Karl Jaspers, did everything in their power to keep the legacy of

18   Craig, 106.

Auschwitz in the public eye. One strategy was focused on efforts to create distance from Auschwitz using economic, juridical and administrative means, the other on efforts to expose the extent of the collective implication in the fascist legacy. Kantsteiner has examined West Germany's postwar politics in light of the traffic between these two diametrically opposed mentalities which sediment to equally different memory registers. On the one hand, the conservative wing of

> the political and cultural elite dealt with the Nazi past in order to leave it behind as quickly as possible. Many politicians, historians, and artists (mis-)identified victims and perpetrators, settled claims for compensation, and sought explanations for the German catastrophe so that they could return to a world that no longer bore any sign of twelve years of Nazi rule. On the other hand, part of the elite did everything in its power to prevent such a return to a state of historical innocence and plastered reminders of Germany's original sin all across the media. The first mind-set invented anti-totalitarianism and the economic miracle and integrated the Federal Republic into the West. This attitude was particularly pronounced among the conservative members of the war generations who had experienced the Third Reich as adults. The second mind-set reflects the historical taste of the liberal members of the postwar generation who were born during or after the war.[19]

The cultural and political tensions that shape disparate ways of mediating the Nazi past become visible through the novel's multidirectional narrative texture, narrative tectonics that toggle back and forth between a focalizer, as well as various narrative instances which not only deliberately distort, forget but also obsessively remember and confess. Oskar's hyperbolic confessions of guilt are often followed by equally overstated protestations of innocence. In the chapter, 'Er liegt auf Saspe' ['He Lies in Saspe'], for instance, he confesses to being responsible for the death of Jan Bronski (his mother's lover) by dragging him into the fight against Hitler's troops at the Polish post office. Prefaced by multiple references to his 'three-year-old innocence' (BT 297, 298; TD, 227, 228), he declares 1 September 1939 – the day of Hitler's invasion of Poland – to be the moment when he can no longer deny his full-fledged implication in the death of his parents and his uncle. 'Ich kann es mir nie, selbst bei

---

19   Kantsteiner, 3.

wehleidigster Stimmung nicht verschweigen: meine Trommel, nein, ich selbst, der Trommler Oskar, brachte zuerst meine arme Mama, dann den Jan Bronski, meinen Onkel und Vater ins Grab.' (BT, 299) [Even when I feel most sorry for myself, I cannot deny it: it was my drum, no, it was myself, Oskar the drummer, who dispatched first my poor mama, then Jan Bronski, my uncle and father, to their graves. (TD, 229–30)] This confession is followed by an equally full-throated claim of ignorance. Oskar, reminiscing in his hospital bed, notes that not unlike many of his contemporaries, he simply did not and, in fact, could not have known what was going on: 'Doch wie jedermann halte ich mir an Tagen, da mich ein unhöfliches und durch nichts aus dem Zimmer zu weisendes Schuldgefühl in die Kissen meines Anstaltsbettes drückt, meine Unwissenheit zugute, die damals in Mode kam und noch heute manchem als flottes Hütchen zu Gesicht steht.' (BT, 300) [But on days when an importunate feeling of guilt, which nothing can dispel, sits on the very pillow of my hospital bed, I tend, like everybody else, to make allowances for my ignorance – the ignorance which came into style in those years and which even today quite a few of our citizens wear like a jaunty and oh, so becoming little hat. (TD, 230)] He not only constantly rehearses possible confessions but also cleverly reverses historical cause-and-effect and ultimately comes away as a 'schlaue[r] Unwissende[r]' [sly ignoramus], a victim of circumstance, 'ein unschuldiges Opfer polnischer Barbarei' (BT 300) [an innocent victim of Polish barbarism (TD, 230)]. This entanglement of professions of innocence, followed by confessions of guilt which, in turn, are suspended by denials, captures the texture of a tension between a memory collective that willingly displays contrition and admits to a sense of guilt and individual citizens who refuse to acknowledge their support for the Nazi regime. Put differently, the rhetoric of this passage mimics strategies of guilt management based on collective acts of contrition that serve to relieve the individual of his or her personal responsibility. Oscar's rhetoric, however, is bound by his 'work on the drum', that is, a more critical recall. Rather than mimicking a particular discourse, this kind of memory work categorically rejects the possibility of historical innocence or the possibility of *Wiedergutmachung* [restitution].

To sum up Grass's 'writing the child': Oskar is conceived as a character who is physically detached from the world, yet intellectually keen and socially marginal. His social detachment translates into a piercing gaze from below and is explained by his second birth – his fall through the trapdoor into the cellar. Thus, satirizing the biblical fall into flawed human existence and knowledge, the text makes plausible the implausible, ascribing a fantastic subject position to an act of volition. As Oskar puts it, he wants to present the facts 'die zwar meine anhaltenden Dreijährigkeit nicht erklären, sich aber dennoch – und von mir herbeigeführt – ereigneten.' (BT, 65) [Even if they do not explain why I continued to be three years old, there is no doubt that they happened – and what is more, that I made them happen. (TD, 47)] The poetic logic invoked by this metaphor characterizes this focalizer/protagonist as an exquisitely cunning performer of childhood. He defies rational explanation and invites a poetic exploration of history sharpened by the marginal perspective of a faux-child ignored by the adults. In other words, the text deploys rational explanations in order to justify the irrational, celebrating its narrator as a quasi-removed witness of history who seeks to expose social landscapes of hypocrisy, complicity, ideological naiveté and cruelty. As Amir Eshel puts it poignantly, 'Oskar [...] enters the stage as a powerful representative of doubt', above all, he represents 'a new lexis of substantial doubt, of distrust in social norms and in the ruling ideologies – in short, in the mental and institutional universe that surrounds Oskar while growing up in Nazi Germany'.[20]

Because laws of causality and rational explanation are suspended in this 'lexis of doubt', moral registers of guilt and responsibility come into play as mere affectations. The line between truth and untruth is blurred – a mere matter of faux negotiation between various narrative voices – and all witnesses clamour to represent the past objectively. Hence, in Grass's staging of a childlike eyewitness, the Nazi past comes into view as an absurd and unpredictable chain of events, brought about and supported by the collective, yet denied by all those individually involved. In what follows, I

20 Amir Eshel, *Futurity: Contemporary Literature and the Quest for the Past* (Chicago: University of Chicago Press, 2013), 40–41.

recalibrate this conclusion through the lens of the author's autobiography *Beim Häuten der Zwiebel*.

Memory Games, or Hide-and-Seek

Die Blechtrommel exposed individual and collective pretensions of the newly founded Federal Republic with merciless irony and sarcasm. When the Swedish Academy awarded Grass the Nobel Prize for Literature in 1999, explicitly honouring his 'frolicsome black fables [that] portray the forgotten face of history',[21] this novel established the author's reputation as 'the nation's moral conscience'. However, Grass's belated admission of his membership in the Waffen-SS caused considerable public outrage and tarnished this image.[22] In his confessional 2006 interview in the *Frankfurter Allgemeine Zeitung*, Grass refers back to his first novel and – speaking as a member of the *Flakhelfer* generation dragged into the war as adolescents – asserts that he sought to expose the complicity of a people who, in retrospect, falsely claimed to have been victimized by Hitler, seduced by his ideology and pomp. 'Es wurde so getan, als wäre das arme

---

21   Quoted in Roger Cohen, 'Günter Grass wins the Nobel Prize for Literature', *The New York Times,* 30 September 1999, <https://archive.nytimes.com/www.nytimes. com/library/books/100199grass-nobel.html>, accessed 3 February 2021.

22   In his article on Günter Grass and the Waffen-SS, Michael Braun points to the role the media played in sensationalizing the author's confession. Many critics had early access to Grass's autobiography *Beim Häuten der Zwiebel* and read the chapter that describes his membership in the SS but it was Frank Schirrmacher's article in the *Frankfurter Allgemeine Zeitung* which initiated the debate about the author's hypocrisy. Grass's membership in the SS had not been kept secret; it was recorded in an official army file from January 1946, managed by the 'Wehrauskunftstelle' [office of military information]. See Michael Braun, 'Günter Grass und die Rolle der Literatur in der deutschen Erinnerungsliteratur', *Der Deutschunterricht* 58/6 (2006): 88. See also Neal Ascherson's remarks after the death of the author. 'Günter Grass, the man who broke the silence', *The Guardian*, 18 April 2015, <https://www. theguardian.com/books/2015/apr/18/gunter-grass-tributes-man-broke-silence>, accessed 3 February 2021.

Volk von einer Horde schwarzer Gesellen verführt worden. Und das stimmte nicht. Ich habe als Kind miterlebt, wie das alles am hellen Tage passierte. Und zwar mit Begeisterung und mit Zuspruch.'[23] [It became fashionable to claim that the poor people had been seduced by a gang of dark fellows. And that was not true. I saw as a child what happened in broad daylight. With enthusiasm and encouragement.]

Almost half a century later, in his autobiography *Beim Häuten der Zwiebel*, Grass publicly confronts his own seduction by Hitler's propaganda. 'Die doppelte Rune am Kragen war mir nicht anstößig.' (HZ, 126) [I did not find the double rune on the collar repellent. (PO, 110)] He admits that his voluntary enlistment in the service of the Waffen-SS left him with an enduring sense of shame (HZ, 127, PO, 111). This confession fundamentally reframes the author's historical identity from involuntary conscript to enthusiastic volunteer, from adolescent bystander to SS accomplice. Not surprisingly, in light of his reputation as Germany's most rigorous cultural critic who spoke for the liberal left, the author's delayed admission was met with anger and disdain. Yet Grass was certainly no exception; many of his generation believed blindly in the *Führer* and the ideology of National Socialism.[24] Anne Fuchs points out that

> after 1945, these young men and women had to come to terms with the experience of Germany's total defeat and with a biographical caesura that divided their lives into a delegitimized past, on the one hand, and a legitimate concern for a radical present, on the other. Also known as the 'sceptical generation', its members were the first to reject the apologist victim discourse in the Germany of the 1950s. They became the prime advocates of a critical engagement with Germany's national past, criticizing, in particular, the political continuities in the postwar period.[25]

23   Günter Grass, 'Warum ich nach sechzig Jahren mein Schweigen breche', *Frankfurter Allgemeine Zeitung*, 11 August 2006, <http://www.faz.net/aktuell/feuilleton/buec her/guenter-grass-im-interview-warum-ich-nach-sechzig-jahren-mein-schweigen-breche-1357691.html?printPagedArticle=true#pageIndex_2>, accessed 5 March 2021.

24   Ulrike Jureit notes that Grass had been open about his SS membership until the mid-1960s but 'harmonized' his war story later to that of an expellee. See Ulrike Jureit, Christian Schneider, *Gefühlte Opfer. Illusionen der Vergangenheitsbewältigung* (Stuttgart: Klett-Cotta, 2010), 30–32.

25   Fuchs, 161–99.

Grass has always made it clear that his youth was overshadowed by National Socialism and that this, in turn, had formed his subsequent scepticism about a memory culture saturated with refutations and reversals of guilt. In 1985, in fact, he describes himself as a member of the 'sceptical generation' – a term made famous by sociologist Helmut Schelsky in a seminal book with the same title. 'Ich gehöre zu einer Generation, die noch durch den Nationalsozialismus geprägt wurde, die nach dem Kriegsende desillusioniert und skeptisch den beginnenden Frieden erlebte.' (STG, 326) [I belong to a generation that was still shaped by National Socialism, who emerged from the initial period of peace after the end of the war disillusioned and skeptical.] In light of this statement and his belated confession about his SS membership, we need to re-examine *Die Blechtrommel* as animated by two contradictory impulses. While the novel narrates the nation's burden of guilt in discontinuous memory fragments encapsulated in a self-reflexive memory register, it also guards a staunchly repressed sense of personal complicity. As Grass puts it in retrospect, 'So beflissen ich im Laub meiner Erinnerung stochere, nichts finde ich, das mir günstig wäre.' (HZ, 26) [No matter how zealously I rummage through the foliage of my memory, I can find nothing in my favour. (PO, 19)]

In contrast to autobiographies written by members of the same generation, Joachim Fest, for instance, *Beim Häuten der Zwiebel* does not flaunt the authority of the confident eyewitness. To the contrary, this self-deprecating text explores the psychological codes of retrospection and the hard-to-admit (self-serving) gaps between life and fiction, truth and lies. Moreover, bounded by the ethical obligation to remember the crimes of the Nazi past, Grass's late and most personal memory writing admits to protective screen memories and self-reflexively comments on face-saving omissions and protestations. The author leaves no doubt that his memoires are less faithful than duplicitous: 'die Erinnerung liebt das Versteckspiel der Kinder. Sie verkriecht sich. Zum Schönreden neigt sie und schmückt gerne, oft ohne Not. Sie widerspricht dem Gedächtnis, das sich pedantisch gibt und zänkisch rechthaben will.' (HZ, 8) [Memory likes to play hide-and-seek, to crawl away. It tends to hold forth, to dress up, often needlessly. Memory contradicts itself; pedant that it is, it will have its way. (PO, 3)]. He makes no secret of the fact that such strategies are guided by an opinionated and faux-heroic self-righteousness that mirrors the attitude of his famous memory protagonist, Oskar Matzerath. Grass reveals the moment that inspired the creation of Oskar. He recounts how, during a dinner party with friends, the young son of the hosts marched through the living room beating his drum and refused to stop drumming, despite attempts to bribe him into silence with chocolate (HZ, 384, PO 341). Taking his cue from this determined child drummer, Oskar was conceived as an alter hero, a voice of glorious wit and sharp insight the author fervently wished he had possessed back then (HZ, 351, PO 312). Looking back, he admits, 'Oskar verstand es, schöne Worte zu drechseln; ich war wie aufs Maul gefallen. [...] Ach, wäre ich doch frech wie Oskar gewesen! Ach, hätte ich doch seinen Witz gehabt!' (HZ, 300) [Oskar knew how to make the most of words; I seemed almost at a loss for them. [...] If only I had been as brave as Oskar! If only I had had his wit! (PO, 266)]. This frank retrospective lament indicates the intersection of the autobiographical voice of *Beim Häuten der Zwiebel* as conceived in Grass's late work and the voice of his most famous protagonist in his early work. Wrestling with a sense of collective and personal implication, but staged to provide a protective shield, both voices are infused with feelings of personal shortcomings and regrets. How, then, does Grass's autobiography present the fantasy of historical innocence claimed by the *Flakhelfer* generation?

Noting how easy it was for him and the majority of Germans to remain in denial about Nazi crimes, Grass reflects on the vicissitudes of history through the lens of his 15-year-old self. It was preferable, he asserts, 'ganz und gar vom eigenen Versagen abzusehen, ersatzweise nur die allgemeine Schuld einzuklagen oder nur uneigentlich in dritter Person von sich zu sprechen: Er sah, hat, sagte, er schwieg [...] Und zwar in sich hinein, wo viel Platz ist für Versteckspiele' (HZ, 36) [to discount one's own silence, or to compensate for it by invoking the general guilt, or to speak about oneself all abstractly, in the third person: he saw, had, said, he kept silent [...] and what's more, silent within, where there is plenty of room for hide-and-seek. (PO, 28–9)] The metaphor of the childhood game, of course, evokes a re-membering subject who knows that the 'discovered' episodes put forth in the text are anything but the 'lost' episodes of past experiences. Rather, they signify substitutions; they were 'found' precisely in order to 'hide' what was otherwise too difficult to face. This game of hide-and-seek may be a metaphor for what Freud has examined as the constant dialogue between adult and childhood self. As noted earlier, this dialogue finds expression in narrative fragments that, while palatable to a vigilant, yet conflicted self, provide creative screens for unresolved personal experiences. While the remembering subject is not fully aware of the displacements as they occur, the auctorial voice of the autobiography most certainly is. Looking back from a distance of well over half a century, this voice knows both the impulse and the temptation to hide behind the voice of a child. In fact, he exposes this childhood self as a cunning innocent, caught in the act of running to his mother and crying: "'Ich war doch nur ein Kind, nur ein Kind'" (HZ, 37) "I was just a child, just a kid" (PO, 29)]. At the end of his life Grass admits that his early writing efforts were creative strategies used to guard, conceal and ultimately disavow his life's inconvenient 'truth'.

As discussed in the previous chapter, fictions of memory draw on the dialogue between disparate temporal plains and seek to make difficult life experiences productive. Like the focalizer of Forte's novel, the narrative perspective of *Die Blechtrommel* reveals the stance of a 'concealed first generation' to use Sigrid Weigel's terminology. Yet in contrast to contemporaries like Dieter Forte, Martin Broszat and Helmut Kohl, Grass does not feel 'lucky enough *not yet* or only marginally, having been dragged into political business and responsibility, but [...] *old enough* to be affected emotionally and mentally by the morally confusing suggestive power that the NS-Regime had, at least in the area of educating the youth'.[26] The fact that *Beim Häuten der Zwiebel* is focused on the years between the outbreak of the Second World War and 1959, when *Die Blechtrommel* was published, suggests the author regards this period to be foundational to his identity, a rupture to which he returns time and again in his fiction. The text critiques a particular postwar mentality, yet at the same time fails to reveal a sense of personal shortcoming, a tension between the collective and the personal brought to light half a century later. Nothing, Grass notes, 'konnte meine Einsicht, einem System eingefügt gewesen zu sein, dass die Vernichtung

---

26   Quoted in Sigrid Weigel, "'Generation" as a Symbolic Form: On the Genealogical Discourse of Memory since 1945', *Germanic Review* 77/4 (Fall 2002): 272.

von Millionen von Menschen geplant hat, [...] verschleiern. Selbst wenn mir tätige Mitschuld auszureden war, blieb ein bis heute nicht abgetragener Rest, der allzu geläufig Mitverantwortung genannt wird.' (HZ, 127) [could [...] blind me to the fact that I had been incorporated into a system that planned, organized and carried out the extermination of millions of people. Even if I could not be accused of active complicity, there remains to this day a residue that is all too commonly called joint responsibility. (PO, 111)] Fifty years earlier, Oskar Matzerath deftly acts out what use of the passive tense of the authorial confession above implies: an exculpatory mindset of seemingly powerless Germans, seduced by fascism united in their refusal to acknowledge their 'Mitverantwortung' [joint responsibility].

Generational Palimpsest

Since the narrative premise of *Die Blechtrommel* suspends the logic of cause-and-effect, questions of guilt, remorse, responsibility and culpability are also suspended. In her insightful analysis of Grass's work, Elizabeth Krimmer argues that in the novel questions of guilt and suffering are at once buried and exposed beneath an inflated discussion of guilt and suffering that challenges the binary categories of victim and perpetrator. She predicates her reading on the change in focus shaping the memory regime of the Berlin Republic. 'Rather than ask whether or not it is appropriate to discuss German suffering', she points out, 'one might ask *how* to acknowledge the suffering of individual Germans without denying or minimizing their responsibility and culpability on the personal and national level'.[27] Oskar, Krimmer notes, is 'both a victim and a perpetrator, but most of all he is the quintessential bystander', a witness who categorically refuses to intervene, which ultimately defines him as someone who is unwilling and (in some instances egregiously) fails to act.[28] The fact that Oskar is a knowing bystander to Nazi crimes is most

27   Krimmer, 257.
28   Krimmer, 278 f.

obvious during Grass's oblique military career spent with Bebra's front theatre when he observes the casual murder of a group of nuns (BT 404–24, TB 310–27). Oskar's unwillingness to engage becomes more and more problematic as time goes on.

While it is easy to see Oskar as an aesthetic transposition of the moral character of Adenauer's postwar Germany, that is, a condensation of a savvy but ultimately hypocritical guilt management, it takes a very attentive reader to see the degree to which this *Kunstfigur* performs what could be called a deliberate and convenient infantilism. This attitude of political indifference skirts personal responsibility by pointing to socio-political forces beyond anyone's control which inevitably immobilize the individual. In a speech from 1970, given a year after the Social Democrats gained power under the leadership of Willy Brandt, Grass parses childlikeness as the prevalent, collective stance in the first postwar generation, a stance that both frames and deconstructs the notion of heroic yet passive resistance (the stance of Forte's protagonist). The 'Jungbürgerrede: Über Erwachsene und Verwachsene' [Speech to Young Citizens: Concerning Adults and Mishappen Adults] addresses the first generation of voters born after the war (in 1949, the year the country was divided) and reminds them of their political obligations in light of Germany's history. Drawing on the idiolect of his 4-year-old son Bruno, Grass diagnoses a particular social, psychological and generational form of escapism. He tells his audience that Bruno likes to call 'Erwachsense' [adults], 'Verwachsnige', [stunted or mishappen grown-ups], a term that recognizes adulthood as a kind of failed childhood. The accidental neologism of his son evokes childhood as a source of both power and powerlessness. On the one hand, it suggests that adults have lost a child's immediate access to primary truths, the gift of intuitive insight that lives on in spontaneous acts of political activism. On the other hand, it refers to a child's cognitive limitations, vulnerability and lack of historical agency, the very limitations which, as I pointed out in the introduction, make a child subject *to* but not yet subject *of* the political arena. Grass leaves no doubt that all adults, himself included, need to critically rethink historical and political agency as fundamentally 'verwachsen' when he asks

inwieweit Erwachsene Verwachsene sind und warum sie es sind und warum sie meinen, es sein zu müssen. Deshalb heißt meine Rede: Über Erwachsene und

Verwachsene. Was immer ich zu diesem Prozess des Verwachsens sagen werde, ich bin eingeschlossen in diesen Prozess, stehe nicht außerhalb oder oberhalb; allenfalls bin ich mir tauglichstes Objekt zur Beobachtung allgemeiner Symptome. (JB, 431)

[to what extent and why adults are stunted and why they think they must be that way. For that reason, my speech is called: 'Concerning Adults and Mishappen Adults'. Whatever I might say about this process of becoming stunted, I include myself in this process, I am neither outside nor above it; in all events I consider myself a most suitable subject for studying its general symptoms.]

Speaking from the point of view of the war generation or, more precisely, the *Flakhelfer* generation, he examines the ubiquitous stance of political deflection and social resignation. 'Es ist die kindliche Ohnmachtsbezeugung, die infantile Geste, mit der Erwachsene ständig Schuld und Verantwortung außerhalb des eigenen Bereichs vermuten und mystifizieren: Die Gesellschaft ist schuld, die Verhältnisse sind schuld.' (JB, 431) [It is a child's gesture of powerlessness, the infantile gesture whereby adults continually assume guilt and responsibility to be outside their own purview, a gesture of deliberate mystification: society is at fault, circumstances are at fault.] However, Grass is not only critical of a postwar generation, presumably caught in between 'puerilem Trotzverhalten und pragmatischen Anpassungsgesten' (JB, 433) [puerile defiance and pragmatic conformity], but equally critical of his own generation's state of moral disarray.

While 'Verwachsnige' could not have been used in *Die Blechtrommel* since it was 'invented' only years later by one of the author's sons, interestingly, a related term, 'verwachsen', is used. Both Oskar and the theatre artist Bebra who, not unlike Oskar, exercises resistance only obliquely as an act of 'inner resistance', are characterized as 'verwachsen'. Here 'verwachsen' refers not only to their physical appearance (childlike) and mindset (sharp, yet not taken seriously) but also to the lack of resistance through means of artistic expression during the Third Reich. It evokes a fictional perspective of sly and 'clair-audient' marginality from which to critique society, yet also indicates an unwillingness to resist or take personal responsibility. Hence, Oskar anticipates the moral and aesthetic indifference of the subsequent generation. In short, *Die Blechtrommel* 'writes the child' less as a developmental stage eventually left behind than as an enduring self-centred stance of defiant exceptionalism expressed by affectations of ignorance, innocence and powerlessness – a stance the novel reveals but also inadvertently repeats.

Grass's capacious critique of Germany's memory culture is particularly evident in the fairy-tale rhetoric of the *Reichskristallnacht* chapter 'Glaube, Liebe, Hoffnung' ['Faith, Hope, Love'] that concludes Part I of the novel. This chapter poignantly rehearses the Nazi mindset and offers a scathing picture of the collusion of Christianity and National Socialism. It deconstructs the biblical trope of 'ewige Hoffnung' [eternal hope] as nothing more than a convenient promise of redemption and miraculous recovery held out by Adenauer's Germany. The war generation's insistence on being innocent, their claim of not-having-known is mocked in endless repetitions of 'I do not know'. In his reading Amir Eshel points out that intricate shifts among past, present and future tense direct the contemporary reader's attention to questions of historical continuity, marking the degree to which the past remains alive in the present. 'Grass's narrative implies that the *Reichskristallnacht* and the subsequent Nazi genocide reverberate in the postwar West German present through obliviousness towards the crimes and the willingness to integrate Nazi functionaries and party members into West Germany's political elite.'[29] The novel's narrative configuration of a focalizer, held in check by different keepers and a self-reflexive play with various temporal layers, recalls Hitler's fascism through the lens of what Eshel calls 'prospection', that is, the interruption of the unidirectional flow of time. From the perspective of 'eternal innocence', the text probes how past and present mutually constitute each other in acts of recall that are shot through with strategic forgetfulness. Oskar simultaneously challenges and amplifies a recall of the Nazi past that draws on obfuscating stories of German suffering. While he remembers certain details of his life rather vividly, the authority of his voice remains in perpetual doubt, called into question not only by the instability of this character but also, more broadly, by the tenuousness of West German national identity. The dialogue between text and extra-textual reality, then, reveals that closure vis-à-vis the Nazi past, or, to use one of the key terms of West German cultural memory, *Vergangenheitsbewältigung* [mastering the German past],

---

29   Eshel, 44.

remains illusory and in constant progress.[30] Like Benjamin, Neumann categorically asserts that 'meaningful memories do not exist prior to the process of remembering and narrating the past, but they are constituted by the active creation of self-narrations'.[31] In 1973, Grass reflected on this aspect of *Die Blechtrommel* when he stated with his signature *caveat lector* of the 'Autor als fragwürdiger Zeuge' [the author as a dubious witness] that he had no interest in mastering the past.

> Mich hat nicht edle Absicht getrieben, die deutsche Nachkriegsliteratur um ein robustes Vorzeigestück zu bereichern. Und auch der damals billigen Forderung nach 'Bewältigung der deutschen Vergangenheit' wollte und konnte ich nicht genügen, denn mein Versuch, den eigenen (verlorenen) Ort zu vermessen und mit Vorzug die Ablagerungen der sogenannten Mittelschicht (proletarisch-kleinbürgerlicher Geschiebemergel) Schicht um Schicht abzutragen, blieb ohne Trost und Katharsis. (RB, 625)

> [I was not driven by the noble intention to enrich German postwar literature with a robust masterpiece. I also did not want to, nor could I, succumb to the rather cheap demand of 'mastering the German past'; attempting to locate my own (lost) place and to take down the sediments of the so-called middle class (the proletarian-petit bourgeois moraine clay), layer by layer, provided neither comfort nor catharsis.]

While refuting the notion of a master narrative *per se*, the author is nonetheless keenly aware that he is writing backwards in time, that his memories are inevitably shaped by shifting historical vantage points. *Die Blechtrommel*, he notes, is not a contribution to the discourse of *Vergangenheitsbewältigung*; instead, it was conceived as a poetic and arch-aeological excavation of the past: 'Vielleicht gelang es dem Autor, einige neu anmutende Einsichten freizuschaufeln, schon wieder vermummtes Verhalten nackt zu legen, der Dämonisierung des Nationalsozialismus mit kaltem Gelächter den verlogenen Schauer regelrecht zu zersetzen, und der bis dahin ängstlich zurückgepfiffenen Sprache Auslauf zu

---

30 For a brief history of this term, see the online *Handwörterbuch des politischen Systems der Bundesrepublik Deutschland* maintained by the *Bundeszentrale für politische Bildung*, <http://www.bpb.de/nachschlagen/lexika/handwoerterbuch-politisches-system/202200/vergangenheitsbewaeltigung>, accessed 4 June 2021.

31 Neumann, 337ff.

schaffen; Vergangenheit bewältigen konnte (wollte) er nicht.' (RB, 625) [Maybe the author succeeded in excavating some seemingly new insights, to expose behaviour already forgotten and covered up, to shatter the demonization of National Socialism with cold laughter and to set free a language that had been cautiously and fearfully restrained until then; he could not (and did not want to) master the past.] Grass claims that he was focused on sifting through 'Ablagerungen' [sediments of the past], trying to uncover 'vermummtes Verhalten' [social masquerades] by means of satire, or 'kaltem Gelächter' [cold laughter] that cuts through the 'Dämonisierung des Nationalsozialismus' [demonization of National Socialism]. While still unwilling to address his own implication in the Nazi past, Grass underscores the power of fictions of memory to unearth how sediments of the past are still lodged in the present and provide a potentially critical register with which to locate and examine one's historical subject position.

In conclusion, from the point of *Nachträglichkeit*, the episodic memories presented in *Die Blechtrommel* about the Nazi past become meaningful as composites which deliberately bring disparate moments in space and time into dialogue in a non-linear fashion. The resulting text evokes Benjamin's notion of 'constellation' that foregrounds an ongoing dialogue between the past and the present – a 'then' that is recognizable only in hindsight as corresponding to a particular 'now'. Moreover, the tension between a self-assured but mendacious childlike focalizer kept in check by multiple narrative instances at once identifies and contests any given 'now' (the 1950s) as the phantasmagoric residue of a 'then' (the Nazi past). Oskar Matzerath is more than just an outrageous *Kunstfigur*; he is a figure of memory that reveals the manipulations and blind spots of a history of perpetration that come into increasing focus in the following chapters. Gisela Elsner's novel *Fliegeralarm* discussed next, ties in with Grass's 'lexis of doubt' by demonstrating that 'writing the child' can offer a paradoxical, agile, self-serving and radically distorting point of address that forces the reader to examine his or her subject position in a more critical light. Published three decades after *Die Blechtrommel*, *Fliegeralarm* uses a rhetoric of elliptical repetition, deliberate omissions and a satirical perspicacity similar to Grass's work. However, this text provocatively presents preschool children as 'Hitler's willing executioners' and categorically refutes any claim of collective innocence, thus establishing an even more radical critique of Germany's memory culture.

CHAPTER 4

'The Disgrace of an Untimely Birth': Gisela Elsner's *Fliegeralarm*

Gisela Elsner published her last novel *Fliegeralarm* (Air Raid Alarm)[1] on the cusp of unification in 1989. In this satirical novel, a band of precocious preschool children create their own homes and a makeshift concentration camp in the bombed-out ruins of Nuremberg, left after British and American air strikes. They enthusiastically follow the directives of National Socialism and see it as their mission to capture and torture to death a neighbourhood boy whom they have declared to be Jewish. Elsner's text offers instructive differences to the two works discussed so far. It aggregates 'writing the child' as a stance of knowing (Forte) and faux-innocence (Grass) to a stance of willing complicity resting on half-knowledge and magical thinking. *Fliegeralarm* turns to the air war at the home front at a historical turning point, but not in the sense represented in *Der Junge mit den blutigen Schuhen*, that is, as a lasting trauma experienced by innocent German civilians. Rather, in no uncertain terms *Fliegeralarm* exposes the shift from denial to reversal of guilt about the

---

1   Elsner's works are cited as follows: FA: *Fliegeralarm* (Berlin: Verbrecher Verlag, 2009); FV: 'Flüche einer Verfluchten', in Christine Künzel, ed., *Flüche einer Verfluchten. Kritische Schriften I* (Berlin: Verbrecher Verlag, 2011), 185–270; ÜMB: 'Über Mittel und Bedingungen schriftstellerischer Arbeit', in Christine Künzel, ed., *Gisela Elsner. Im literarischen Ghetto. Kritische Schriften II* (Berlin: Verbrecher Verlag, 2011) 13–17; BW: 'Bandwürmer im Leib des Literaturbetriebs', in *Im literarischen Ghetto*, 247–53; ALG: 'Autorinnen im literarischen Ghetto', in *Im literarischen Ghetto*, 41–59; AF: 'Antwort auf einen Fragebogen, die Literaturszene in der Bundesrepublik Deutschland seit 1945 betreffend', in *Im literarischen Ghetto*, 115–17; VF: 'Vereinfacher haben es nicht leicht. Ein Gespräch mit der Autorin der Romane *Riesenzwerge* und *Punktsieg*', in *Im literarischen Ghetto*, 33–40. I am grateful to Jan Süselbeck, who has made me aware of Elsner's work and the relevance of *Fliegeralarm* for this study.

Nazi past that occurred during the neoconservative decades of the 1980s and 1990s. Decisively not based on a register of trauma, the text rejects the claim that Germans were victims of Hitler's tyrannical regime, saved by the Allies (as President von Weizsäcker put it in his iconic commemorative speech from 1985). Elsner's portrayal of the air war suggests that she considered this particular point in time (unbeknownst to her on the brink of unification) to be a pivotal interface between the war and the postwar period. She seemed to have recognized that four decades after the war had ended, the cultural memory of National Socialism was, once again, coalescing around mythologies of German innocence and victimization.[2]

Like Grass and Forte, who were ten and two years older than she, respectively, Elsner considers her wartime childhood her 'Zeitheimat' [her 'home in time'] to use W. G. Sebald's poignant neologism. The term *Zeitheimat* suggests that particularly intense biographical experiences inscribe identity with an enduring sense of rupture and subsequently tie a sense of self to a particular point in time ('Zeit') and space ('Heimat'). Like Sebald, Elsner was consistently dogged by such a sense of dislocation in the wake of National Socialism and regards her 'Zeitheimat' to be a 'Fluch' [curse], a curse that affects all subsequent generations.[3] Christine Künzel

2   For more on the symbolic dimensions of the air wars, see Jörg Echternkamp, 'Von der Gewalterfahrung zur Kriegserinnerung – über den Bombenkrieg als Thema einer Geschichte der deutschen Kriegsgesellschaft', in Dietmar Süss, ed., *Deutschland im Luftkrieg. Geschichte und Erinnerung* (Munich: Oldenbourg Verlag, 2007), 13.

3   Reflecting on her motivations to write, Elsner notes, 'Das Problem der Bewältigung des Faschismus hat sich mir immer wieder gestellt, also nicht nur in meinen Erinnerungen, die ich im Buch *Fliegeralarm* zu Papier brachte (BW, 249). [Time and again, the problem of working through fascism became apparent to me, not just in my memories, which I put to paper in *Fliegeralarm*.] Similarly, for W. G. Sebald the legacy of the bombing war remained a pivotal point of identity, 'Es stellt sich das Gefühl einer Identität, eines Ursprungs ein – eines Ursprungs, von dem man sich herschreibt.' [It is a sense of identity, of origin – an origin from which one writes.] Volker Hage, ed., *Zeugen der Zerstörung. Die Literaten und der Luftkrieg* (Frankfurt a.M.: Fischer, 2003), 260–61. Such considerations of the dialogue between personal memory and collective history expressed as intersections between the temporal and the spatial go back to M. M. Bakhtin's 1937 essay 'Forms of Time and of the Chronotope in the Novel'.

observes that Elsner responds with a 'Gegen-Fluch' [counter-curse]. Her prose work, as well as her essays and interviews, rigorously contest the notion of transgenerational innocence central to the memory politics of the 1980s.[4] Not unlike *Die Blechtrommel*, *Fliegeralarm* brings historical reality into relief through satirical exaggerations. However, it establishes a 'lexis of doubt' far more radical and uncompromising than Grass's novel. While Elsner's early prose texts satirize strategies of forgetting evident in the self-satisfied consumerism of the postwar period,[5] her last novel reveals the extent to which the latent legacy of Nazism is still manifest in the nation's guilt management. As opposed to the works discussed so far, *Fliegeralarm* does not rely on the perspective of a hyper-perceptive child in order to assert the authority of a knowing-but-innocent witness. Rather, it deploys child protagonists as savvy actors who mimic innocence and suffering when it serves their savage will-to-know or when it is convenient, to pretend not to know. Although *Fliegeralarm* contends with historical experiences similar to those of *Der Junge mit den blutigen Schuhen*, it differs sharply from Forte's trauma text in that it emphatically rejects empathy for, or identification with, a violated childhood self. In fact, Elsner's child protagonists are anything but traumatized or marginalized victims. To the contrary, stylized to the point of sardonic distortion, they are determined little Nazis who enthusiastically follow the directives of the Nazi ideology with which they have grown up. Like Oskar Matzerath, Lisa Welsner, the novel's focalizer, is a also *Kunstfigur* of memory, but unlike Oskar her protestations of innocence do not rest on a detached spectatorship but on enthusiastic acts of perpetration. Lisa and her friends are unapologetically implicated subjects who exploit the privilege bestowed on them as members

---

4   Christine Künzel, '"Ohne einen Anflug von Mitgefühl". Der Generationendiskurs als "Gegenfluch". Monströse Kriegskinder in Gisela Elsners Roman *Fliegeralarm*', in Jan Süselbeck, ed., *Familiengefühle. Generationengeschichte und NS-Erinnerung in den Medien* (Berlin: Verbrecher Verlag, 2014), 108.

5   The best-known example may be her first novel, *Die Riesenzwerge. Ein Beitrag* [*The Giant Dwarves*] (1969), a sharp social critique of petty bourgeois hypocrisy and the excesses of postwar consumerism viewed through the eyes of a child. Translated into twelve languages, it won the *Prix Formentor* and remained the author's only critical and commercial success.

of the 'master race'. This chapter argues that the novel's metonymic play with the term *Endlösung* [final solution], Hitler's term for dealing with the 'Jewish Question', reveals the notion of historical innocence to be a foundational illusion of German cultural memory. I first contextualize *Fliegeralarm* through the lens of recent re-evaluations of this author's oeuvre and then refract my initial reading through considerations of the political context shaped by Helmut Kohl's neoconservative *Schlussstrich* politics. Finally, I show that, despite the novel's alignment with critical feminist work engaging *Mittäterschaft*, Elsner's fiction of memory once again displaces the fate of Jewish victims and effectively reinforces the very silence it seeks to interrupt.

From Celebration to Castigation

In line with the ubiquitous conflations of aesthetic merit, biographical details and physical looks reserved for female artists, Elsner initially gained prominence less as a serious author than as a flamboyant woman who flaunted an outrageous hairstyle, used makeup in unusual ways and, in the eyes of male critics and colleagues, was notably 'sexy'. She was introduced to the 'Group 47' (a platform for predominantly male authors dedicated to finding new literary registers after the breakdown of artistic integrity under Hitler) through her first husband Klaus Roehler (known as an editor and friend of Günter Grass). Along with Ilse Aichinger and Ingeborg Bachmann, Elsner was one of the few female authors who participated in (some of) the group's meetings.[6] After the initial success of her first novel *Die Riesenzwerge* [*The Giant Dwarves*] (1961), Elsner's oeuvre was quickly sidelined by the literary establishment, not least due

---

6   Filmmaker Oskar Roehler, Elsner's son, emphasizes the iconographic status of his
     parents. He notes that they quickly became the 'dream couple of the Group 47. No
     meeting, no party without Klaus and Gisela.' Tilmann Krause, 'Geschichte ist die
     einzige Quelle', *Die Welt*, 6 May 2000, <https://www.welt.de/print-welt/article513
     060/Geschichte-ist-die-einzige-Quelle.html>, accessed 3 June 2021.

to its ideological slant. Summarily judged as unseemly, her satires were considered unsuitable for a woman author. In fact, her writing style represented the extreme opposite of the kind of subjective interiority celebrated as the hallmark of women's writing in the 1970s and 1980s. Her characters do anything but invite empathy or identification, yet as I discuss later in this chapter, her concerns about women's complicity in crimes of National Socialism overlap with those expressed by other female authors such as Bachmann and Elfriede Jelinek.[7]

In defiance of her upper-bourgeois background and its excesses (she was chauffeured daily to her convent school), Elsner joined the Communist Party in 1977. Although essentially a bourgeois intellectual defying the values of her upper-class upbringing, she remained committed to the ideals developed by Marx, Lenin and Engels for the rest of her life. This left her ideologically and socially isolated at the time of the publication of *Fliegeralarm*. Her books no longer sold, she had difficulties finding a publisher and was in financial distress, a situation that may well have contributed to her suicide in 1992. While contemporary critics promoted the image of Elsner as a disturbed, hopeless and drug-addicted woman who suffered mental distress and could not be taken seriously, more recent re-evaluations of her work have significantly revised these clichéd reductions.[8]

Not surprisingly, the representation of Nazi children in *Fliegeralarm* was vehemently rejected when it first came out. Critics accused Elsner not only of 'bad writing' but also of 'a terrible historical falsification' and dismissed the text wholesale.[9] To quote just one of the contemporary reviewers,

An diesem Text stimmt einfach gar nichts: Weder kann die Erzählung als hypertrophierte Parabel gelten noch als radikale Satire. Dieses Buch der Gisela Elsner

---

7   Künzel, 'Einmal im Abseits, immer im Abseits? Anmerkungen zum Verschwinden der Autorin Gisela Elsner', in *Die letzte Kommunistin. Texte zu Gisela Elsner* (Hamburg: Verbrecher Verlag, 2009), 16.

8   See for instance Mathias Meyer, 'Gisela Elsner und die Kommunisten', in *Flüche einer Verfluchten*, 375–94.

9   Elisabeth Endres, 'Braune Riesenzwerge: verunglückt', *Süddeutsche Zeitung*, 30 August 1989.

ist bloß blind und wütig. Früher hat sie an ihren Texten noch gearbeitet – dieses Buch ist eines der fahrlässigsten und sorglosesten, das ich seit vielen Jahren gelesen habe.[10]

[Nothing is right in this text. The story cannot be understood as a hypertrophied parable nor as a radical satire. This book of Gisela Elsner is simply blind and angry. Earlier, she actually worked on her texts – but this book is one of the most careless and frivolous I have read in years].

While certainly a careless overstatement, Ludwig Arnold's assessment nonetheless accurately reflects the fact that Elsner's oeuvre was and remains provocative. Her hypotactic prose, often punctured by slogans and phrases in all caps, is informed by the author's conviction that literature first and foremost performs an important social function. Thus, many of her texts present stylized and foreshortened abstractions of Germany's postwar culture. However, when *Fliegeralarm* was republished in 2009, it found a much different reception because the novel's satirical register now offered an instructive contrast to the trauma texts of the *Kriegskind* narrative.[11] Furthermore, the novel's narrative perspective is now received in alignment with the shift in the focus of German memory studies from the inter- and intragenerational to transgenerational aspects of the legacy of Nazi perpetration.[12] In the following, I argue that the text not only

10   Heinz Ludwig Arnold, 'Gisela Elsners *Fliegeralarm*. Nichts als Ruinen', *Zeit Online*, 25 August 1989, <https://www.zeit.de/1989/35/nichts-als-ruinen>, accessed 6 June 2021.

11   In her editorial notes, Christine Künzel remarks that the original manuscript had been handled very carelessly. Instead of correcting numerous spelling and grammatical mistakes, the editors added to them. In some instances, sentences were transposed as incomplete and unintelligible fragments. Elsner's work is currently being re-evaluated thanks in large part to the dedication of Künzel, who edited subsequent editions of Elsner's works for the independent *Verbrecher Verlag* and has written extensively on this author. See for instance '*Ich bin eine schmutzige Satirikerin*'. Zum Werk Gisela Elsners (1937–1992) (Roßdorf: Ulrike Helmer, 2012), as well as the edited volume *Die letzte Kommunistin. Texte zu Gisela Elsner*.

12   For more on this, see Tanja Röckemann, 'Die "Wiedervereinigungsflickschusterei". Zur Rezeption von Gisela Elsners Roman *Fliegeralarm* in den deutschen Verhältnissen von 1989/2000', *undercurrents. Forum für linke Literaturwissenschaft* (October 2013), <https://undercurrentsforum.com/index.php/undercurrents/article/view/37>, accessed 4 July 2021.

rejects the neoconservative premise of liberation from the Nazi past but, more foundationally, marks as absurd the possibility of an innocent historical subject position. The text's stylistic provocations (endless run-on sentences, punctuated by Nazi slogans and propaganda terms) highlight the absurd premises and conclusions of Nazi ideology. Elsner's much-maligned style, rather than an example of overwrought prose, efficiently exposes the web of half-knowledge, inspired co-perpetration, and protestations of innocence that defined reality for most Germans during the last years of the war.

Writing the Final Solution

Fliegeralarm portrays preschool children as ardent followers of the ideological directives they (over-)hear in their hometown of Nuremberg (Elsner's hometown).[13] Told from the perspective of 5-year-old Lisa Welsner, the text describes their 'wunderbare Kindheit' [wonderful childhood] (FA, 11), made exciting by a 'großartige[n] Weltkrieg' [an astounding world war] (FA, 22). This war keeps giving 'Geschenke aus dem Himmel' [gifts from above] (FA, 11), that is, bomb fragments that the children – savvy capitalists that they are – covet and trade. Lisa and her friends use the ruins created by Allied bombs to make their own home, their 'Zuhaus' (FA, 10), intent to please their *Führer*. Lisa declares, 'Ich habe zum Spielen überhaupt keine Zeit.' (FA, 170) [I have no time to play.] Instead, she and her younger brother Kicki have joined their own private division of the SS created by Wolfgang Wätz, a boy who has 'honoured' Lisa by making her his 'wife'. His rather clueless leadership, however, is countered by the manipulative and increasingly cruel directives

---

13   As noted in the previous chapter, enthusiasm among children for Hitler's project was quite common. Margarete Dörr provides an extensive collection of letters and diary entries in which ardent support of the war is evident. See *'Der Krieg hat uns geprägt'. Wie Kinder den Zweiten Weltkrieg erlebten*, I (Frankfurt, New York, 2007), in particular Chapter 3, 'Fasziniert. Indoktriniert. Im Zwiespalt?', 69–102.

of the only other girl in the group, Gaby Glotterthal. Since they need a Jew for the *Endlösung* – without really knowing what *Endlösung* means or what it means to be Jewish – they capture Rudi, a (non-Jewish) neighbourhood boy whose communist father has been sent to a concentration camp. Gaby, the daughter of a high-ranking physician, steals scarce and precious medication and medical instruments with which they 'treat' their prisoner in a bombed-out ruin, their makeshift concentration camp. The band haphazardly torments Rudi until he confesses to be what they accuse him of being: an *Untermensch* [of inferior race] until he finally begs to die in order to be released from his 'well-deserved' suffering (FA, 182–86). Taken aback when their victim does indeed die of maltreatment and neglect, the children are relieved shortly thereafter when his body is buried during the next bombing attack.

While these are anything but realistic or psychologically calibrated child characters, the text nonetheless accurately reflects the reality of the home front, portrayed in some *Kriegskinder* memoirs as a time of adventure that turned the war into child's play and children into fighters for the *Führer*. After their KZ is destroyed, 4-year-old Kicki wants to fight at the *Ostfront* [Eastern front] (FA, 229–41) and join Hitler's warriors, a ridiculous wish that accentuates the extent to which children were inundated with manipulative slogans, the belief in the absolute authority of the Führer and the final victory.[14] Hitler's motto for children and youth, 'Hart wie Kruppstahl, zäh wie Leder, flink wie Windhunde' [Hard as Krupp steel, tough as leather, agile as greyhounds], shorthand for the omnipresent Nazi propaganda efforts of the time, is repeated over fifty times throughout the text, visually distinct in capital letters. Elsner's child characters embody Hitler's infamous vision for German children and youth: 'Eine gewalttätige, herrische, unerschrockene, grausame Jugend will ich. Jugend muss das alles sein. Das freie, herrliche Raubtier muss erst wieder aus ihren Augen blitzen. [...] Sie sollen mir in den schwierigsten Proben die Todesfurcht

---

14   Hilke Lorenz, *Kriegskinder. Das Schicksal einer Generation* (Berlin: List, 2007), 116. Also see the companion book to the ARD TV show, Yury and Sonya Winterberg, eds, *Kriegskinder, Kriegskinder. Erinnerungen einer Generation* (Berlin, 2009), 19–25.

besiegen lernen.'[15] [I want a violent, imperious, undaunted, cruel youth.
Youth has to be all that. The free magnificent predator has to again radiate
out of their eyes. [...] They shall learn to conquer fear of death for me in
the most difficult trials.]

Not only did German children indeed play in the ruins and craters
left behind by Allied bombs and avidly collect bomb fragments, they also
fervently believed in the glory of Hitler's war. Lisa rigorously detests her
parents for being critical of the *Führer*; she despises her father for not
fighting in Hitler's war. Hence, rather than distorting reality, the novel
puts it into sharp relief. It highlights the effects of the Nazi propaganda
war, which aimed to secure the home front with the help of fearless citizens
willing to give everything for the *Endsieg* [final victory],[16] effectively pitting
children against parents. In fact, repeatedly evoking the *Gräuelmärchen*
[violent warning (fairy) tale] of the 'Story of the Youth Who Went Forth
to Learn What Fear Was', the novel juxtaposes the children's fearlessness
with the fear of their parents. While this accurately reflects the swagger
of the early war years war portrayed in *Kriegskinder* letters of the time,
it represents an absurd contrast to the reality of children traumatized by
the bombing war of the last war years.[17] As a whole, the text dramatizes
children's expert mimicry of the fascist project which, based on unwitting
shifts from play to reality, underscore a child's sense of uncompromising
agency and lack of nuance. In satirical reversal of historical reality, the
last passage of the text characterizes the contemporary mis/remembering
German public, when it celebrates the children as war heroes, unreformed
innocents whose violence is neither believable nor traceable in the future.

The children's innocence rests on an all-too-convenient confusion: the
common portrayal of the Allied bombing as attacks on innocent German
victims disregarding historical causality (see for instance Hans Rumpf's *The
Bombing of Germany* and Jörg Friedrich's *Der Brand* discussed in Chapters

---

15   Hermann Rauschning, *Gespräche mit Hitler* (Zurich: Europa Verlag, 1940), 237.

16   Dörr's account of *Kriegskinder memories* includes the story of Michael F., who as a
      13-year-old refused to give up his air rifle because he wanted to shoot every GIs as
      they walked by his house. Dörr, 78.

17   See Dörr's chapters on 'Kriegsspiele – Kriegshelden', 47–68, and 'Keller, Bunker,
      Bomben', 103–55.

1 and 2). But even more fundamentally, *Fliegeralarm* deconstructs the very notion of innocence as a meaningful category in any recollection of the Third Reich. Refuting claims of the neoconservative *Wende* politics, which cast all Germans as victims of Nazi tyranny, *Fliegeralarm* does not so much distort, as carefully unpack the effects of Nazi indoctrination. The reader is forced to become aware that children were neither just helpless and traumatized witnesses to Hitler's war nor merely its innocent victims. In short, the novel insists that there simply is no transcendent space from which to neatly delineate the victim–perpetrator imaginary. Elsner's recall of the Nazi past leaves no doubt that Germans were and remain implicated, both synchronically and diachronically, in the Third Reich.

Central to Elsner's aesthetic critique of Germany's memory culture is her portrayal of the children's struggle to grasp the meaning of certain words – in particular certain propaganda terms. The difference between not-knowing, half-knowing and knowing circumscribes the still-contested space of what exactly German civilians did know, what they chose not to know, and what they did not, or could not know. While the children can confidently negotiate the meaning of Hitler's propaganda terms – that is, *Herrenmenschen* [those belonging to the master race], *Untermenschen* [those who are racially inferior] and *Endsieg* – they betray their age when they come up with ridiculous ways to understand the function of their bodies and sexuality, the feeling of fear and the meaning of death (FA, 15, 26, 88). However, not surprisingly, they possess a deep knowledge of the instruments and weapons of war but have absolutely no idea what peace means. Based on their ideologically slanted imagination, they grasp at the meaning of unknown concepts by acting them out, evident, for instance, in their grotesque game of 'Vergaserlenz' [gassing game], which consists of turning on the stove and breathing in gas (FA, 38). But in contrast to this breezy and playful appropriation of a murderous reality, they struggle with key terms of Hitler's policies of annihilation – not only abstract concepts like *Endlösung*, but also concrete objects perverted as instruments of mass murder, such as 'Verbrennungsöfen' [incinerators]. In other words, they see the world according to a half-knowledge distorted by Nazi propaganda. In the end, they triumphantly declare that the physical burial of their 'Wätz-KZ' [Wätz Concentration Camp] during a bombing attack had to be the *Endlösung*.

The last – and impossibly convoluted – sentence of the novel mimics the equally convoluted web of assertions and ideological justifications. This passage explains Hitler's demand for an 'eternal war' in light of one of the many bombing attacks that pulverized German cities in the last phase of the war, including the bodies of those previously 'nur verwundeten, nur verstümmelten, nur verkrüppelten, oder nur sterbenden deutschen Soldaten' (FA, 260) [only wounded, only mutilated, only crippled or only dying German soldiers] An almost nonsensical syntax celebrates the *Endlösung* as an event that permanently eradicates all traces of Rudy's death and implicitly the complicity of civilians in Hitler's murderous regime. I quote in full the last paragraph of the novel – one long run-on sentence – to convey the full force of the novel's idiosyncratic language.

> Das ist die ENDLÖSUNG, erklärte schließlich außer seinen fünf HEIL HITLER brüllenden SS Männern, außer meiner zur FRAUENSCHAFTSFÜHRERIN ernannten Freundin Gaby Glotterthal, die jetzt im Begriffe war, dabei zuzusehen, wie die Körperfetzen der vor dem letzten Bombenangriff nur verwundeten, nur verstümmelten, nur verkrüppelten oder nur sterbenden deutschen Soldaten in jene besagten Blechsärge, so heftig, dass diese schepperten, geworfen wurden, sowie außer meinem immerzu SCHADE UM MEINE WUNDERBARE, GARANTIERT ECHTE RUSSISCHE KUGEL jammernden Bruder Kicki nicht zuletzt auch mir, seiner von ihm zur Mutter seiner Kinder erkorenen FRAU, die kein [sic] Hehl aus ihrer Freude darüber machte, dass sie jetzt endlich wusste, was die Endlösung war, kein anderer als mein MANN, der SS Oberscharführer und künftige Nachfolger unseres Führers, der mir, wenn er erst mal unser Führer war, einen Weltkrieg zu führen versprochen hatte, der selbst diesen von Adolf Hitler geführten, ohnehin sattsam großartigen Weltkrieg in den Schatten stellen sollte. (FA, 259–60)

> [That is the FINAL SOLUTION, explained finally in addition to his 5 HEIL HITLER screaming SS men, in addition to my friend Gaby Glotterthal, who was declared to be LEADER OF THE WOMEN'S LEAGUE, who just now was about to watch as shreds of bodies of German soldiers – before the last bombing raid only wounded, only mutilated, only crippled or only dying – were thrown into those aforementioned tin coffins so strongly they clattered, as well as in addition to my forever whining PITY ABOUT MY WONDERFUL, GUARANTEED GENUINE RUSSIAN BULLETS brother Kicki, last but not least to me, his WIFE chosen by him to be the mother of his children, who made no bones about her joy that she

finally knew now what the final solution was, no one other than my HUSBAND the SS Technical Sergeant and future successor of our Führer, who promised to me to lead a world war, destined to overshadow even this amply magnificent world war, led by Adolf Hitler, once he became our Führer.]

This explanation of the *Endlösung* is uttered by Wolfgang Wätz, the children's leader. However, a syntax of endless delays circumscribes his authority as illusionary. Circumscribed as 'no other than my HUSBAND', he is identified in affiliation to Lisa as the subject of the sentence in the last clause. Mimicking the social coherence of the group, this run-on sentence seems to perform the process through which the band members begin to understand what *Endlösung* means. It celebrates Allied acts of retaliation since they completely erasure German acts of violence. The drawn-out construction of this sentence/paragraph implies that participation, or even complicity in Nazi crimes was conceived in such a way that those at home did not *have to* know, while others truly could not or did not want to know (as described by Reinhart Koselleck, see Chapter 2).[18] After the bombing attack that levels their 'Wätz KZ' the children know that their crime is not only guaranteed invisibility, but also plausible deniability. They consider this to be a brilliant premise for a future envisioned as an eternal extension of Hitler's power. Descriptions of the violence suffered by German soldiers, embedded as an aside and associated with Gaby, the cruellest character in the novel, make the sentence close to incomprehensible. The lamentations of Kicki about the loss of his precious Russian bullets express how weapons of war and dynamics of market competition intersect. This paragraph, at once childlike in its repetitive structure and well beyond a (preschool) child's grasp of language, underscores the power of ideological distortions. But it also points to the equally intense reality of suffering and death, disavowed as the children's final commitment to an eternal war of annihilation, a war Lisa enthusiastically describes as 'destined to overshadow even this amply magnificent world war'.

18   Reinhart Koselleck, 'Die Diskontinuität der Erinnerung', *Deutsche Zeitschrift für Philosophie* 47/2 (1999): 217.

To come back to earlier observations about the text's grounding in the reality of 1944–45: *Fliegeralarm* leaves no doubt that these fictional children experienced a 'normal' childhood. Those who grew up during the last years of the war did not know anything else; for them peace was truly a foreign country.[19] Elsner's children are curious but, as noted, also clueless about what peace means; they rave about Hitler's war and rigorously condemn anybody not in line with his directives – including their parents. Strikingly, they are also strategic actors who know when to pretend innocence (FA, 153–55). (I return to this aspect in more detail in the last part of this chapter.) In contrast to Forte's descriptions of Allied bombing attacks through the eyes of a traumatized boy, a child who always feels supported by his family and his mother's courage, Elsner describes the air war through the eyes of a young girl who rejoices in the violence around her and rejects her family's opposition to Hitler. Lisa is an ardent fan of the bombing war over Nuremberg and has nothing but disdain for her cowardly father whom she considers to be a 'feige[r] Zivilist und ruchlose[r] Vaterlandsverräter' (FA, 29) [cowardly civilian and nefarious traitor] afraid of the bombs. Instead of being concerned about his family's welfare, he is obsessively concerned about the integrity of his wife's sewing box (FA, 30, 251) – an irrelevant object standing in for his outsized concern for all their material possessions. Disgusted by their parents' fear, both Lisa and her brother feel invigorated by the ongoing destruction. 'Die draußen vonstatten gehende Zerstörung entfachte in uns eine Zerstörungswut, die Trümmer, Schutt, Asche, Ruinen und Verschüttete in Hülle und Fülle forderte. Mit bösartig funkelnden Augen saßen wir in unseren Feldbetten und lauschten, berauscht von den Klängen einer wunderbaren Musik, den

---

19   Many *Kriegskinder* have testified to this. To quote only one example, Dietmar Hoffmann-Axthelm (born three years after Elsner) notes, 'Im übrigen ist die Kriegskindheit eine ganz normale Kindheit. Da ist kein Grund, sich zu beklagen. Wenn der erste Lebenstag schon ein Kriegstag ist, dann gibt es eben nichts anderes. Das Kriegskind vermisst nichts, kann nichts vergleichen.' [War childhood is a completely normal childhood. There is no reason to complain. When the first day of your life is a war-day, then there simply is nothing else. The *Kriegskind* does not miss anything, has no comparison.] Hellmut Lessing, ed., *Kriegskinder* (Frankfurt a.M.: extrabuch, 1984), 124.

Bombendetonationen.' (FA, 38) [The ongoing destruction outside kindled a fury of destruction within us which demanded bountiful rubble, debris, ash, ruins and people buried under the rubble. With maliciously sparkling eyes we sat in cots and listened, intoxicated by the sound of this wonderful music, the detonation of bombs.]

In comparison to Forte's child witness – a traumatized victim of circumstances beyond his control – and Grass's childlike protagonist – a picaresque bystander to the unfolding Nazi violence – Elsner's *Kriegskinder* are determined and implicated agents of Hitler's project. They inhabit contradictory yet at times overlapping subject positions: too young to grasp the historical context or ideological violence of the NS propaganda, they are victims seduced by Nazi rhetoric; as ardent executioners of Nazi directives, however, they are at once perpetrators, accomplices, bystanders and witnesses. (These intersections come into even sharper focus in the postmemory works discussed in the last two chapters of this study.) Elsner's 'writing the child' rests on satirical exaggerations and fantasies about domination and privilege that align with the subject position Michael Rothberg explores in the context of systemic perpetration. Elsner's *Kriegskinder* not only contribute to but also profit from a system of domination without fully understanding, let alone controlling it. Cast as direct co-conspirators and perpetrators, they are folded into the insidious structure of Nazi violence in a provocative text that probes historical agency in search of a language or a paradigm with which to expose indirect, structural and collective forms of agency. These forms of intersectional agency are not always manifest as direct perpetration but nonetheless enable violence and domination.[20]

Elsner skilfully draws on personal experiences and historical facts and offers the reader personal and biographical details discernible only in distorted ways. Protagonists and plot are simultaneously oversaturated by, and different from, biographical truth. That is to say, attempts to locate

20   In different ways, this complicity is apparent in the mother's behaviour. Although no supporter of Hitler, when at the end of her rope, she threatens to dump the children into a 'KINDER-KZ AM WALDESRAIN' (FA, 239) [children's concentration camp in the forest]. Mirroring the attitude of many citizens about Nazi crimes, she dismisses Kicki's confession about their horrible deed as a horror fairy tale and thus inadvertently allows them to continue (FA, 195).

the author in the text are frustrated by a strategy that, as Bernhard Jahn puts it poignantly, 'transparently veils' reality.[21] The city of Nuremberg was indeed Elsner's hometown and her father – in the text barely masked as Dr Welsner, an executive at DIEMENS – was indeed a manager at Siemens. Yet in the novel he is neither powerful nor competent but riven with anxiety and obsessive fear. The children's fictional GAGFA neighbourhood refers to the real GAGfAH (now called Vonovia), a non-profit corporation for employee housing. According to the company's current website, this organization seeks to offer more than affordable living space: it aspires to support the spirit of 'community and welfare'.[22] *Fliegeralarm*, however, describes the very opposite. In the text, the GAGFA is a neighbourhood deeply contaminated by petty grievances, mutual surveillance, the constant threat of denunciation and violent child-rearing practices (FA, 15, 195). The air raids are, of course, the most central historical fact; Nuremberg was bombed from 1940 to the end of the war, most heavily from 1943 to 1945, a period of time Elsner was old enough to remember.[23] And finally, both the age and the name of the narrator also suggest biographical proximities. In short, Lisa Welsner seems to be the author's satirically distorted alter ego. By superimposing historical and autobiographical fact the text undermines a rhetoric of historical verisimilitude, effectively both drawing on and challenging the authority of the *Kriegskinder* narrative that begins to emerge in the late 1980s.

The novel's aesthetic framework interrogates West Germany's pre-1989 cultural memory of National Socialism.[24] While, on the plot level,

21   Bernhard Jahn, '*Fliegeralarm* oder die Freilegung der bösen Familie mit Hilfe von Bomben', in *Die letzte Kommunistin*, 64.

22   Vonovia's website presents the 100-year history and concept of the GAGfAH, <https://www.vonovia.de/ueber-vonovia/ueber-uns/historie?sc_lang=en>, accessed 5 June 2021.

23   Radio Bayern recently described how Nuremberg tried to protect its citizens from air raids by building air raid shelters, <https://www.br.de/radio/bayern2/sendungen/zeit-fuer-bayern/licht-ins-dunkel-nuernbergs-bunker-heute-100.html>, accessed 5 June 2021.

24   See Kathrin Schödel, 'Radikale Umkehrungen von Gedächtnisdiskursen und das politisch Subversive in Gisela Elsners Roman *Fliegeralarm*', in Ari Sepp and

it shows the violent effects of hateful rhetoric and ruthless manipulation, as a fiction of memory it critiques contemporary memory politics by radically rewriting the *Kriegskind* experience. Put differently, rather than another autobiographically inspired reckoning with a childhood under Hitler, *Fliegeralarm* is fiction in Nünning's sense. It recalls the Nazi past through a fictional embellishment and exaggeration and simultaneously reveals an underlying culture of denial which half a century after May 1945 remains unwilling to confront the full degree of collective implication. Had *Fliegeralarm* been given the attention it deserved in 1989, the central metaphor of the text – the revelation that the German 'Zuhause' remains a buried crime site – would have raised the question of when and how lingering discriminatory violence would again erupt into the present. In fact, critique of this lingering violence and its attendant authoritarian order mobilized the student movement of the late 1960s. Yet, as I describe in the next section, the 1968ers rely on the very victimologies they seek to expose when they regard themselves to be the 'Jews of their parents'. Understanding the historical backdrop to Elsner's novel is pivotal since it brings into relief the contestatory scope of her critical project. Before I turn to the memory politics of the 1980s, as articulated in speeches by Chancellor Helmut Kohl and President Friedrich von Weizsäcker, I consider differences in the *Kriegskinder* narrative, from early expressions to more recent publications.

Intergenerational Victimologies: The *Kriegskinder* and the 1968ers

Since *Fliegeralarm* critiques postwar victimologies as inherently false, it is instructive to take a closer look at the ways in which stories about collective suffering buttressed German national identity after the change of political

---

Gunther Martens, eds, *Gegen den Strich. Das Subversive in der deutschsprachigen Literatur nach 1945* (Berlin: Lit Verlag, 2017), 10.

leadership in 1982. As discussed in previous chapters, in the immediate postwar decades, Germans had found convenient ways to cast themselves as victims of a war they themselves had started. Yet under the leadership of Willy Brandt and in the wake of the political activism of the 1960s and 1970s, West German memory culture shifted its focus to the victims who had been programmatically targeted under National Socialism. This did not mean, however, that those who grew up under Hitler had completely changed their mindset. In fact, many *Kriegskind* parents continued to be deeply marked by the ideological and traumatic fallout of the war. As a consequence, their children felt abandoned by emotionally distant or intensely authoritarian parents and saw themselves as victims of tyrannical structures reinforced by a rigid educational system. This frustration, channelled into the student movement of the 1960s and 1970s, was transposed into a fight against the legacy of National Socialism as manifest in structures of capitalist hegemony and continued political oppression. Ironically, the next generation not only identified *with* the Jewish victims but identified *as* being Jewish. In fact, in 1968, during a demonstration in Paris, victimization fantasies turned into a racist slogan when one of the banners proclaimed, 'We are all German Jews'. This claim, French philosopher Alain Finkielkraut observes, in effect posits that 'Jewish identity was no longer for Jews alone. The event taking place put an end to such exclusivity. Every child of the postwar era could change places with the outsider and wear the yellow star.'[25] Similarly, Peter Schneider, a former member of this cohort, reflects on this troubling identification with Holocaust victims. In retrospect, he comes to the conclusion that at this particular political moment, sweeping accusations buttressed a rigid

25   Quoted in Ruth Wittlinger, 'Taboo or Tradition? The "Germans as Victims" Theme in the Federal Republic until the mid-1990s', in Bill Niven, ed., *Germans as Victims: Remembering the Past in Contemporary Germany* (New York: Palgrave Macmillan, 2006), 69. Wittlinger parses the trope of the 'new Jew' in more detail. Also see Robert G. Moeller, *War Stories: The Search for a Usable Past in the Federal Republic of Germany* (Berkeley, Los Angeles, London: 2001), 69, 180, as well as Ulrike Jureit, Christian Schneider. *Gefühlte Opfer: Illusionen der Vergangenheitsbewältigung* (Stuttgart: Klett-Cotta, 2011), 26–28.

victim–perpetrator binary which conveniently bracketed one's own implication in the legacy of racist perpetration.

> '68 – das war in Deutschland die Zeit des Schuldigsprechens. Es war der rabiate
> Versuch der Nachgeborenen, sich aus der Verstrickung mit der 'Täter-Generation'
> zu lösen und sich durch die Identifikation mit den Opfern des Nazi-Faschismus
> ihre Unschuld zu erobern. Deutsche aus der 'Täter-Generation', die Opfer wurden,
> Deutsche, die gar zivilen Mut bewiesen und Juden gerettet hatten, störten die Wucht
> der Anklage.[26]

> ['68 – in Germany, that was the time of accusations of guilt. It was the brutal attempt
> of those born afterwards to free themselves from the involvement with the 'perpe-
> trator generation' and to proclaim their own innocence through identification with
> the victims of Nazi Fascism. Germans from the 'perpetrator generation' who were
> victims, let alone Germans who showed civil courage and saved Jews, disrupted the
> momentum of denunciation.]

This seemingly reflexive claim of historical innocence and indeed historical victimhood asserted by both the *Kriegskinder* and their children
also comes to light in *Kriegskinder* memories written in the wake of the
anti-war and feminist activism of the 1970s and 1980s. Social historian
Klaus Latzel compares two *Kriegskinder* memories, published in 1984
and 2005, one edited by Hellmut Lessing and the later one by Hilke
Lorenz. Despite the same title, they show instructive differences between
the pre-unification *Kriegskinder* narrative (the backdrop to *Fliegeralarm*)
and their reconfiguration post-unification (the backdrop to *Der Junge
mit den blutigen Schuhen*). Both publications describe similar historical
events, that is, the effects of traumatic ruptures as a result of air raids and
the experience of flight. Yet due to differing biographical, political and
socio-historical premises they express distinctly different *experiences*. The
later volume, edited by Hilke Lorenz, has the generalizing subtitle *Das
Schicksal einer Generation* [*The Fate of A Generation*] and weaves eyewitness interviews into the common narrative about repressed childhood
war traumas (examined in Chapter 1). Lorenz's book ties in with the

---

26   Peter Schneider, 'Deutsche als Opfer? Über ein Tabu der Nachkriegsgeneration', in
      Lothar Kettenacker, ed., *Ein Volk von Opfern? Die neue Debatte um den Bombenkrieg
      1940–1945* (Berlin: Rowohlt, 2003), 163.

trauma culture of the 1990s and seeks to work through collective psychological wounds going back to the Second World War. By contrast, the autobiographical essays in Hellmut Lessing's compilation frame Nazi childhood memories through the lens of political and social activism. Many contributors critique the ideological premises of the military-industrial complex. Moulded by the anti-military and anti-war stance of the 1980s, they express the anxiety of living at once in a post- and in a pre-war period.[27] *Fliegeralarm* is animated by political critiques that animate both the activism of the 1960s and its subsequent articulations expressed in Lessing's volume. Yet instead of presenting the grievances of traumatized *Kriegskinder*, Elsner's satire offers children who are energized and thrilled by what they experience. While they are no anti-war activists, they are also not ready to move on. These children do not consider themselves 'blessed' by what journalist Günter Gaus termed the 'Gnade der späten Geburt' [blessing of a late birth]: 'zu jung, um den Versuchungen des Nationalsozialismus widerstehen zu müssen; alt genug, um die letzte Kriegszeit und die Besinnungsjahre danach bewußt aufzunehmen'[28] [too young to have been tempted by the seductions of National Socialism, but old enough to have experienced the impact of the last years of the war and its aftermath].

The 'Gnade der späten Geburt' became the signature phrase of Helmut Kohl's politics. Born in 1930, Kohl was Elsner's peer, although as noted before, at that time, a 7-year age difference made a big difference. Initially,

27 For more on this, see Klaus Latzel, 'Kriegskinder, Kriegsopfer und kriegskompetente Mädchen', in Hans-Heino Evers, ed., *Erinnerungen an Kriegskindheiten: Erfahrungsräume, Erinnerungskultur und Geschichtspolitik unter sozial- und kulturwissenschaftlicher Perspektive* (Weinheim: Juventa, 2006), 209.

28 The entire quote reads: 'Die *Gnade der späten Geburt*, unter der diese Jahrgänge leben – um 1930 geboren; zu jung, um den Versuchungen des Nationalsozialismus widerstehen zu müssen; alt genug, um die letzte Kriegszeit und die Besinnungsjahre danach bewusst aufzunehmen – schließt einiges aus.' (271) [The blessing of a late birth enjoyed by this cohort, born around 1930, exempts them in many ways: too young to have been tempted by the seductions National Socialism, but old enough to have experienced the impact of the last years of the war and its aftermath.] Günter Gaus, *Wo Deutschland liegt. Eine Ortsbestimmung* (Hamburg: Hoffmann Campe, 1983), 271.

this adage may have circumscribed Kohl's gratitude for having survived the violence of the war while his older brother died in an air raid.[29] In fact, his politics, packaged and sold as a 'geistige und moralische Wende' [moral and spiritual change], may have expressed the chancellor's desire for a *Schlussstrich*, a break with the past driven by the need to leave behind the trauma of his youth. However, the determined promotion of a return to normality also denotes a mentality centred on deflection and driven by the need to assuage a lingering sense of collective guilt. Sociologist Jeffrey Olick observes that 'Kohl's style of normalization was more aggressive [than that of his predecessors], embodied in an ideological program for cultural change which included pride in German history, the celebration of heroes, national museums and monuments, and a distancing to past misdeeds, which [...] have lost their specificity – all victims are the same.'[30] Not unlike the cultural tensions of the 1950s described in *Die Blechtrommel*, the Kohl era of the 1980s and 1990s was shaped by two diametrically opposing trends: on the one hand, the desire to move on and return to a state of historical innocence and on the other an almost obsessive need to remember

29   Jürgen Leinemann describes Kohl as a typical *Kriegskind* who vividly remembered the bombing war as a series of traumatizing events he witnessed as a *Flakhelfer*. 'Ab 44 hab ich schon sehr konkrete Erinnerungen. Wir hatten dauernd Fliegerangriffe in Ludwigshafen. Ich war beim Schüler-Löschtrupp – und das war keine Kindheit, wie man sie sich heute beim einem 14-Jährigen vorstellt. Wenn Sie Tote nach einem Fliegerangriff geborgen haben, sind Sie kein 14-Jähriger mehr. [...] Es gab ja solche Wahnsinnstaten am Ende, das hat mich schon geprägt. [I have very distinct memories from '44 onward. We had continual air raids in Ludwigshafen. I was with the students' fire brigade – and that was not the childhood of a 14-year-old that one imagines today. If you've retrieved corpses after an air raid, you are no longer a 14-year-old. [...] There were just such incredible acts at the end that really left a mark on me.] Jürgen Leinemann, *Höhenrausch. Die wirklichkeitsleere Welt der Politik* (Munich: Karl Blessing, 2004), 200.

30   Jeffrey K. Olick, 'What Does it Mean to Normalize the Past? Official Memory in German Politics since 1989', *Social Science History* 224 (Memory and the Nation) (Winter 1998): 265. More recently, the legacy of politics based on this displacement of historical responsibility in the name of national pride is carried on by the AfD, Germany's right-wing party. See for instance the 2017 speech by Alexander Gauland, the co-founder of the AfD (cited in Introduction, Note 30), in which he asserts pride in the efforts of German soldiers during two world wars.

the nation's guilt. Seemingly focused on the Nazi past, the Kohl administration used the politics of memory rather strategically, commissioning
monuments and orchestrating events of remembrance, which in effect
'outsourced' the memory of Nazi history and thus relieved the individual
citizen of the burden to remember.[31]

In contrast to the spontaneity of Willy Brandt, famously captured in
his impromptu decision to kneel in honour of the victims of the Warsaw
Ghetto, Kohl's political gestures remained abstract by design. This strategy
is introduced in his first speech to the German parliament on 13 October
1982, in which he frames the history of National Socialism with counter-
examples of German civil fortitude and disobedience. Avoiding the question of shared collective responsibility for the death of millions, he refers
to National Socialism only abstractly as the 'German dictatorship that led
towards catastrophe'.[32] He projects a West Germany that has a distinct history, forged in the shadow of 'the catastrophe', yet is no longer shaped by
it.[33] Three years later, President Richard von Weizsäcker countered Kohl's

31   The Memorial to the Murdered Jews of Europe in the heart of Berlin may be most
      representative of Germany's 'institutionalized' memory sites that are dedicated to
      the victims of National Socialism. Going back to a citizens' initiative in the 1980s, it
      took shape through decades of public discussion and controversy. Initially funded
      in 1999 and finally inaugurated in 2005, this commemorative site is installed in
      the previous no-man's-land just south of the Brandenburg Gate. Although meant
      to be experienced up close as a walking labyrinth-like expanse, it remains an ab-
      straction of history. This memorial shares a history of public controversy with the
      Neue Wache (re-)dedicated by the Kohl administration to the Victims of War and
      Dictatorship in 1993. As mentioned in the introduction, in 2017 the Memorial to
      the Murdered Jews of Europe became a flashpoint for the radical right when AfD
      politician Björn Höcke, referred to it as 'monument of shame', intentionally leaving
      open whether the monument itself or what it stands for is shameful. <https://
      www.welt.de/politik/deutschland/article161286915/Was-Hoecke-mit-der-Denk
      mal-der-Schande-Rede-bezweckt.html>, accessed 15 July 2021.
32   Helmut Kohls Regierungserklärung, 13 Oktober 1982, <https://www.1000do
      kumente.de/pdf/dok_0144_koh_de.pdf>, accessed 4 June 2021.
33   Bill Niven observes that Kohl's commemorative speeches had the 'tendency to pin
      sole responsibility for the war on Hitler or the Nazi Party, while implicitly exoner-
      ating the broad mass of Germans.' *Facing the Nazi Past: United Germany and the
      Legacy of the Third Reich* (New York: Routledge, 2002), 109.

Schlussstrich politics with exhortations of moral fortitude resting on a sense of accountability for Nazi crimes. Kohl, emphasizing the 'knowing innocence' of his generation, sought *Vergangenheitsbewältigung* [*mastering* of the past], he wanted to 'close the book on the past'. Von Weizsäcker, on the other hand, underscored 'Vergangenheitsbewahrung' [pledge to commemorate the past]. And yet, not unlike the neoconservative recasting of the Nazi past, the president's moral pledge also rests on the projection of a victimized people. He paints Hitler as a dictator who allowed little room for resistance and needed to be defeated by the Allies. The end of the war, von Weizsäcker declares emphatically, 'liberated all of us from the inhumanity and tyranny of the National Socialist regime.'[34] Not only does this statement imply that all Germans were ultimately victims of the Nazi tyranny, it also gives permission to appreciate the fate of those who suffered the consequences of a war they did not support, or of those who were too young to be held accountable. Thus, von Weizsäcker's speech, often quoted as paradigmatic for a new moral imperative in Germany's cultural memory, in fact opened and validated the space for the German sense of victimhood expressed by the *Kriegskinder* voices in the decades that followed.

When seen in light of these political recalibrations of historical accountability, that is, the sense of victimhood expressed by the 1968ers and Kohls' universalizing assertions of generational innocence, it becomes clear that *Fliegeralarm* not only echoes, but also sharply critiques the political premises of the 1980s. Ironically, the fact that Rudi, the child targeted by the children, is not Jewish but the son of a communist, betrays Elsner's political convictions and mirrors the victimhood claims of the 1968ers. (I elaborate on this displacement of the Jewish victim in the conclusion to this chapter.) But the text rejects projections of normalization cast as 'liberation from Hitler's rule' and instead reveals the extent to which the legacy of Nazi violence remains hidden in the everyday. In this respect, the novel aligns with the perspective promoted by the *Geschichtswerkstatt* [History Workshop] movement. Inspired by the Scandinavian 'Dig Where

34   Speech by Richard von Weizsäcker, President of the Federal Republic of Germany, on 8 May 1985 to commemorate the 40th Anniversary of the End of the War in Europe and of the National Socialist Tyranny, <http://deferred-live.net/muse/ari Uploads/pdfs/speechRichardvonWeizsacker.pdf>, accessed 10 June 2021.

You Stand' project, which seeks to understand history as refracted in local practices of 'Alltagsgeschichte' [everyday history], this grassroots movement gained momentum in the 1970s and 1980s as a fresh way to understand the local legacy of the past. In striking dialogue with the *Geschichtswerkstatt*, Elsner's text 'digs up' the compromised foundations of one German town and relocates the killing of innocent citizens deemed inferior by Nazi propaganda to the home front, the domestic space of homelife and child's play.

Elsner has consistently written against the enduring legacy of fascism, both in her prose work and even more pointedly in her essays and articles. Sceptical of proclamations that Germany has successfully left behind the Nazi past, in the 1980s she sees the country locked in the same kind of ideological blindness that led to Hitler's rise in the first place. In this respect her work dialogues with the critical memory work of women authors of the 1970s and 1980s. Like Ingeborg Bachmann, Barbara Duden and Elfriede Jelinek, Elsner addresses women's unacknowledged complicity in regimes of oppression – a *Mitwisserschaft* or *Mittäterschaft* [shared knowledge or co-perpetration, a term I have parsed in Chapter 2].[35] Hence, before concluding this chapter with a more detailed analysis of how the novel refutes the notion of collective innocence, I want to place *Fliegeralarm* in the context of feminist work that traces the contradiction that subjugated subjects are at once enfolded into structures of domination and readily perpetuate the very structures that control them.

Writing (against) Women's Complicity

Elsner consistently wrote about topics reserved for women authors – children, the family and the domestic sphere in a register reserved for male authors. The cruelty of young girls in *Fliegeralarm* is a calculated

---

35   In *Women and National Socialism in Postwar German Literature* (Rochester, New York: Camden House, 2017), Katherine Stone addresses the complications of gender and memory work that are negotiated as various forms of implication in the work of women authors.

provocation which violates unwritten rules of the male-dominated literary establishment. Distorted by Nazi directives, Lisa degrades everybody who does not follow Nazi ideals or directives (her father, her
brother and Rudy), while Gaby's ruthless will-to-know ultimately tor-
tures Rudy to death. In her assessment of 'women's writing' (a genre
that emerged in the context of the women's movement in the 1970s and
was well established by the late 1980s), Elsner reminds the reader that
women are supposed to write about 'Kindheit, Liebe, Schwangerschaft,
Erziehungsfragen, häusliche Sorgen, Familien- und Ehealltag' (ALG,
42) [childhood, love, pregnancy, questions of child-rearing, domestic
matters, family and marital life]. With 'einer an Hysterie grenzende[n]
Sensibilität' (ALG, 42) [an attitude of sensitivity bordering on hysteria]
women should express 'Emotionalität, Inkonsequenz und Irrationalität'
(ALG, 42) [emotions, inconsistencies and the irrational]. In fact, to her
mind the label 'women's literature' itself expresses a kind of censorship. In
an interview from 1978 she observed poignantly that in Germany women
are not allowed to employ a satirical tone.

> Im Gegensatz zu Frankreich oder England […], wo man mit einem faschistischen
> Frauenbild nicht zurande kommen musste, gestattete man hier einer Frau, wenn sie
> schon das Schreiben nicht lassen konnte, mit einer unverhohlenen Gönnerhaftigkeit
> trübe Metaphern über Geburt, Liebe und Tod, ja sogar mal einen surrealistischen
> Seitensprung. Satiren hingegen galten wie ein Bordellbesuch ausschließlich als
> Männersache. (VF, 33–34)

> [In contrast to France or England […], where one did not have to deal with a fascist
> view of women, if she could not actually forego writing, in a blatantly patronizing
> manner a woman was permitted to handle dull metaphors about birth, love and
> death and, yes, even the occasional surrealistic infidelity. Satires, however, were seen
> exclusively as a man's purview, just like a visit to the brothel.]

In a questionnaire solicited three years later, Elsner asserted that 'in der
Bundesrepublik findet eine Literaturzensur statt' (AF, 115) [the literature
of the FRG is censored]. In short, Elsner was well aware that social critique, let alone writing satire, was taboo for a (German) woman writer.
    Elsner's work, although different in style, is conceptually aligned with
the work of Bachmann, Duden and Jelinek. Her critique of patriarchal

and capitalist structures of exploitation, deepened by violent *Kriegskind* experiences and sharpened by her female (outsider) perspective, is circumscribed by what Barbara Duden defines as *Mitwisserschaft* (a term that, denotes not only a sense of shared knowledge, as noted above, but also a pact of subsequent silence). For Duden, *Mitwisserschaft* means 'als Kind von Tätern, der Tätergeneration, involviert zu sein, ohne involviert zu sein' [to be involved without being involved – as a child of perpetrators, as a member of the perpetrator generation].[36] Bachmann is one of the first German-speaking women authors to explore the dimensions of this subject position in her literary work. She parses women's complicity, as a kind of 'verschwiegene Erinnerung' [concealed memory] which, in contrast to Forte's use of the term, indicates less traumatic childhood memories, than the awareness of a lingering fascist mindset manifest as women's voluntary subjugation to the patriarchal order.[37] In the wake of Auschwitz, Bachmann describes human agency along radically new lines: 'Die erste Veränderung, die das Ich erfahren hat, ist, dass es sich nicht mehr in der Geschichte aufhält, sondern dass sich neuerdings die Geschichte im Ich aufhält.' [The first change the subject has experienced is that it no longer resides in history; rather, history now resides in the subject.][38] This deceptively simple statement acknowledges the extent to which the history of fascist perpetration continues, both synchronically and diachronically, to permeate the modern subject. To my knowledge, Bachmann is also one of the first authors to understand that post-1945 historical subject positions can no longer fully be grasped within the victim–perpetrator imaginary. She maintains that post-1945, beyond individual agency, every subject is foundationally enfolded into structures of racial, social and gendered discrimination and/or subjugation. This insight aligns with Rothberg's more recent observation that being at a temporal or geographic distance from

---

36   Alexander von Bormann, 'Besetzt war sie durch und durch'. Traumatisierung im Werk von Anne Duden', in Stephan Braese et al., eds, *Deutsche Nachkriegsliteratur und der Holocaust* 6 (Frankfurt a.M., New York: Campus, 1998), 252.

37   Christine Koschel et al., eds, *Ingeborg Bachmann. Werke*, 3 (Munich: Piper, 1982), 23. Also see my chapter on *Malina* in *Erklär mir Liebe. Weibliche Schreibweisen von Liebe in der Gegenwartsliteratur* (Hamburg: Argument Verlag, 1995), 44–93.

38   *Bachmann. Werke*, 5, 230.

the production of suffering only draws attention to the ways in which we are folded into past histories of domination – histories which do not seem on the surface to concern or shape our individual agency. From the perspective of different generations, the work of (white) female authors like Bachmann (who was born in 1926 and like Grass belongs to the war generation) and Anne Duden (who was born in 1942 and belongs to the *Kriegskinder* generation) identifies and explores the tension inherent in the female subject. Their fictions of memory work reflect on structural discontinuities that shape women's lives and underscore that, depending on race and socio-economic status, real *women* may well be aligned with power and privilege. Yet the performance of gender, as denoted by the referent *woman*, points to a systemic exclusion from both power and privilege.[39] Bachmann's and Duden's critical engagement with the Nazi legacy interrogates the paradoxical confluence of *women's* distance from (women's relative absence from political leadership positions) and *woman's* proximity to (the symbolic appropriation of *woman* as mother of the nation, for instance) regimes of oppression. Recognizing that the shared cultural memory of Austria and Germany largely fails to acknowledge this kind of female *Mittäterschaft,* women authors attempt to articulate the burden of a received 'guilt', a trauma that paralyses their protagonists and turns them into witnesses who lack a language of identity. (I address this kind of paralysis further when discussing *Der Verlorene* in the next chapter.) Knowing that 'die Wahrheit ist dem Menschen zumutbar' [we can bear the truth], Bachmann's prose work reckons with a sense of (female) complicity and implication that resists easy articulation yet demands uncompromising honesty. It is based on the insight 'dass man ent-täuscht und das heißt ohne Täuschung zu leben vermag' [that we can live disappointed, dis-illusioned, and that means without illusions]. Elsner, like Bachmann, posits that we can bear the truth of our 'verschwiegene Erinnerung'. Hence *Fliegeralarm* exposes the extent to which West Germany's post-Shoah memory culture rests on political *Täuschungen* [illusions] and reframes the subject position

39   See for instance Ingeborg Bachmann, *Malina* (1971) and *Der Fall Franza* (1978), as well as Anne Duden, *Das Judasschaf* (1985).

of the *Kriegskinder* by exposing an underlying web of knowledge, denials and disavowals. In conclusion, I return to the novel in light of these findings.

Staging Innocence

In earlier chapters, I have examined the ways in which the *Kriegskinder* narrative, unmoored from historical context and circumstance, draws on equivocations between persecutors and persecuted. Elsner's text rejects this equivocation by provocatively reversing the roles of perpetrators and victims. In *Fliegeralarm*, the claim of innocence rests on the calculated and opportunistic acts of preschool girls. Most notable in this respect is the character of Gaby Glotterthal – besides Lisa Welsner, the only other female character in the whole text. Introduced as unattractive yet sly and devious, she is an expert at dissimulation and pretence. Time and again, her carefully calibrated air of innocence helps her to escape responsibility for her actions since no matter what she steals from her father's surgery, she remains her father's beloved 'Engelskindchen' [little angel child] (FA, 48–49). Her last name, Glotterthal, is also telling. It refers to Glottertal, the location of *Die Schwarzwaldklinik*, a German medical TV drama, popular in the 1980s. Well known to the contemporary reader, it evokes what Jan Süselbeck called 'die seltsam aseptische Sacha Hehn- und Klaus-Jürgen Wussow-Erotik, die in den 1980er Jahren bis zu 28 Millionen deutsche Frührentner und privatversicherte Helmut-Kohl-Wähler in Aufregung versetzte.'[40] [the strangely aseptic Sacha-Hehn-and-Klaus-Jürgen-Wussow-language of erotic titillation, which in the 1980s entertained up to twenty-eight million early retirees and privately insured

---

40 Jan Süselbeck, 'Verfluchung einer Kriegskinderbiografie. NS-Geschlechtsbilder und Generationenkritik in Gisela Elsners Roman *Fliegeralarm*', in Christian Poetini, ed., *Gender im Gedächtnis. Geschlechtsspezifische Erinnerungen in der deutschsprachigen Gegenwartsliteratur* (Bielefeld: Aisthesis, 2015), 204. Forty years after its first broadcast *Die Schwarzwaldklinik* is rebroadcast on German public TV; evidently, the show has not lost its broad appeal.

Helmut-Kohl-voting-Germans.] Gaby's savvy performance of innocence and medical 'expertise' coupled with her willingness to experiment on her victim, gives the novel its incisive diachronic charge, sardonically fusing the shallow seductions of a TV soap opera with the historical shadow of Josef Mengele, the sadistic SS officer and physician known as 'the angel of death'.

Since *Fliegeralarm* is focalized consistently through the unfiltered, if unchildlike, immediacy of Lisa's thoughts and observations, Gaby's last name is the only instance in the text that evokes the contemporary context, that is, the only instance that interrupts the fusion between a narrating 'I' and an experiencing 'I'. This only slightly veiled reference to a contemporary TV show represents an intermedial and self-referential break in the textual diegesis. It draws attention to the difference between narrated time and narrating time. In her analysis of the rhetoric of memory in literature, Birgit Neumann points out that the 'synchronous plurality of culturally circulating media of memory and versions of the past' create what Barthes called an 'echochamber' of the past, a space of temporal reverberation 'in which the complex cultural heritage continues to resonate up to the present'.[41] In *Fliegeralarm*, this echochamber effect is most obvious when the children *act* either as traumatized victims or as victims coarsened and numbed by bombing attacks. Here, Elsner's choreography of childhood innocence uncovers what Bachmann termed 'Täuschungen', in this case illusions reinforced in debates about Germany's *Kriegskinder* as the 'forgotten victims of war'. The novel makes unmistakably clear that perpetrators are perfectly capable of playing the victim for their own gain, that the nation's cultural memory rests on wilful manipulations and deflections. This victim and perpetrator reversal uncomfortably borders on victim-blaming, a strategy of guilt displacement which, as Adorno pointed out in 1962, is a common trick used by anti-Semites: 'sich als Verfolgte darzustellen; sich zu gebärden, als wäre durch die öffentliche Meinung, die Äußerungen des Antisemitismus heute unmöglich macht, der Antisemit eigentlich der, gegen

---

41   Birgit Neumann, 'The Literary Representation of Memory', in Astrid Erll and Ansgar Nünning, eds, *A Companion to Cultural Memory Studies* (Berlin, New York, 2010), 339.

den der Stachel der Gesellschaft sich richtet'[42] [to represent themselves as persecuted; to act as if the anti-Semite is the one discriminated against, denounced by public opinion which makes anti-Semitic speech impossible today]. As discussed above, in the Kohl era, responsibility for the Nazi past was increasingly outsourced to public acts of commemoration which turned victims and perpetrators into abstractions. In the mid-1990s, events like the 'Wehrmachtsausstellung' [Wehrmacht exhibition], a critical look at the mentality promoted in Hitler's military, which is further exposed in Daniel Goldhagen's book *Hitler's Willing Executioners* (discussed in more detail in Chapter 5), reverse this trend by focusing on the role individuals played in Hitler's project of annihilation. More recently, Germany's right-wing parties such as the AfD, use the time-honoured strategies Adorno identified in 1962, that is, the shift 'von Schuldabwehr zu Schuldumkehr' [from denial to reversal of guilt]. Alexander Gauland, co-founder of the AfD, asserts that all Germans are first and foremost Hitler's victims, 'Ja, Hitler hat viel mehr zerstört als die Städte und die Menschen, er hat den Deutschen das Rückgrat gebrochen, weitgehend.'[43] [Yes, Hitler destroyed far more than cities and people, he broke the back of the German people – to a great extent]. Gauland's assertion is representative of the recent trend in German politics to embrace victim–perpetrator reversals. On the one hand, the far right relies on anti-Semitic projections supported by concrete denials of guilt and accountability vis-à-vis Nazi perpetration, and on the other hand, it decontextualizes and mythologizes the past in order to forge a sense of national belonging based on collective victimhood.[44]

By fluidly trading positions of perpetrator and victim, Elsner's *Kriegskinder* not only mirror the illusions that obscure collective *Mitwisserschaft* in the 1980s and 1990s but also anticipate the victimology reasserted by the contemporary right-wing rhetoric. Moreover, while certainly a provocative social critique in this respect, the novel may also express

---

42   Theodor W. Adorno, 'Zur Bekämpfung des Antisemitismus heute', Rolf Tiedemann, ed., *Adorno. Vermischte Schriften I*, 20–1 (Frankfurt a.M.: Suhrkamp, 1997), 363.

43   Quoted in Samuel Salzborn, *Kollektive Unschuld. Die Abwehr der Shoah im deutschen Erinnern* (Berlin: Hentrich & Hentrich, 2020), 112.

44   Salzborn, 83.

a personal sense of victimization felt by a writer sidelined and marginalized as a communist.[45] Despite the novel's sharp rejection of exculpatory
memory cultures, it is not without irony that (like the two works discussed
so far) *Fliegeralarm* also displaces the Jewish victim – yet again, there are
no Jewish victims. Not surprisingly, Rudy, the German boy and designated
'Jewish' victim, is the only rational voice in the text, he represents the better
German. Raised as the son of a Hitler-critical communist, he deftly calls
out the ideological distortions, false claims and irrational explanations put
forth by his captors (FA, 81–85). The fact that Rudy's father is the only
character sent to a concentration camp reflects Elsner's own sense of mar-
ginalization. In the 1980s, no longer recognized as an author, cultural critic
or relevant political voice in the Communist Party, she feels maligned and
misunderstood.[46] Alienated from her community and frustrated by party
functionaries, she regards herself to have been 'murdered' by the public
and members of the Communist Party alike. Thus, *Fliegeralarm* at once
reveals structural illusions of cultural memory and, not unlike the postwar
fictions of memory discussed so far, perpetuates them: again, the fate of
a German child obscures the fate of Jewish children, in effect reinforcing
a collective silence about the Nazi perpetration that fictions of memory
seemingly seek to interrupt.

In conclusion I want to come back to the dynamics of curse and
counter-curse in Elsner's oeuvre. As a *Kriegskind* and communist, Elsner
felt emotionally and politically aligned with the voice of the victims. In fact,
the story of inadvertent victimhood (a randomly killed German boy) articulates a sense of estrangement typical for members of a generation who could
not publicly work through the psychological wounds of their childhood, let
alone integrate them into a coherent story that made sense in the present.
She shares this sense of estrangement with Helmut Kohl. Curiously, both

---

45   Jahn, 'Fliegeralarm', in Künzel, *Die letzte Kommunistin*, 73.
46   For more on Elsner's struggle with the Communist Party, see her letter to Herbert
     Mies, in which she lays out why she is leaving the party (which she joins again four
     months later). 'Brief an Herbert Mies', in *Flüche*, 357–74, as well as the afterword by
     Matthias Meyers in the same volume, 375–93. See also Künzel, 'Einmal im Abseits',
     and in the same volume, Werner Preuß, 'Von den Riesenzwergen direkt ins Abseits.
     Gisela Elsner und ihre Kritiker', 31–46.

Elsner and Kohl acknowledge their *Kriegskind* (dis-) locations using biblical tropes, albeit diametrically opposed ones: while Kohl speaks of a 'blessing', Elsner refers to the corresponding opposite, a 'curse'. While perpetuating illusions it seeks to uncover, *Fliegeralarm* nonetheless categorically rejects exculpatory generalizations. In many ways, this aesthetic refutation of historical innocence dialogues with Adorno's social critique expressed thirty years earlier. In his 1959 essay 'Was bedeutet: Aufarbeitung der Vergangenheit' ['The Meaning of Working Through the Past'], Adorno observed that the memory politics of the 1950s foundationally rested on avoidance of the Nazi past and a reversal of guilt. '[M]an will einen Schlussstrich darunter ziehen und womöglich es selbst aus der Erinnerung wegwischen. Der Gestus, es solle alles vergessen und vergeben sein, der demjenigen anstünde, dem Unrecht widerfuhr, wird von den Parteigängern derer praktiziert, die es begingen.' [There is the intention 'to close the books on the past and, if possible, even remove it from memory. The attitude that everything should be forgotten and forgiven, which would be proper for those who suffered injustice, is practiced by those party supporters who committed the injustice.']⁴⁷ Seven years into Kohl's 'geistig-moralische Wende' and on the cusp of the *Kriegskinder* wave, Elsner's prescient text affirms that National Socialism remains very much alive and challenges the reader with the same question that prompted Adorno's essay in the first place:

> Der Nationalsozialismus lebt nach und bis heute wissen wir nicht, ob bloß als Gespenst dessen, was so monströs war, daß es am eigenen Tode noch nicht starb, oder ob es gar nicht erst zum Tode kam, ob die Bereitschaft zum Unsäglichen fortwest in den Menschen wie in den Verhältnissen, die sie umklammern.

> [National Socialism is very much alive, whether it is merely the ghost of what was so monstrous that it lingers on after its own death, or whether it has not yet died at

---

47 Theodor W. Adorno, 'Was bedeutet: Aufarbeitung der Vergangenheit', in Rolf Tiedemann, ed., *Adorno: Kulturkritik und Gesellschaft*, 10–2 (Frankfurt a.M.: Suhrkamp, 1997), 555. 'The Meaning of Working Through the Past', in Henry W. Pickford, trans., *Critical Models: Intervention and Catchwords* (New York: Columbia University Press, 1998), 89–90.

all, whether the willingness to commit the unspeakable survives in people, as well as in the conditions that enclose them.][48]

This concludes my analysis of fictions of memory written by authors of the 'Erfahrungsgeneration', that is, the war and *Kriegskinder* generations. All three texts examined so far 'write the child' as a potent focalizing lens that transposes visceral and immediate historical experiences into fictions of memory. Seen from the turn of the millennium and in dialogue with the *Kriegskind* narrative, they define (Forte), stylize (Grass), or satirize (Elsner) the child as a figure of memory through which to illuminate core tenets of cultural memory. While Forte's novel rests on the imagination of the 'innocent child', this trope of the heroic child witness has no traction in the works of both Grass and Elsner. In the 1980s, Grass's knowing child gives way in Elsner's novel to the implicated child and further exposes the shift from denial to reversal of guilt in the memory politics of West Germany. In the last part of this study, I turn to postmemory texts written from the perspective of subsequent generations that use a child focalizer as a lens through which to inspect a generational belatedness, a received *Mitwisserschaft* about the Shoah. Their texts offer critical engagements with the increasingly ubiquitous web of narrative tropes, metaphorical condensations and iconic abbreviations, a web that offers redemptive negotiations between the horrors of a history that remains uncontainable while producing ever more strategies of narrative containment.

48   Adorno, 'Was bedeutet: Aufarbeitung', 555; 'The Meaning of Working Through the Past', 89–90.

PART II

The *Kriegsenkel* Generation

CHAPTER 5

'The past does not want to disappear':
Hans-Ulrich Treichel's *Der Verlorene*

In the second part of this volume, I turn to works by second- and third-generation authors. Born well after 1945, they have received the history of National Socialism as mediated through family stories and an increasingly dense web of cultural and aesthetic representations. More than half a century after the end of the Second World War, the Holocaust is a firmly established paradigm for a trauma memory that draws on ubiquitous tropes, metaphors and narrative choreographies. Its 'genrefication' has been critiqued as an aesthetic encoding that not only rests on, but in some instances also serves to screen out the gravitas of the unresolved questions at its core. In previous chapters, I have traced how 'writing the child' both mirrors and refutes strategies of encoding primary wartime experiences, how authors of the *Kriegskind* and the war generation navigate questions of generational complicity. In these last two chapters, I examine more broadly how authors 'born after' 'rewrite the child' in order to address questions of transgenerational implication. While the fictions of memory examined so far deal with this question synchronically, that is, based on personal experiences of the Second World War, the two chapters that follow examine works that address them diachronically across a widening generational and temporal gap.

Due to a greater degree of historical and generational distance from the originary event, Hans-Ulrich Treichel's *Der Verlorene* (1998)[1] and Rachel

---

1   Hans-Ulrich Treichel's works are quoted as follows: DV: *Der Verlorene* (Frankfurt a.M.: Suhrkamp, 1999); L: *Lost*, Carol Brown Janeway, trans. (New York: Vintage, 2000); VLS *Von Leib und Seele* (Frankfurt a.M.: Suhrkamp, 1992); HK: *Heimatkunde* (Frankfurt a.M.: Suhrkamp, 1996); and EA: for *Der Entwurf des Autor: Frankfurter Poetikvorlesungen* (Frankfurt a.M.: Suhrkamp, 2000). Since

Seiffert's *The Dark Room* (2001) turn to the Nazi past from the position of *Nachträglichkeit*. Their work trains the childhood lens on a sense of identity shaped, if not ruptured, by 'inherited' experiences of historical trauma. Writing both through and against the grain of a lexis of the Holocaust, Treichel and Seiffert deploy the child witness as an unwitting agent of received but not always overtly articulated family stories. In that sense, their work belongs to the German family or generational novel which searches for an adequate language for what Marianne Hirsch has termed (affiliative) postmemory: 'a very powerful and very particular form of memory, precisely because its connection to its object or source is mediated not through recollection but through an imaginative investment and creation'.[2] This kind of memory resonates for a generation of writers who, as Kirstin Gwyer notes, is less concerned 'with the historical events, themselves, than the secondary effects on those inheriting them in the form of a legacy of trauma or guilt and a burden of memory, or, conversely, as repressed or absent memory'.[3] Instead, they address the persistent presence of an inherited history. As I show in this chapter, the 'German family novel' reacts to the historical caesura of unification as either a historical turning point or a reopening of as-yet-unhealed wartime wounds and offers powerful imaginative explorations of a received history, in particular its gaps, misrepresentations and mythologies.[4]

---

the existing translation does not do justice to the wit and irony of Treichels' text, I offer adjustments when necessary.

2   Marianne Hirsch, *Family Frames: Photography, Narrative, and Postmemory* (Cambridge, London: Harvard University Press, 1997), 22.

3   Kirstin Gwyer, 'Beyond Lateness?: "Postmemory" and the Late(st) German Language Family Novel', *New German Critique* 42/2 (2015): 140. The title of this chapter refers to a remark by the author in 2004: 'Auch ich habe – trotz des gegenwärtigen Hangs zur bloßen Gegenwärtigkeit – irgendwann gemerkt: die Vergangenheit will nicht vergehen. Alles ist in uns aufgehoben als nachwirkender Konfliktstoff.' [Even I noticed that – despite the current trend to remain in the present – the past does not want to disappear. Everything is stored within us as an enduring site of conflict.] Jane V. Curran, Steve Dowden, '"Ostwestfalen ist überall". Gespräch mit Hans-Ulrich Treichel', *Colloquia Germanica* 37 3/4 (2004): 315.

4   Examples of German family novels include Marcel Beyer, *Spione* (2000), Rachel Seiffert, *The Dark Room* (2001); Günter Grass, *Im Krebsgang* (2002); Tanja Dückers, *Himmelskörper* (2003); Stephan Wackwitz, *Unsichtbares Land* (2003);

Der Verlorene, written in the wake of unification, is inscribed by a 'Verlustgeschichte' (EA, 46) [history of loss], both on the personal and the national level. In his Frankfurt lectures *Der Entwurf des Autors* [*Conceptualizing an Author*], Treichel reflects on 1989 as an incisive moment of collective disorientation and personal revelation.

> Ich habe den Verlust Westberlins, wenn ich die Wiedervereinigung mal so nennen darf, in gewisser Weise verschoben verarbeitet, in dem sich mir plötzlich der Verlust meines ältesten Bruders im Jahr 1945 aufdrängte. Er wurde nun für mich, das heißt für meinen damaligen Schreibzustand, zu einer aktuellen Erfahrung, die verarbeitet werden musste. Und ich schließe nicht aus, dass das Aktuellwerden dieser weit zurückliegenden Verlustgeschichte auch etwas mit den Umbrüchen der damaligen deutschen und Berliner Gegenwart zu tun hatte. (EA, 46–47)

> [I worked through the loss of West Berlin, if I may describe unification in this way, by way of displacement, in that all of a sudden, I felt the need to address the loss of my brother in 1945. For me, for my former writing self, this loss became an immediate experience which demanded to be worked through. And I suspect that this acute immediacy of a history of loss was connected to the historical changes of 1989 and living in Berlin.]

When his mother died shortly after reunification, he began slowly to work through the papers his parents had left behind, including documentation from the Red Cross about their search for their first-born son. Although Treichel knew about the loss of an older brother, he did not know that his parents had actively searched for him. In fact, he had been told that his brother had died as a 14-month-old baby during the family's flight from their first home in Rakowiec (now Poland) in January of 1945. Thus, the cultural moment of German unification – a foundational shift in the fabric of the nation – uncannily converged with a shift in his own family story, the moment when a dead brother all of a sudden became a

---

Uwe Timm's *Am Beispiel meines Bruders* (2003); Thomas Medicus, *In den Augen meines Großvaters* (2004); Wibke Bruhn's *Meines Vaters Land* (2004); Hans-Ulrich Treichel, *Tagesanbruch* (2016); Susanne Fritz, *Wie kommt der Krieg ins Kind* (2018); Nora Krug's graphic novel *Heimat. Ein deutsches Familienalbum* (2018); and most recently, Jürgen Wiebicke, *Sieben Heringe: Meine Mutter, das Schweigen der Kriegskinder und das Sprechen vor dem Sterben* (2021).

'lost' brother who might well be alive. In ways more complex than the trauma at the centre of the *Kriegskind* narrative, but nonetheless in its wake, *Der Verlorene* is premised on this confluence of the collective and the personal.

In 1995, four years before the publication of *Der Verlorene*, the traveling exhibition *Verbrechen der Wehrmacht 1941–1944* [Crimes of the Wehrmacht 1941–1944] contested the myth of Germany's clean *Wehrmacht*;[5] a year later, Daniel Goldhagen's book *Hitler's Willing Executioners* (1995) questioned the humanity of German soldiers who 'willingly' committed heinous crimes at the Eastern Front. Unlike abstract historical studies about Nazi perpetration which attract little interest from the general public, the Wehrmacht exhibit and Goldhagen's book led to agitated discussions about how to understand the role of German soldiers and civilians in Hitler's war. Both offered what Harald Welzer described as 'emotionale Anschlussfähigkeit' [emotional connectivity], stories about individual perpetrators and individual victims, not statistical facts or abstract theoretical explanations.[6] Furthermore, as I noted in Chapter 1, media representations of the Bosnian War (1992–95) and the Kosovo War (1998–99) triggered repressed memories for the *Kriegskind* generation. For the *Kriegskinder*, televised images of women and children fleeing war zones brought back their own trauma of flight, expulsion and the bombing war – hence the second wave of childhood war memoires at the end of the millennium. *Der Verlorene* negotiates this visceral return of the Nazi past, albeit from the *Kriegsenkel* [grandchild of war] perspective. In contrast to the material discussed thus far,

5   For more on this exhibit, see for instance Bernd Ulrich, ed., *Besucher einer Ausstellung: Die Ausstellung 'Vernichtungskrieg: Verbrechen der Wehrmacht 1941–1944': Interview und Gespräch* (Hamburg: Hamburger Institut für Sozialforschung, 1998).

6   For more on the reception of Goldhagen's book, see Michael Schneider, 'Die "Goldhagen Debatte": ein Historikerstreit in der Mediengesellschaft', Friedrich Ebert Stiftung, Gesprächskreis Geschichte, 17, Bonn 1997, <https://www.fes.de/ fulltext/historiker/00144.htm>, accessed 10 August 2021. For more on the debate about its merits, see Jochen Böhmer, '*Hitlers willige Vollstrecker* und die Goldhagen Debatte in Deutschland', *Zukunft braucht Erinnerung*, <https://www.zukunft­ braucht-erinnerung.de/hitlers-willige-vollstrecker-und-die-goldhagen-debatte-in­ deutschland/>, accessed 10 August 2021.

this text does not offer yet another story about the last war years. Rather, it represents what W. G. Sebald described as a 'Schmerzensspur' [trace of pain] and what Treichel identifies as 'eine sehr späte Reaktion eines Nachgeborenen auf ein nicht sehr oft erzähltes Leiden' [the rather belated reaction of someone 'born after' to a story of suffering that was rarely told] or 'die Wirkungen der Wirkungen' [the effects of the effects].[7] Conceived post-1989, in the wake of agitated national conversations about the Nazi past, Treichel works through details of his own life in light of recalibrations of a German national identity that was caught between celebrating the end of the postwar era, on the one hand, and acknowledging unresolved wartime legacies, on the other. His text, a postmemorial pastiche, weaves together a web of private family legends, historical facts and collectively curated memory narratives, in which the child features as a symptomatic site of memory, a site of received secrets, unacknowledged feelings, inadvertent disclosures and sullen resistance. In the following, I first consider Treichel's staging of the child's voice and then examine how the text performs palimpsestic memory work. The last part of the chapter is focused on the vicissitudes of German postmemory.

Modulating the Child's Voice

The text – more a psycho-sociological vignette of dysfunctional postwar life in the 1950s than a plot-driven narrative – describes the dynamics of a family caught in obsessive, yet futile attempts to undo the irreversible loss of a child. The narrative has minimal typographical demarcations and the whole text consists of four long paragraphs that describe how the search for a child lost during the flight from the family's first home in the former eastern territories deepens a sense of dislocation and displacement in the 'replacement' child born after. Initially, the parents of the nameless

7   Rhys W. Williams, '"Leseerfahrungen sind Lebenserfahrungen": Gespräch mit Hans-Ulrich Treichel', in David Basker, ed., *Hans-Ulrich Treichel* (Cardiff: University of Wales, 2004), 22.

narrator claim that their first-born son Arnold (the only character who has a name) has died. Later they revise this story and reveal that Arnold was lost when the mother, in a moment of impending rape and mortal danger, hands her baby to a stranger and later is unable to locate him. For the narrator, Arnold becomes 'der untote Bruder' (DV, 17) [my un-dead brother (L, 10)], an increasingly disturbing irritant who erases his sense of existence. The more desperately his parents search for their lost child, the more the remaining child feels lost.

The text starts rather abruptly with a description of baby Arnold, 'Mein Bruder hockte auf einer weißen Wolldecke und lachte in die Kamera. Das war während des Krieges, sagte die Mutter, im letzten Kriegsjahr, zuhaus. Zuhaus, das war der Osten, und der Bruder war im Osten geboren worden.' (DV,7) [My brother squatted on a white blanket and laughed into the camera. That was during the last year of the war, at home. Home was the East and my brother had been born in the East. (L, 30)][8] Arnold's presence in the family album is emphatically set apart from the narrator's pictorial absence: 'Während mein Bruder Arnold schon zu Säuglingszeiten nicht nur wie ein glücklicher, sondern auch wie ein bedeutender Mensch aussah, war ich auf den meisten Fotos meiner Kindheit zumeist nur teilweise und manchmal auch so gut wie überhaupt nicht zu sehen.' (DV, 8–9) [While my brother Arnold looked not just happy but important, even when he was a baby, in most of the photos from my childhood I am either only partly visible or sometimes not really visible at all. (L, 4)]. Similar to what Barthes has called a 'referent', Arnold is a figure who is 'both present (implied in the photograph) and absent (has been here but is not here now). The referent haunts the picture like a ghost: it is a revenant, a return of the lost and dead other.'[9] The indexical trace of this photograph, that is, the fact that the narrator cannot deny that his brother has been there but does not recognize him, creates the palimpsestic space of temporal superimposition, which Barthes has described as the *ça-a-été* of a photograph. 'In photography', Barthes writes, 'I can never deny that *the thing has been there*. There is a superimposition here: of reality, and of the past', an incontrovertible

---

8   The translation erroneously reads: 'my mother had been born in the East'.
9   Hirsch, *Family Frames*, 5.

ça-a-été [what-has-been].[10] In other words, the photograph of this unknown brother is a ghost witness to history. The opening of the text, then, unfolds history as a faded image of unknown people, 'a time when we were not yet born', as Hirsch puts it, inscribed by family mythologies which rest on the narrative and imaginary power of family photographs. 'Photographs', she suggests, 'locate themselves in the space of contradiction between the myth of the ideal family and the lived reality of family life.'[11] In this case, however, there is no (coherent or inclusive) family photo to uphold a family myth, only an array of isolated and detached pictures of children who never encountered each other. Yet the mother's continued contemplation of Arnold's picture nonetheless represents the focus of the family gaze and sustains this family's mythology. That is to say, her gaze establishes Arnold's presence and erases that of her second son. The narrator's life is evacuated – not by stories, but by photographs of an omnipresent phantom brother.

In this family, acts of looking are a source of permanent discomfort. 'Vom Tag meiner Geburt an herrschte ein Gefühl von Schuld und Scham in der Familie, ohne dass ich wusste, warum. Ich wusste nur, dass ich bei allem, was ich tat, eine gewisse Schuld und eine gewisse Scham verspürte.' (DV, 17) [From the day of my birth, guilt and shame had ruled the family, without my knowing why. All I knew was that whatever I did, I felt guilty and ashamed as I did it. (L, 10–11)] Treichel's child witness shoulders an emotional burden that does not belong to him – a burden he increasingly resists when Arnold threatens to become all too real. Wise beyond his years, in sometimes sad and sometimes defiantly hilarious ways, the idiosyncratic voice of this child witness is a character in its own right. Insistent observations flaunt precocious insights that expose contradictory parental statements and behaviours. On one hand the narrator, nurturing sadistic revenge fantasies, adopts the voice of a hurt child plagued by sibling rivalry; on the other hand, he offers more mature retrospections than his teenage self would allow. Not unlike *Fliegeralarm*, the text mimics the single-mindedness of children's thought and speech patterns. The narrator's

10 Roland Barthes, Richard Howard, trans., *Camera Lucida: Reflections on Photography* (New York: Hill and Wang, 2010), 76–77.
11 Hirsch, *Family Frames*, 8.

diction displays elliptical repetitions in which recurring elements within a string of enumerations return, but in slightly displaced and reconfigured form. Refracted through the subsequent mediations of his older adolescent self, this voice is shot through with broader discourses about the war (in this case, about flight and expulsion) that betray a sense of personal belatedness and collective resentment. When his father shares with his son that Arnold is not dead but 'only lost', the son first patiently repeats what he hears, and then spins his own reflections using the same verbiage his father had used. I quote an extensive passage to illustrate the son's verbal mimicry and reflections.

> 'Arnold', sagte ich, 'ist gar nicht verhungert, Arnold ist verlorengegangen.' Als der Vater nicht reagierte, sagte ich noch einmal, 'Arnold ist gar nicht verhungert. Arnold ist verlorengegangen.' Der Vater reagierte immer noch nicht und schien irgendwelchen Gedanken nachzusinnen. Vielleicht hätte ich ihm auch noch sagen sollen, dass ich gar keinen Verlust verspürt hatte. Schließlich hatte ich ja auch niemanden verloren. Ich hatte nur erfahren, dass die Eltern jemanden verloren und doch nicht verloren hatten. Und als ich erfahren hatte, dass Arnold nicht verhungert, sondern nur verloren gegangen sei, hätte ich höchstens insofern einen Verlust erlitten, als ich nun gewissermaßen einen toten und zumal einen auf der Flucht vor den Russen gestorbenen Bruder verloren hatte. Statt des toten hatte ich nun einen verlorengegangen Bruder. Das war für mich allerdings kein Gewinn. Doch wie sollte ich das dem Vater erklären? (DV, 49)

> ['Arnold', I said, 'didn't starve to death, Arnold was lost.' When my father didn't react, I repeated, 'Arnold didn't starve to death. Arnold was lost.' My father still didn't react and seemed to be turning thoughts over in his mind. Perhaps I should have told him that I hadn't felt any loss at all. When you came right down to it, I hadn't lost anyone anyway. I had only learned that my parents had lost and yet not lost someone. And when I discovered that Arnold hadn't starved, but had just been lost, the only loss I could be said to have suffered was that I'd lost a dead brother, who'd died what's more while fleeing the Russians. Now I didn't have a dead brother, I had a lost one. That was hardly a plus for me. But how could I explain this to my father? (L, 35)]

These repetitive utterances denote the enormity of both a personal loss and a historical rupture beyond the grasp of a child. While the use of complex past tense and subjunctive constructions, as well as the paratactical syntax, are incompatible with the speech pattern of a child (not unlike the voices of all child focalizers examined so far), the reiterative rhetoric at

once mimics a child's penchant for repetition and underscores the intensity of Arnold's ghostlike presence. Permeated by dry irony and humour,
it indicates the growing confusion of a child gripped by sibling rivalry.
Addressing a non-listening parent, the narrator describes his own state of
mind to the reader and discloses that he is already in the know. Hence, he
keeps repeating the key facts and terms of the Arnold story: 'verhungert'
[starved to death] and 'verlorengegangen' [lost]. The use of the German
phrase 'verlorengegangen' stands out as particularly provocative, since it
levels the difference between objects and people. Objects can end up as
'verlorengegangen'; people, however, go missing or disappear. Yet for the
narrator, the unknown brother does signify a lost 'object' that frames and
ultimately empties his own sense of self. This shift in the parental story
from a dead (and hence unthreatening) brother he vaguely feels proud of
(DV, 11, L, 6) to a lost brother he is competing with delineates the foundational loss at the core of postwar German identity and evoked by the
title of the book.

The story unfolds as a more expansive story of loss deeply inscribed
onto the psychopathology of his family. Eric Santner, referring to Margarete
Mischerlich's remarks about the effect of inherited Nazi structures passed
on to successive generations, speaks about the 'ghosts, the revenant objects
of the Nazi period [...] transmitted to the second and third generations at
the sites of the primal scenes of socialization, that is, within the context
of the psychopathology of the postwar family'.[12] *Der Verlorene* exposes
how contemporary discourses about the 'Vertriebenen' (German civilians
displaced from the eastern territories by the war) cohere around the long-
standing victimology going back to the 1950s (the narrated time frame)
and continue to rest on assertions of innocence, yet fail to completely
erase a paradoxical sense of guilt. Permeated by a sense of complicity in a
history that came before, the text simultaneously evokes and disputes the
presumption of childhood innocence.[13] As mentioned above, this child
always feels guilty.

12   Eric Santner, *Stranded Objects: Mourning, Memory and Film in Postwar Germany*
      (Ithaca, NY: Cornell University Press, 1990), 35.
13   Here, my reading builds on the work of Serena Grazzini and Christoph Parry
      who argue that *Der Verlorene* reveals the extent to which acts of recall are

Ich fühlte mich schuldig, weil ich aß, und ich schämte mich, weil ich aß. Wohl spürte ich sehr genau, dass ich mich schuldig fühlte und dass ich mich schämte, aber es war mir gänzlich unerklärlich, warum ich, der ich doch nichts weiter als ein unschuldiges Kind war, mich eines Stückes Fleisch oder einer Kartoffel schuldig fühlen musste. (DV, 17–18)

[I felt guilty to be eating, and ashamed to be eating. I absolutely knew that I felt guilty and ashamed, but I could not explain to myself why the innocent child that I was should be shamed by a piece of meat or a potato or should feel guilty. (L, 11)]

This passage makes legible the transgenerational legacy of a perpetrator history permeated by unacknowledged trauma. Haydée Faimberg has described this transference of emotions as the 'telescoping of generations', a symbiotic but paradoxical connection between traumatized parents and their children. She examined how a traumatic history that does not belong to the child is transmitted across generations as a secret to be shouldered. This 'inheritance' creates a 'double, contradictory condition of a psyche that is *empty* and at the same time *"overfull"* [...] weighed down by an excessive or never absent object'.[14] Arnold, the lost brother, is this 'excessive or never absent object'; his omnipresence leads to rivalry with a phantom, a tension that only reinforces the younger brother's sense of guilt and shame. In the next section, I read the narrative choreography of *Der Verlorene* as a textual superimposition of disparate historical layers, outlined in the introduction as the 'Nach-Geschichte' [post-history] of Nazism in the wake of post-*Wende* agitations.

---

permeated by strategies of disavowal. Serena Grazzini, 'Erinnerte Vergangenheit und subjektive Wahrnehmung. Hans-Ulrich Treichels Der Verlorene', in Manuel Maldonado-Alemán and Carsten Gansel, eds, *Literarische Inszenierungen von Geschichte. Formen der Erinnerung in der deutschsprachigen Literatur nach 1945 und 1989* (Stuttgart: Metzler, 2018); Christoph Parry, 'Die Rechtfertigung der Erinnerung vor der Last der Geschichte. Autobiographische Strategien bei Timm, Treichel, Walser und Sebald', in *Grenzen der Fiktionalität und der Erinnerung* (Munich: Iudicum, 2007), 98–111.

14   Haydée Faimberg, *The Telescoping of Generations: Listening to the Narcissistic Links between Generations* (London, New York: Routledge, 2005), 8.

Palimpsestic Configurations

For Treichel, the war trauma of his parents only becomes legible decades after the war.

> Wobei es für mich selbst symptomatisch ist, dass ich dieses Buch erst in den neunziger Jahren geschrieben habe und nicht etwa zehn oder fünfzehn Jahre früher, was ja vom Lebensalter durchaus möglich gewesen wäre. Insofern stellt das Buch eine sehr späte Reaktion eines Nachgeborenen auf ein nicht sehr oft erzähltes Erleiden dar.[15]

> [The fact that I wrote the book only in the nineties and not ten or fifteen years earlier – which I could have done given my age – is symptomatic, to my mind. The book is a belated reaction to a story of rarely told suffering from the perspective of someone born after.]

The voice and perceptual stance of an overdetermined childlike witness in *Der Verlorene* thus represents the 'späte Reaktion eines Nachgeborenen' [delayed reaction of someone born afterwards].[16] The narrated time frame of the 1950s and 1960s offers a diagnosis of the 1990s based on superimpositions of disparate temporal and semiotic layers which, rather than dissolving different points in time, reconfigure both. Referring to Benjamin's notion of constellation, Maxim Silverman has described this kind of memory work as a poetic composite that does not simply combine different temporal moments, that is, past and present. Rather, by evoking a number of disparate moments, it effectively creates new chains of signification which bring into dialogue previously distinct spaces and times and as a result transform the perception of both present and past.[17] Toggling between 1945 and the 1990s, *Der Verlorene* does not draw on the gap between narrated time and narrating time in the way *Die Blechtrommel* does (by bringing temporal moments into dialogue but nonetheless keeping

---

15	Williams, 22.
16	Ibid.
17	Maxim Silverman, *Palimpsestic Memory: The Holocaust and Colonialism in Francophone Fiction and Film* (New York, Oxford: Berghahn, 2013), 3.

them distinct) but unfolds how temporal differences dissolve on the experiential and psychological level.

On the plot level, unresolved aspects of the war come to light first and
foremost in the intrinsically futile search for a child who is paradoxically
saved (to the world) by being lost (to his parents) and whose existence leads
the child born after to feel lost. Amir Eshel has observed, on a more existential level, the trope of the lost child evokes the Christian symbolism of the
sacrificed child and points to the symbolic loss of historical continuity.[18]
This discontinuity is etched into the psyche of all involved: for the parents
it translates into never-ending grief, guarded by denials of guilt; for the
son, it manifests as psychosomatic symptoms and an inherited sense of
shame. But there are also concrete external manifestations of a past 'that
does not want to go away'.[19] Some, like the secret attic that served for the
narrator as 'Zauberort, aber auch mein Angstort' (DV, 46), ['my magical
forest but also my place of terror' (L, 33)], are removed during the frantic
rebuilding efforts of the 1950s. Others remain visible, like the bullet holes
in the ceiling of the examination room at the Institute of Forensic Medicine
in Heidelberg, where the family has come to determine their biological
connection to Arnold, designated as 'foundling 2307'. When the narrator
sees these visible traces of war, he is stunned – he has never seen bullet
holes. Catching his curious gaze, the head scientist at the institute, Baron
von Liebstedt, makes clear to him that these remnants of the Second World
War are utterly irrelevant. 'Das sind Einschusslöcher [...] vom Krieg, [...]
aber das tut nichts zur Sache.' (DV, 114) [They are bullet holes [...] from
the war, [...] but they are irrelevant. (L, 87)][20] In fact, just the opposite is
the case: the bullet holes have everything to do with the war. Not only are
they physical reminders of a war that was lost at great cost, but they also

18   Amir Eshel, 'Die Grammatik des Verlusts: Verlorene Kinder, verlorene Zeit
      in Barbara Honigmanns *Soharas Reise* und in Hans-Ulrichs *Der Verlorene*', in
      Hartmut Steinecke and Sander Gilman, eds, Beiheft zur *Zeitschrift für deutsche
      Philologie: Deutsch-jüdische Literatur der neunziger Jahre: Die Generation nach der
      Shoah* (Berlin: Erich Schmidt, 2002), 63.
19   Curran, Dowden, 315.
20   My translation.

signify that Hitler's war rages on in those who survived – evident in the Nazi mindset of von Liebstedt and the father.

The father's words and perceptions betray the kind of reductive racism propagated during the Third Reich. When he muses about the intimate connection between a pig's physiognomy and its value, he is obliquely repeating pseudo-racial hierarchies established in Hitler's physiological taxonomies: 'Ein schöner Kopf komme zwangsläufig immer auch von einem schönen, also muskulär und fettmäßig harmonisch entwickelten Schwein' (DV, 39) ['A fine head is always connected to the body of a fine, that is to say muscular, pig with an even distribution of fat.' (L, 27)]. During his conversation with von Liebstedt about the lost eastern territories and their superior soil quality, the father readily agrees with the professor that the Poles are dirty and disorganized, and the Russians are equally inferior: 'die Russen [...] konnte man nicht mal als Knechte gebrauchen.' (DV, 110–11) ['You couldn't [...] even use the Russians as labourers.' (L, 84)] The father feels fundamentally displaced and is afraid of travelling; leaving one's home remains intrinsically dangerous: 'Ein Bauer aus Rakowiec verlässt sein Haus nicht. Wer sein Haus verlässt, dem lauern die Russen auf. Wer sein Haus verlässt, dem wird sein Haus geplündert und zerstört.' (DV, 122) [A farmer from Rakowiec doesn't abandon his house of his own free will. He who abandons his house will be ambushed by the Russians. He who abandons his house will have his house plundered and destroyed. (L, 93)] Not only are the parents incapable of travelling, they are also 'unfähig zur Erholung' (DV, 19) [incapable of relaxation].[21] In fact, the son keenly understands his father 'büßte durch Arbeit. Er hätte in Frieden leben können, aber es gab keinen Frieden.' (DV, 45) [did his penance in work. He could have lived in peace but there was no peace. (L, 32)] He knows that he is living in an enduring 'Nach-Krieg' [postwar era]: 'es gab keinen Frieden.' (DV, 45) [There was no peace. (L, 32)] The politics of restitution promoted under Adenauer through the 1952 'Lastenausgleichsgesetz' [Equalization of Burdens Act], a legislative initiative to compensate those who had 'lost property or suffered damage during the war', is very present in this family who lost everything after their flight. Yet for the son, the meaning of 'Lastenausgleich' remains

21 Ibid.

nebulous. 'Ich wusste nicht genau, was der Lastenausgleich war, hatte das
Wort aber schon so oft gehört, dass es zu den häufigsten Worten meiner
Kindheit gehört.' (DV, 163) [I wasn't exactly sure what compensation for
their suffering was, but I'd heard the expression so often that it was one of
the most familiar of my childhood. (L, 127)]

Most importantly, the narrator's confused sense of identity straddles
various historical subject positions without finding traction. Feeling humiliated by the ways his parents demand his participation in their search
for Arnold, he emphatically resists being photographed for the purpose
of bio-genetic comparison with 'foundling 2307'. When his father forces
him to have his hair cut very short for the photo shoot, he compares himself to a Holocaust victim: the 'Kurzhaarfrisur' [short haircut] makes him
feel like 'eine Art Lagerinsasse[n] [...] Ich wurde gleichsam kahlgeschoren
und dann von allen Seiten abgelichtet.' (DV, 66) [a sort of camp inmate.
I was shaved almost bald and then photographed from all sides. (L, 48)]
Feeling overlooked and victimized, the son suffers from perpetrator and
guilt fantasies. After the break-in at the family's storage unit, he is convinced of his guilt. 'Ich fühlte mich schuldig, obwohl ich wusste, dass das
völlig unsinnig war.' (DV, 129) [I suddenly imagined that I'd done it. I felt
guilty, even though I knew it was completely mad. (L, 99)] On the psychological level, this unresolved sense of identity documents a 'narcissistic
wounding', common in children of traumatized parents. In her seminal
study of transgenerational war trauma, Anita Eckstaedt draws on Faimberg's
findings about the telescoping of generations. She focuses on the psychological symptoms of children born to parents who had internalized Nazi
ideals and whose childhood was framed by an expressive silence. Pregnant
with the weight of affirmations, rejections or devaluations, this silence,
she argues, distorts the perceptions and communication between parents,
who do not speak and children abandoned into this silence. Drawing on
D. W. Winnicott's concept of the 'false self', his concern that one's sense
of vitality can be jeopardized by pressure to comply with the demands of
others, Eckstaedt observes that 'Nazi children' (here meaning *Kriegskinder*)
often develop a 'false self'. 'Im "falschen Selbst" ist nun das umgekehrte Bild
des vom Objekt Gewünschten enthalten, ein Negativ; in Reaktion auf das
Objekt ist ein Anti-Entwurf entstanden. Diese Form des "falschen Selbst"

möchte ich als "abwehrendes falsches Selbst" bezeichnen.'[22] [The "false self" contains the opposite image of that desired by the object [here meaning the parent, S.B.], a kind of negative; an anti-image evolves in reaction to the object. This kind of "false self" I would like to call the "resisting false self".][23] The resisting 'false self' has difficulty differentiating between inner and outer reality since it contends with an internalized reality shaped by the (traumatic) memories of fathers and mothers, including their false hopes and illusions. In other words, descendants of traumatized Nazi parents struggle with illusionary, unmourned and unnamed fragments of a past which, in fact, do not belong to them but to their parents. As a result, Eckstaedt finds, they are more than just lost and more than just alienated; they suffer a powerful sense of 'Enteignung' [expropriation], as a consequence of serving as a replacement for someone irreplaceable (I return to this below).[24]

When seen in light of these psychological dynamics, the permeable boundaries between victims and perpetrators described in *Der Verlorene* reveal the narrator's sense of expropriation based on the telescoping of generations.[25] On the level of its narrative choreography, however, the escalating slide across disparate subject positions represents a poignant and self-reflexive traversal of cultural mediations of the Holocaust. The narrator assumes the perspectives of the confused outsider, the hurt witness, the guilty culprit, the angry perpetrator and the traumatized victim. In this respect, the text draws on aesthetic approximations and appropriations of the Shoah which remain resonant because they are open to multiple meanings. However, as I show in the next section, in this instance

22　Anita Eckstaedt, *Nationalsozialismus in der 'zweiten Generation'. Psychoanalyse von Hörigkeitsverhältnissen* (Frankfurt a.M.: Suhrkamp, 1989), 22.

23　Note that in object relations theory, the object is a person, in particular a significant person (here the mother) who is the target of another's (here the child's) feelings or intentions.

24　Eckstaedt, 24.

25　For more on this aspect, see Katja Stopka, 'Vertriebene Erinnerung: Transgenerationelle Nachwirkungen von Flucht und Vertreibung im literarischen Gedächtnis am Beispiel von Hans-Ulrich Treichels *Der Verlorene*', in Wolfgang Hartwig and Erhardt Schutz, eds, *Keiner kommt davon. Zeitgeschichte in der Literatur nach 1945* (Göttingen: Vandenhoeck & Ruprecht, 2008), 166–84.

the slide across multiple subject positions is anchored in the perspective of the *Kriegsenkel*, that is, a distinctly German refraction of postmemory.

Postmemorial Transpositions

Treichel's 'writing the child' neither apologetically rewrites nor unilaterally focuses on the effects of a perpetrator legacy. Instead, it translates generational distance to an originary event into the self-reflexive and critical language of postmemory. Marianne Hirsch has defined postmemory as 'distinguished from memory by generational distance and from history by deep personal connection'.[26] It expresses an existential form of 'belatedness', not in a temporal but in a conceptual sense, similar to the layered postmodern pastiche created through borrowing and cross-referencing. Instead of being an identity *position*, postmemory is conceived of as a generational *structure* of transmission that generates a dynamic of familial belonging. Postmemory brings the family into focus as an overdetermined site, a space of belonging 'entrenched in a collective imaginary shaped by public, generational structures of fantasy and projection and by a shared archive of stories and images that inflect the transmission of individual and familial remembrance'.[27] While similar, German and Jewish expressions of postmemory draw on distinctly different historical premises. Descendants of Jewish survivors are tasked with creating and guarding a family memory shaped by persecution and murder; descendants of Nazi families also hear stories of suffering and deprivation but tend to disavow a memory riddled with acts of persecution or complicity. In the first case, based on a deep commitment to remember, a legacy of suffering is *guarded* and *preserved* as part of a collective identity. In the second case, similar stories of blameless suffering *distort* and *displace* a legacy of perpetration.

26   Hirsch, *Family Frames*, 22.
27   Marianne Hirsch, 'The Generation of Postmemory', *Poetics Today*, 29/1 (Spring 2008): 114.

How, then, does *Der Verlorene* register these differences and intersections between Jewish and German postmemory?

Treichel's 'writing the child' accentuates generational belatedness in meta-reflexive passages and in the use of irony and laconic humour. The narrator feels overjoyed when he is no longer forced to participate in the family Sunday walks and excursions. He describes them as 'Schuld- und Schamprozessionen' (DV, 19) [processions of shame and guilt (L, 12)] and remembers the moment of release as one of his 'schönsten Kindheitserinnerungen' (DV, 23) [happiest memories of my whole childhood (L, 15)]. The child knows there is no joy in these outings; feelings of joy or pleasure are impossible.

> Ich begriff auch, dass Arnold verantwortlich dafür war, dass ich von Anfang an in einer von Schuld und Scham vergifteten Atmosphäre aufgewachsen war. Vom Tag meiner Geburt an herrschte ein Gefühl von Scham und Schuld in der Familie, ohne dass ich wusste, warum. Ich wusste nur, dass ich bei allem, was ich tat, eine gewisse Schuld und Scham verspürte. (DV, 17)

> [I also understood that Arnold was responsible from the very beginning for my growing up in an atmosphere poisoned with guilt and shame. From the day of my birth, guilt and shame had ruled the family without my knowing why. All I knew was that whatever I did, I felt guilt and ashamed as I did it. (L, 10–11)]

In this instance, the self-ascribed innocence indicates the retrospective distance between narrated time and narrating time, focalizer and narrator. But more importantly, this deflection also highlights an ironic distance between focalizer and narrator, hallmark of the German family novel (a genre which I discuss in more detail below).[28] This gap dissolves,

---

28   Less angry and more even in tone, the family novel extends and expands the genre of *Väterliteratur* [Fathers' Literature], a body of memory texts which in the late 1970s and early 1980s recalled the psycho-social legacy of the Nazi past from the perspective of disillusioned sons and daughters. Centred on authoritarian father figures, who represent the continued influence of Nazi values within the postwar German family, *Väterliteratur* reveals an enduring sense of moral and psychological injury. For a re-evaluation of this genre, see Anne Fuchs, *Phantoms of War in Contemporary German Literature, Films, and Discourse: The Politics of Memory* (Houndmills, Basingstoke: Palgrave Macmillan, 2008), 20–44.

however, when it comes to the language of bodily symptoms. Not unlike trauma symptoms in survivor children, the body of this vicarious witness to the Nazi past performs involuntary memory work, expressing a kind of psychosomatic resistance to what is, because what is is always already contaminated by what is not. Repeating his parents' deeply ingrained fear of travel, the boy develops 'eine spezielle Form von Reisekrankheit' (DV, 21) [a special form of travel sickness (L, 13)], 'Hauptsymptom der Reisekrankheit war eine körperliche Unverträglichkeit von Bewegung' (DV, 21) [the chief symptom of which was a physical inability to tolerate movement (L, 13)]. Tellingly, he regularly throws up in the family car, an ostentatiously flashy vehicle bought to show off the family's material success. As manifestations of an inherited memory of guilt and shame, the boy's symptoms speak the language of postmemory; they 'approximate memory in its affective force and its psychic effects'.[29] Weighed down by a received sense of shame, his body acts out, repeats and ultimately performs an unresolved relationship to the Nazi past. His body performs a postmemorial truth; 'the index of postmemory (as opposed to memory) is the performative index, shaped more and more by affect, need, and desire as time and distance attenuate the links to authenticity and "truth".[30]

Not surprisingly, his symptoms only intensify as he grows older and develops a painful trigeminal neuralgia causing uncontrollable facial contortions, a 'bösartige[s] Grinsen' (DV, 170) ['evil grin' (L, 132)], met with harsh rebukes by the adults. The father's metaphorical manner of speech, asserting that he looks like his lost brother, triggers an intense physical reaction in his son:

> 'Der Junge,' sagte der Vater, 'ist dir wie aus dem Gesicht geschnitten.' Eine Vorstellung, die mir so großes physisches Unbehagen bereitete, dass ich mich zwar nicht übergeben musste, wohl aber eine Art Magenkrampf bekam, der auch mein Gesicht erfasste, die Wangen durchzog und hinter der Stirn endete. Fast schien es, als würde ich die Schnitte spüren, mit denen mir Arnold aus dem Gesicht geschnitten wurde, wobei sich die Schnitte auch in Stromschläge und Schmerzblitze verwandeln konnten, die durch mein Gesicht fuhren und mir ein krampfartiges Grinsen aufnötigten. (DV, 56)

29   Hirsch, *Family Frames*, 31.
30   Hirsch, *The Generation of Postmemory: Writing and Visual Culture after the Holocaust* (New York: Columbia University Press, 2012), 48.

['The boy,' said my father, 'looks as if he were carved out of your face.' An idea which made me so physically queasy that although I didn't have to throw up, I got some kind of stomach cramp that reached up to my face, shot through my cheeks, and ended behind my forehead. It was almost as if I were feeling the cuts as Arnold was being carved out of my face and stabs of pain ran through my face and caused me to grimace. (L, 40)][31]

All too aware that his trigeminal neuralgia is caused by the family ghost, his lost brother, or more precisely, the striking similarity to this brother, the living son feels increasing resentment towards himself.

[I]ch war sicher, dass die Gesichtskrämpfe mit Arnold und speziell mit dem zu tun hatten, was der Vater eine verblüffende Ähnlichkeit nannte. Ich wollte niemandem ähnlich sein, und schon gar nicht meinem Bruder Arnold. Die angeblich verblüffende Ähnlichkeit hatte die Wirkung, dass ich mir selbst immer unähnlicher wurde. Jeder Blick in den Spiegel irritierte mich. Ich sah nicht mich, sondern Arnold, der mir immer unsympathischer wurde. (DV, 57)

[I was sure that my facial twitches were connected with Arnold, and in particular with what my father called an amazing likeness. I didn't want to look like anyone, particularly not my brother Arnold. The supposedly amazing likeness made me feel less and less like myself. Every look in the mirror grated on my nerves. I didn't see me, I saw Arnold, and he was getting less appealing all the time. (L, 41–42)]

In this case, the language used thoughtlessly by his father turns on itself and talks back as a physical symptom in the son; his somatic protestations disrupt the already fragile communication even further. In her analysis of current theories of cultural memory, Anne Fuchs underscores the limits of narrativity for working through and representing historical trauma. Any linear representational and narrative code, she argues,

fails to take into account alternative modes of cultural transmission that communicate through the unsaid, the *sous-entendue*, through innuendo, and silence. [...] this

31 As in other passages, the translation does not do justice to the nuance and force of Treichel's language. In this instance, the original passage builds on the violent metaphor of 'wie aus dem Gesicht geschnitten sein' [as if carved out of [one's] face] and escalates into a pain likened to electric shocks and the force of lightening [*Stromschläge und Schmerzblitze*].

latent type of memory work speaks a language of gesturing that defies representation. [...] This other code upsets the rules of discourse by turning the body into a stage for a performance that offers ghosts and phantoms of the past.[32]

As an exquisitely sensitive stage for unresolved tensions, the language of the body contests the cohesion of narrative representation and brings to light a somatic underbelly, 'a frightful appearance of bodily phantoms [...] both excessive and elusive: excessive because it punctuates the flow of language, and elusive in that it thwarts signification'.[33] In this case, the narrator's body language quite literally displays a phantom presence threatening to evacuate his identity. Treichel's 'writing the child' articulates the existential impasse experienced by 'replacement children' – a phenomenon particularly common after violent histories such as the Holocaust and other genocidal wars.

Children born into a legacy of violent loss are often burdened with the role of (an inherently insufficient) replacement of a lost brother and a lost home, as in *Der Verlorene*. Ironically, since the body does not know the facts of historical cause-and-effect, children of perpetrators and children of survivors suffer similar symptoms. Gabriele Schwab has examined the legacy of transgenerational trauma as experienced by replacement children. Based on her personal experience – she herself is the daughter of parents who lost a child during the war – she comes to recognize that she 'always felt guilt for owing [her] life to the death of an infant brother who was killed during the war'.[34] After consulting psychoanalytic literature about replacement children, she found that these children share a common problem. 'Children born after such wars may feel more than the burden of having to replace the child or children whom their parents lost during the war: they grow up with a sense that their generation must replace the entire generation that was meant to be exterminated.'[35] While equally unrelenting, this

32   Anne Fuchs, 'Towards an Ethics of Remembering: The Walser–Bubis Debate and the Other of Discourse', *The German Quarterly* 75/3 (2002): 236.

33   Fuchs, 241.

34   Gabriele Schwab, *Haunting Legacies: Violent Histories and Transgenerational Trauma* (New York: Columbia University Press, 2010), 120.

35   Ibid.

burden of having to stand in for a lost sibling is framed somewhat differently for children of perpetrators than for children of survivors. Children born to perpetrator parents do not feel the pressure to replace an entire generation, yet nonetheless grow up in a similar atmosphere of silence, denial and splitting off. In fact, a 'family frame' of silence and denial perfectly describes the psychopathology of the narrator's family. Forever displaced by a war and shamed by a sense of failure (to protect their son), all characters 'speak' in symptoms – the visceral language Eva Hoffman, a child of Holocaust survivors, calls the 'most private and potent of family languages – the language of the body'.[36] But in contrast to survivor children, who are tasked with what Hoffman describes as having to become guardians of a 'cargo of awesome knowledge',[37] Treichel's child protagonist rejects this 'cargo'. Feeling trapped by an unacknowledged sense of shame and guilt that is not his to acknowledge, this German child deeply resents what came before. The Jewish survivor child is tasked with the mission to *preserve* the story of lost family members, both for the individual family album and as a contribution to a collectively shared history of survival. In this case, the memory of the past is sacred, even 'salutary',

> the salutary balm most needed by those who have been targets of brutality and injustice. [...] The past cannot be healed or cured. But full and exact acknowledgement – of what happened, of the wrongs inflicted, of the suffering that continues to wind the soul – can act as a form of affective, symbolic justice. It can, crucially, serve to restore for the victim a world of shared meanings and common assumptions after such a world has been wilfully destroyed.[38]

This possibility of remembering in order to restore 'a world of shared meaning' is categorically not available to a German child who experiences the family story of loss as an evacuation of identity. Treichel's narrator, the son of traumatized German expellees, cannot 'fully and exactly acknowledge' the existence of his lost brother, let alone find him and share his life with him. His resistance to Arnold circumscribes the outlines of a

---

36   Eva Hoffman, *After Such Knowledge: Memory, History, and the Legacy of the Holocaust* (New York: Public Affairs, 2004), 9.
37   Hoffman, 14.
38   Hoffman, 57.

memory intimately bound up with received guilt and shame, in this case 'guarded' by silent parents who are paralysed by their own sense of humiliation and defeat. In fact, the moment of truth-telling about Arnold, ominously labelled the 'Aussprache' (DV, 12) [discussion (L, 6)][39] and accompanied by the mother's plea for his help with finding Arnold (DV, 50, L,36), represents a re-wounding for the son and leads to sadistic perpetration fantasies. 'Um ihn doch noch verhungern zu lassen, wünschte ich mir einen dritten Weltkrieg.' (DV, 58) [I longed for a Third World War so that he would starve to death after all. (L, 42)]

Against the backdrop of the psychology of the replacement child and the agitated memory debates of the 1990s – in particular the more rigorous engagement with the perpetrator legacy by a younger generation – Treichel's 'writing the child' offers a picture of the cultural dilemma of this decade. The text unpacks the German child's feelings of resentment about and rejection of a received memory of guilt at odds with broader collective efforts to recalibrate cultural memory in light of a more nuanced knowledge about German perpetration and complicity in Hitler's war of annihilation. *Der Verlorene* belongs to the body of memory texts written around the turn of the millennium that illustrate why Hirsch's notion of postmemory translates into the German context with a twist. Persistent family silences about the Nazi past have compelled German authors to carefully craft postmemory narratives that reflect the dissonance between the family album and the fact-based lexicon. Hence, the German family novel often revolves around the tension between stories of family suffering and stories of family heroism. Helmut Schmitz argues that this tension represents both the premise and the core of German postmemory.[40] *Der Verlorene* registers postmemory as *resistance* to a family story centred around a sense of victimization (the parents lose their child), feelings of guilt and shame (they failed to protect their son, the mother was raped), as well as complicity (their mindset betrays

39   The German term *Aussprache* implies the need to resolve an issue and carries the more ominous ring of 'we need to talk'.

40   Helmut Schmitz, 'Postmemory. Erbe und Familiengedächtnis bei Hanns-Josef Ortheil, Thomas Medicus, Wibke Bruhns, Uwe Timm und Dagmar Leupold', in Hans-Peter Preusser, Helmut Schmitz, and Dominick Orth, eds, *Autobiografie und historische Krisenerfahrung* (Heidelberg: Universitätsverlag Winter, 2010), 275.

a belief in Nazi ideals), an unsavoury entanglement of subject positions German family legends readily omit. The narrator toggles between moments of acknowledgment and moments of disavowal, choreographed as a dialogue between two disparate, but adjacent voices: the voice of childish self-centred focalizer shaped by the resentment of a replacement child, on the one hand, and the auctorial voice of a narrator which frames this resistance with meta-reflective observations, on the other. Hoffman describes the language of her survivor family as 'a form of expression that is both more direct and more ruthless than social or public speech. [...] it was a chaos of emotion that emerged from their words rather than a coherent narration. [...] the 'past broke through in the sounds of nightmares' yet was also sealed into silence.'[41] As painful as it was, for the child of survivors this chaotic language preserved an 'awesome' knowledge in the service of a sacred guardianship of memory. Although in Treichel's text, the narrator, a child born to expellees, also grows up with a family language built on fragments, repetitions and silences, in this case, the silence is based on the desire to avoid accusations and expresses an unacknowledged sense of guilt and shame. As Aleida Assmann puts it poignantly,

> Während die Nachkommen der Holocaust-Überlebenden von dem heimgesucht werden, was ihre Eltern gesehen und erlebt haben, werden die Kinder der Nationalsozialisten von dem heimgesucht, was ihre Eltern nicht gesehen und aus der Erinnerung verdrängt haben. Sie stehen unter dem Zwang, die blinden Flecken und Lücken im Bewusstsein ihrer Eltern nachträglich auffüllen zu müssen.[42]

> [While the descendants of Holocaust survivors are haunted by things their parents *saw* and *experienced*, children of National Socialists are haunted by things their parents *did not see* and *suppressed in their memory.* They are forced to retrospectively fill in the blanks in the consciousness of their parents.]

This foundational lack of memories encapsulates the premise of Treichel's postmemorial work, what he calls 'die Erfindung des Autographischen' [the invention of the autobiographical]. In conclusion, I turn to his

---

41   Hoffman, 9, 10.
42   Aleida Assmann, *Generationsidentitäten und Vorurteilsstrukturen in der neuen deutschen Erinnerungsliteratur* (Wien: Picus, 2006), 49.

poetological programme as paradigmatic for a new generation of authors struggling to find a 'narrative Identität' [narrative identity], a voice for the subject position of those born after, yet nonetheless deeply entangled with what came before.

Auctorial Dislocations

In *Der Entwurf des Autors*, Treichel offers a brief autobiographical sketch. Tellingly titled 'Lektionen der Leere' ['Lessons about Emptiness'], he premises his reflections with a long-standing trope of classic fictions of memory: idealized childhood memories which authenticate auctorial identity. 'Die vergehende und vergangene Zeit gehört zu den wichtigsten Besitzständen eines Schriftstellers. Und der Teil einer vergangenen Zeit, der vielen als der wertvollste erscheint, ist die Kindheit.' (EA, 11) [Time that is passing and past time are among an author's most important possessions. And the part of the past many cherish most is childhood.] In this register, childhood figures as 'das sonnenbeschienene Griechenland auf der Landkarte der eigenen Lebensgeschichte, ursprungsnah und hoffnungsfroh zugleich.' (EA, 11) [the sun-drenched Greece on the map of one's own life history, simultaneously close to one's roots and yet hopeful for the future]. As a kind of *Urszene* (EA, 12) [primal scene] of personal and collective identity, this vision promises social coherence and belonging. In his case, however, there is no utopian promise, just a sense of emptiness and loss. His motivation to write is inscribed with a sense of displacement and dislocation:

> Das, was den Schreibwunsch hat heranbilden lassen, war ganz offensichtlich eine Erfahrung jenseits von Glück und Unglück. Ein unbekanntes Drittes, von dem ich bis heute nicht sicher weiß, was es der Substanz nach war, und an das ich mich heute vor allem als seine Erfahrung der Abwesenheit erinnere. Als ein eigentümliches Nichts sowohl im Bereich des äußeren wie auch des inneren Lebens. (EA, 15–16)

> [What created the desire within me to write was obviously an experience beyond happiness and unhappiness. An unknown third element, the substance of which I

still do not know, and which I remember today as an experience of absence. As a curious nothingness of both my inner and my outer life.]

He grows up with 'Eltern ohne Vergangenheit' [parents without a past], 'Eltern ohne Eltern' (EA, 21) [parents without parents], a profound lack of family memory transposed into a kind of existential nihilism.[43] 'Der Mensch ist ein voraussetzungsloses und zugleich rückhaltloses Wesen, das keine Kindheit hat und nichts erzählt. Der Mensch ist ein Vertriebener, der aus dem Osten kommt und Angst vor den Russen hat.' (EA, 22) [Man is both outside of history and lacking support, he has no childhood and does not tell stories. Man is an expellee who comes from the East and fears the Russian.] As a child of emotionally homeless parents, Treichel writes from the unresolved belatedness of postmemory. He has to im-aginatively fill in the gaps of an incoherent history transmitted through seemingly inexplicable emotions and reactions.

Treichel underscores time and again that he, himself, did not inherit a family memory. 'Mich zu erinnern, gehört nicht zu den Dingen, die ich gelernt habe. Die Erinnerung ist kein Familienerbe, obwohl sie beinah das einzige ist, was die aus dem Osten vertriebenen Eltern hätten bei sich haben können, als sie sich in Westfalen niederließen.' (EA, 21) [Remembering is not one of the things I learned. Memory is not a family inheritance, although it is almost the only thing that my parents, who were expelled from the East, could have had with them when they settled in Westfalia.] In striking contrast to Forte, who inherited a wealth of family stories, this author feels eminently, literally 'story-less': 'Ich hatte mich immer als ein Mensch empfunden, dem nichts erzählt wurde. Schon gar nicht von Angehörigen einer anderen Generation.' (EA, 69) [I had always seen myself as a person who was never told stories. Certainly not by members of a different generation.] The lack of (family) memory seems to repre-sent a sense of dislocation which created a perennial 'Unmut', a sense of irritation – 'eine Mischung aus Verzagtheit und aufkommender Wut'[44] [a mixture of discouragement and emergent anger] – which may well have

---

43   In his prose collections *Heimatkunde* and *Von Leib und Seele*, Treichel also reflects on this foundational sense of displacement that defines his family identity.
44   Curran, Dowden, 312.

motivated his desire to become an author.[45] Hence, Treichel frames his writing project as 'die Erfindung des Autobiographischen'[46] [the invention of the autobiographical], as a very deliberate poetic play with historical reality (also manifest in the works discussed in previous chapters, albeit in divergent aesthetic registers). Repeatedly confronted with questions about the autobiographical veracity of his works, he reflects on what 'autobiographical' actually means for him and points out that there is an implicitly false assumption about biographical veracity.

> Sie setzt voraus, dass ich über eine eigene, längst in meinem Innern ausformulierte Lebenserzählung verfüge, auf die ich je nach Bedarf zurückgreifen kann. Dem ist aber nicht so. [...] Ich bin sozusagen auch selbst nicht autobiographisch. Mir fehlt das, was man eine narrative Identität nennt. Ich verfüge über meine eigene Lebenserzählung nicht. Ich kann zu mir nichts sagen. Ich muss mir meine eigene Lebenserzählung fortlaufend erarbeiten.[47]

> [It implies that I have access to my own, long internally articulated life story, which I can use whenever needed. But this is not the case. [...] I am, so to speak, not auto-biographical. I lack what is called a narrative identity. I do not have a personal life story. I am unable to speak to who I am. I have to continuously work on the narra-tive of my own life.]

What Treichel calls his lack of 'narrative identity', then, constitutes the deep sense of psycho-social disruption felt by those born into the Nazi legacy and transmitted through transgenerational memory entangle-ments which, as mentioned above, have found expression in the German family novel.

For this generation of authors historical identity is not a given but a text to be written, and rewritten, a continuous and imaginative memory project which Susanne Fritz, another author of the *Kriegsenkel* generation, describes as a home made of words: 'Ein Papierhaus. Ein Buchstabenhaus. Ein Traumhaus aus dem Alptraumhaus: viel Geschichte auf wenig

---

45   Ibid.
46   Jeannette Stickler, '"Was ich betreibe, ist die Erfindung des Autobiographischen": Ein Gespräch mit dem Lyriker, Librettisten, Prosautor und Dozenten Hans-Ulrich Treichel', *Frankfurter Rundschau*, 4 March 1998.
47   Hans-Ulrich Treichel, 'Das Autobiographische', *Allmende* 26/78 (2006): 8.

Quadratmetern.'⁴⁸ [A house made of paper. A house made of letters. A
dream house from the nightmare house: lots of history spanning just a few
square feet.] When asked why he did not write memoirs instead of fiction
(a question also put to Forte), Treichel replied,

> Von Anfang an ergab sich eine Distanz zum Realen, und von Anfang an setzte ich
> Fiktionssignale. Und dies nicht nur für einen möglichen Leser, sondern vor allem
> für mich selbst. Denn die Arbeit am Autobiographischen war für mich erst dann
> wirklich reizvoll und vielleicht auch möglich, wenn ich das Autobiographische in
> den Bereich des Fiktionalen rückte – und umgekehrt.⁴⁹

> [From the beginning there was a distance from reality, and from the beginning I en-
> coded my texts as fiction. Not only for a potential reader but, above all, for myself.
> Because for me the work on the autobiographical only became interesting, and maybe
> also possible, when I fictionalized the autobiographical and vice versa.]

Treichel's child witness in *Der Verlorene* represents such an alter ego, a fic-
tionalized self that is occupied by indirectly transmitted parts of German
history writ large. By this point in time, then, 'writing the child' has
evolved into a capacious lens through which to make legible traces of the
past in the present. Treichel's postmemorial negotiation of his postwar
identity contends with the interdependence of private family legends,
historical facts and collectively curated memory narratives. Importantly,
Der Verlorene does not release its nameless protagonist with a sense of
identity, rather he remains in a state of diasporic displacement. While
this feeling of displacement indicates an enduring sense of temporal and
spatial exile, it is not the diaspora described by descendants of Jewish survivors who, as Henri Raczymow puts it, are orphans of a world they never
knew.⁵⁰ Rather, Treichel's text brings into relief a culture of 'Schuld*abwehr*'
[collective denial] that – in contrast to *Fliegeralarm,* but not unlike to
Die Blechtrommel – rests on the tension between 'Schuld*zugabe*' [rhet-
oric of confession] and its opposite 'Schuld*umkehr*' [protestations of

---

48   Susanne Fritz, *Wie kommt der Krieg ins Kind* (Munich: btb, 2019), 155.
49   Curran, Dowden, 308.
50   Henri Raczymow, 'Memory Shot Through with Holes', *Yale French Studies* 85
     (1994): 103.

innocence]. Put differently, Treichel's 'writing the child' performs the work of resistance against an unwanted 'German' truth. It straddles emphatic assertions to 'never forget', yet at the same time resents the intrusion of a received memory of shame. Instead of constructing a palliative screen, the voice of the self-absorbed, contrite and angry focalizer in *Der Verlorene* exposes intrafamilial and transgenerational tensions between overt and covert forces of avoidance. His defiant stance – representative of a collective sensibility shared by the second and third generation – captures a memory culture that, post-1989 is again permeated by an identification *with* and *as* Hitler's victims. This stance, however, is countered by auctorial distancing devices that underscore the vicissitudes of such identification. In the final chapter of this study, I examine more closely this form of ironic complicity in Rachel Seiffert's story 'Lore'.

CHAPTER 6

'Lore', or the Implicated Subject: Rachel Seiffert's Postmemory Work

'Lore', the story under examination in this chapter, is the middle piece of Rachel Seiffert's *The Dark Room* (2001),[1] a collection of three independent but interrelated stories. Written from the perspective of the third generation, it traces the lasting impact of National Socialism on familial memory, not unlike *Der Verlorene*. Yet in contrast to Treichel's belated discovery of hidden parental truths, Seiffert writes with the distinct knowledge that her grandparents were committed Nazis. Unlike Treichel's literary engagement with National Socialism, *The Dark Room* is not based on (repressed) family secrets. Rather, from different generational vantage points the stories seek to imaginatively understand a legacy contaminated by familial complicity or transgenerational implication in the Nazi past. Since Seiffert was born and raised in the United Kingdom by an Australian father and a German mother, the truths produced by these stories are refracted by both a cultural and a linguistic distance. 'Lore', the final text under examination in this study is written in English and exemplifies not only the transcultural poignancy of the topic as a whole, but also an instructive shift towards the perpetrator perspective.

Treichel and Seiffert, descendants of parents or grandparents who were either victimized by their flight from eastern territories (in the case of Treichel) or convinced Nazis (in the case of Seiffert) belong to a generation of authors who contend with received family histories in which the personal and the political converge surreptitiously. Treichel examined this intersection as the 'loss of West Berlin'; Seiffert addresses it through the lens

---

1   All text quotations refer to Rachel Seiffert, *The Dark Room* (New York, Pantheon, 2001).

of characters who find themselves caught 'on the wrong side of history'.[2] In her work she explores historical conflicts through the limited perspective of those caught up in events that are still unfolding. Speaking about her novel *A Boy in Winter* (2017), she notes that Britain has been spared many of the horrors of the Second World War but, she asks (as the daughter of a German mother), 'how does it feel to be on the wrong side of history? Questions like this spark my urge to write. [...] I have found myself turning again and again to the question above. When power changes hands, when the mood of the country shifts, how far is too far?'[3] Anticipating push-back against her comparison between the present-day and Hitler's Germany, she emphatically insists:

> But I reserve the right to do this – and neither do I take it lightly – because I have a special interest here. My grandparents were Nazis. I can't remember a time when I didn't know this. Opa – my grandfather – was in the Brownshirts and was later a doctor with the Waffen SS; Amfi, my grandmother, was an active party member. I owe a great debt to my mother Gretchen for never hiding these uncomfortable facts from me.

> She was born on the wrong side – the year after Hitler came to power, and into a National Socialist household – but she was still young at the end of the war, and thankfully she and her siblings grew to see the world very differently from their parents. My grandparents also came to regret their past, even if rather more slowly, and although my mother came to Britain in the late 1960s, she never cut ties with home. So while I grew up here in Britain, I knew my Hamburg family well.[4]

Her autobiographical reflections make clear that she is not only acutely aware of her family's role in National Socialism but also haunted by it. Footage from the camps overwhelmed her, not surprisingly: she knew 'what it had to do with my family; my mother had made sure of that.'[5] As a consequence, her literary work, shaped by affection towards her

---

2   Rachel Seiffert, 'My grandparents were Nazis. I can't remember a time when I didn't know this', *The Guardian*, 27 May 2017, <https://www.theguardian.com/books/2017/may/27/grandparents-nazis-inspired-my-novel-about-holocaust>, accessed 4 September 2021.

3   Ibid.

4   Ibid.

5   Ibid.

Nazi grandparents, does not attempt to exculpate her family or others seduced and implicated by Hitler's project. Rather, across national and generational boundaries, it seeks to understand historical culpability within the framework of a quotidian reality that allowed for thousands to be driven from their homes by the SS in broad daylight with no intervention by onlookers. As historian Ian Kershaw put it poignantly, 'the road to Auschwitz was built by hate, but paved with indifference'.[6] Seiffert speaks about just such common acts of complicity committed by bystanders when she relates a childhood memory of her mother. Her mother remembers 'looking out of a window in the family apartment and watching Roma families being rounded up and bundled into trucks'. At once vivid and vague in detail, this maternal memory fragment gains even more salience from the fact that the little girl watching this deportation is admonished by her mother to simply 'Look away'.[7] The grandmother's exhortation to 'look away' paradigmatically captures the perspective of a 'half-knowledge' that is central to all the stories in *The Dark Room*. Seiffert's mother, a *Kriegskind*, belongs to a community of half-blind eye-witnesses who were aware enough to see and to remember but too young to understand what went on in broad daylight. This averted gaze modulates the authority of the 'concealed first generation' by bringing into relief the charge of the bystander. In different ways, all protagonists of *The Dark Room* embrace or confront acts of Nazi perpetration. In that respect, it touches on aspects discussed in previous chapters. Since it is as much about looking as it is about looking away, as much about events playing out in plain sight as about secrets, as much about acknowledgement as about denial, this story collection parses gradations of implication. As such, 'Lore' challenges the reader to reflect on his or her own degree of implication in legacies of systemic historical violence or injustice.

The Dark Room belongs to the growing body of transnational memory work that rests on the relatively recent shift in focus from victim to Nazi perpetrator. Richard Crownshaw has asked if this shift responds to the

---

6   Ian Kershaw, *Hitler, the Germans, and the Final Solution* (New Haven, London: Yale University Press, 2009), 186.

7   Seiffert, 'My Grandparents were Nazis'.

troubling limitations of a wound culture which emphasizes, or even universalizes the perspective of the victim.[8] Warning that a simple reversal from the victim to the perpetrator story is equally problematic, he calls for a more careful reconsideration of trauma narratives. The central question is whether 'the recent theory and practice of cultural memory that is perpetrator-centred makes the perpetrator an appropriable figure available for facile identification across different cultural memories where once the victim figured such availability?'[9] In other words, how are we to investigate the full range and depths of unpalatable subject positions in light of their intricate interconnectedness and intersectionality? How can fictions of memory avoid the pitfall of what Eric Santner has discussed as narrative fetishism, that is, the creation of 'a narrative consciously or unconsciously designed to expunge the traces of the trauma or loss that called the narrative into being in the first place', particularly in light of the presumed 'otherness' of the perpetrator?[10] Film scholar Raya Morag notes that while the triangulation among perpetrators, victims and bystanders inevitably remains central to the ongoing collective and transnational conversation about the ethical legacy of the Holocaust,

> the 'inauguration' of the perpetrator era reflects on the era of testimony as a period which in a particular, temporal aspect has come to its end, rather than as an intellectual-cultural-psychological-social process. Standing as a consecutive as well as a simultaneous period of coming to terms with the past, the perpetrator era is not only being defined by the timing determined by the traumatic calendar of the almost

8   Richard Crownshaw identifies texts by German author Bernard Schlink (*Der Vorleser*, 1995, *Die Heimkehr*, 2006), French American writer Jonathan Littell (*The Kindly Ones*, 2009), Australian writer Kate Grenville (*The Secret River*, 2006), American author Toni Morrison (*A Mercy*, 2008) and Native American author Sherman Alexie (*Flight*, 2007) as perpetrator centred. 'Lore' could be added to this list. Richard Crownshaw, 'Perpetrator Fictions and Transcultural Memory', *Parallax* 17/4 (2011): 75–89.

9   Crownshaw, 75–89. For more on this topic, also see Jenny Adams and Sue Vice, eds, *Representing Perpetrators in Holocaust Literature and Film* (Middlesex, UK: Vallentine Mitchell, 2012), 75.

10   Eric Santner, 'History Beyond the Pleasure Principle', in Saul Friedlaender, ed., *Probing the Limits of Representation* (Cambridge, MA: Harvard University Press, 1992), 144.

seventy-five years that have passed since the end of World War II, but also by giving rise to a few new twenty-first century phenomena.[11]

Morag advocates a revision to the way trauma is transcribed across various media in light of what she calls 'atrocity-producing situations'. She promotes a mnemonic focus less concerned with psychological aspects of the individual perpetrator and trained instead on broader social frameworks that have produced 'soldiers-who-became-perpetrators into these atrocious situations'.[12]

I consider 'Lore' to be part of more recent postmemorial work that takes into sober consideration such contextual factors, meaning 'atrocity-producing situations' and their attendant subject positions. Instead of presenting the interiority of either suffering victims or abhorrent perpetrators, it confronts the reader with characters who reside in moral grey zones, identified with the eponymous character of 'Lore' as being in between 'right and wrong; good and bad, both at the same time' (DR, 152). Evocative of the knowing child, that is, children who remain resistant to the appropriating gaze of the adult, Seiffert's protagonists remain veiled to the reader.[13] Their subject positions unfold in incongruous ways, forged in the contradictions among ideological misperceptions, various degrees of half-knowledge about the Holocaust, and irrefutable photographic evidence of familial complicity and Nazi perpetration. Like *Der Verlorene*, *The Dark Room* belongs to the German family novel premised on a sense of 'belatedness'. Kristin Gwyer notes that in this era 'not only the survivors and their descendants but all of us, at least in the Western Hemisphere, are thought to be living in the shadow of a cataclysmic past that is at once irretrievable and enduring'.[14] My

11   Raya Morag, 'On the Definition of the Perpetrator: From the Twentieth to the Twenty-First Century', *Journal of Perpetrator Research* 2/1 (2018): 14.
12   Morag, 17.
13   Anne Higonnet, *Pictures of Innocence. The History and Crisis of Ideal Childhood* (London: Thames & Hudson, 1998), 210. Higonnet refers to the photographic work of Sally Mann, Courtney Love, Nicholas Nixon, Dick Blau and Judith Black.
14   Kirstin Gwyer, 'Beyond Lateness? "Postmemory" and the Late(st) German Language Family Novel', *New German Critique* 42/2 (2015): 138. For works concerned with the belated witness, see Gary Weissman, *Fantasies of Witnessing* (Ithaca, NY: Cornell University Press, 2004); Alison Landsberg, *Prosthetic*

reading of 'Lore' parses this sense of historical, generational and cultural belatedness. Hence, I first address this text in its larger historical context, a growing discontinuity between the 'Erfahrungsgeneration' [experiencing generation] and the 'Bekenntnisgeneration' [confessing generation]. The following close reading of 'Lore' is focused on the ways in which a sense of implication, approximated through the strained relationship between a young German girl and an imagined Jewish other, extends from the characters to the reader. In sync with Treichel's postmemory work, Seiffert's story, I argue, bears witness to a history of annihilation and its legacy less to *cure* our secondary traumatization than to *draw attention to* dis/continuities between the Nazi past and the present moment.

Belatedness or Familial Complications

The German family novel, which emerged in the 1990s, is inscribed by a perceptual shift from the perpetrator as an isolated and despicable figure to the broader cultural context that supported, demanded and rewarded various shades of violent behaviour. The three distinct but interrelated stories of *The Dark Room* capture two related changes of perspective, not only from victim to perpetrator but also from first-hand experiences of trauma (as seen in *Der Junge mit den blutigen Schuhen*) to their (trans-) generational reverberations (as seen in *Der Verlorene*). Gwyer has argued that the family novel

---

Memory: The Transformation of American Remembrance in the Age of Mass Culture (New York: Columbia University Press, 2004); Michael G. Levine, *The Belated Witness* (Stanford: Stanford University Press, 2006); Michael Rothberg, *Multidirectional Memory: Remembering the Holocaust in the Age of Decolonization* (Stanford: Stanford University Press, 2009) as well as *The Implicated Subject* (Stanford: Stanford University Press, 2019); Michael Heinlein, *Die Erfindung der Erinnerung. Deutsche Kriegskindheiten im Gedächtnis der Gegenwart* (Bielefeld: transcript, 2010); and Angelika Bammer, *Born After: Reckoning with the German Past* (London, Oxford, New York: Bloomsbury, 2019).

seems to indicate a desire, not just on the individual level, but on the broader cultural scale, to move away from the impasse of an incurable primary trauma and in-
surmountable break with the past toward the possibility of effecting a cure of 'our'
own secondary traumatization and of restoring continuity through the inheritance
and transmission of trauma.[15]

What Gwyer describes as curative desire, Susan Sontag critiques as a persistent cultural fantasy which rests on the 'imaginary proximity to the
suffering inflicted on others', and conveniently obscures 'our real relations
to power. So far as we feel sympathy, we feel we cannot be accomplices
to what caused their suffering. Our sympathy proclaims our innocence
as well as our impotence.'[16] Sontag's poignant insight about our vicarious
'consumption' of suffering through photographs trained on the victims
of catastrophe aligns with traumatic complicity. At once a mnemonic
register of transmission, aesthetic lens and social practice, it positions
us largely as traumatized victims of history. This leads to the question of
what those who come after owe the victims (of Hitler's policies of annihilation)? More specifically, what does the guardianship of the stories
of Hitler's victims entail for the descendants of a perpetrator nation, for
those who remain enfolded in the story of National Socialism and continue to benefit from the legacy of violent dispossession, displacement
and murder at the core of Hitler's project?

In a nation where memories of suffering continue to coexist, if not
compete with memories of perpetration, second- and third-generation
writers have to negotiate a family inheritance caught between memories of
private devastation and legacies of familial complicity. As Harald Welzer
has noted, memories of family suffering have great emotional depth but
little historical veracity since the desire to belong to a 'good' German family
readily outstrips the wish to see the objective horrors of participation in
Nazi crimes. While the family novel considers the family album more
critically than represented in many *Kriegskind* memoires, this genre still
rarely focuses on the fate of the Jewish victims, arguably because the latter
does not offer points of identification for the German reader in contrast to

15   Gwyer, 139.
16   Susan Sontag, *Regarding the Pain of Others* (New York: Picador, 2003), 102.

memories about suffering grandparents.[17] How, then, is the affective charge and distorted truth of the family album negotiated in the family novel? In 1989, many claimed that postwar literature, a body of works shaped by a particular historical constellation and its aftermath, had exhausted itself. By this point, a new generation of authors, the so-called *Kriegsenkel*,[18] are recalibrating the memory of the Nazi past centred on the nature of victimization, perpetration and complicity in ways that are less contentious than the 'Väterliteratur' [fathers' literature] conceived by the previous generation. Animated by curiosity instead of accusations, empathy instead of blame, acceptance instead of resentment, the family novel displays a narrative tension based on 'the question of the extent to which empathy with individuals can be reconciled with a more detached contextualization of their suffering within the overarching reality of German perpetration'.[19] Yet in the eyes of those who belong to the war or 'Erfahrungsgeneration', efforts of writers like Treichel and Seiffert, who belong to the subsequent 'Bekenntnisgeneration', are deeply flawed. In an essay about postwar literature published a decade after unification, *Spiegel* literary critic Volker Hage points out that his colleague Klaus Harpprecht (a contemporary of Günter Grass, born in 1927) rejects the memory project of the family novel altogether. He is critical of contemporary fictions of memory since they are no longer grounded in historical experience but instead offer dubious

17   Harald Welzer, 'Im Gedächtniswohnzimmer', *Zeit Online*, 25 March 2004, <http://www.zeit.de/2004/14/st-welzer>, accessed 14 August 2021. There are some notable exceptions, see for instance Kevin Vennemann, *Nahe Jedenew* (Frankfurt a.M.: Suhrkamp, 2005).

18   Like the *Kriegskinder* label, the *Kriegsenkel* label is problematic in that it is purely based on familial genealogy and brackets a multitude of other relevant differences. Nonetheless, the term has become shorthand in works that offer (pseudo) sociopsychological perspectives on a new generation of Germans. Examples are Sabine Bode's book *Kriegsenkel. Die Erben der vergessenen Generation* (Stuttgart: Klett-Cotta, 2009) and Matthias Lohre's more recent book with the strikingly similar title *Das Erbe der Kriegsenkel. Was das Schweigen der Eltern mit uns macht* (Gütersloh: Gütersloher Verlagshaus, 2016).

19   Stuart Taberner, Katharina Berger, 'Introduction', in Stuart Taberner and Katharina Berger, eds, *Germans as Victims in the Literary Fiction of the Berlin Republic* (Rochester, NY: Camden House, 2008), 6.

accounts of historical events the authors never witnessed first-hand. In short, Harpprecht fears, 'die Enkel könnten eines Tages erfinden, was die Großväter und Großmütter erlebt, doch nicht ausreichend beschrieben hätten' [that the grandchildren could one day invent what their grandfathers and grandmothers had experienced but not described sufficiently]. He laments the fact that they are no longer bound by a 'Rest von Takt und Scham' [a remnant of tact and shame] and disqualifies their work as inscribed by 'ruchlose Unschuld'[20] [nefarious innocence]. Harpprecht's somewhat antiquated phrase 'ruchlose Unschuld' is evocative and informative in equal measure. It implies a deliberate distortion of history in literature written by authors 'born after'. Moreover, to summarily call the works of the *Kriegsenkel* shameless representations of history echoes Martin Broszat's narrow understanding of historical authority based on the perspective of the 'secret first generation'. This cohort (as discussed in more detail in Chapter 2) insists that only those who were old enough to have witnessed the war, but too young to be held responsible, are considered to have valid insights into the Nazi past.

In the following close reading, I examine how Seiffert (who by Harpprecht's estimation writes from a position of 'nefarious innocence') negotiates questions of historical veracity through the lens of her historical belatedness yet emotional proximity. Like Treichel, rather than being careless, her work is aligned with the postmodern register in that she not only builds on but also critically traverses mnemonic projections and Holocaust tropes, thus remapping well-established narrative patterns that have come to firmly anchor the Holocaust in the collective imagination. While I agree with Gwyer that the work of second- and third-generation authors illustrates the need 'to testify to what is unintegratable and unintegrated, and to acknowledge the silences in the family history', I do not believe that 'Lore' can be fully explained by 'a desire, on the part of the authors themselves as well as the readers and critical commentators of their work, for a redemptive narrative, for the ruptures to be mended, and for continuity

---

20   Volker Hage, 'Rückblick mit Oskar. Was heißt hier Nachkriegsliteratur?', *Propheten im eigenen Land. Auf der Suche nach der deutschen Literatur* (Berlin: DTV, 1999), 329.

to be restored'.[21] Hence, I focus on the ways in which 'Lore', frustrates a redemptive desire by confronting the reader with grey zones of (moral) undecidability without attempting to integrate the unintegratable.

The Grammar of Complicity and Implication

In order to understand the larger narrative arc of 'Lore' it is helpful to de-scribe briefly the ensemble of three independent but interrelated stories, each featuring eponymous protagonists. The first two stories 'Helmut' and 'Lore' explore the legacy of Nazi perpetration through the eyes of young members of the *Flakhelfer* and the *Kriegskinder* generation, re-spectively. This generational cohort did not have the advantage of his-torical hindsight yet is nonetheless enfolded in the history of the Third Reich. Helmut, born in 1921, is a child when Hitler comes to power; he 'aches and yearns for a uniform, for active service' (DR, 22). Since he is missing a muscle in his chest and does not have full use of his right arm (!) the army rejects him 'because of his arm, his fault, his flaw' (DR, 22). Lore, on the other hand, is a young teenager who struggles to reconcile her belief in Nazi ideals with the reality of defeat.[22] Micha, the protag-onist of the final story, belongs to the *Kriegsenkel* generation. He travels to Belarus in order to find eyewitnesses who knew what exactly his 'Opa Askan' had done while stationed there in 1943 as a member of the Waffen-SS. All protagonists feel decentred and lost; their wish for action (as a soldier for Hitler in the case of Helmut), as well as their involuntary or voluntary travels (across the country in the case of 'Lore', or to the former Eastern front in the case of 'Micha') mirror their desire to understand with greater clarity their place in history at large.

Helmut feels victorious when, in 1945, he can at last join Hitler's army together 'with the fat boys and the boys with the bad teeth, the old men and

---

21   Gwyer, 142. Also see Hunter on the same point. '"To Tell the Story": Cultural Trauma and Holocaust Metanarrative', *Holocaust Studies* 25/1–2 (2019): 12–27.

22   Lore mirrors the perspective of Seiffert's mother, a *Kriegskind* who was 12 in 1945.

amputees' (DR, 16). His sense of victory portrays the illusion of those who refused to accept Germany's inevitable defeat. 'Helmut is standing high on his rubble mountain, over which Soviet tanks will roll with ease, and he is smiling.' (DR 47) Were it not for the congenital condition that limited him to being a frustrated bystander, Helmut would have been an enthusiastic Nazi soldier, more than 'willing to die for Führer and Vaterland' (DR, 22). Ironically, at least in historical hindsight, he is not ashamed on account of Hitler's war or politics but because he was deemed unfit to join Hitler's army. 'Confident of victory' until the last minute, he 'can see nothing beyond the glorious triumph, which he will be part of, and commit to film' (DR, 44). When asked to document how life is changing in Berlin he fails again; this time he is incapable of adequately capturing on film what he witnesses. He feels deeply humiliated when he realizes the truth of what he saw – the violent deportation of a group of gypsies – had eluded him because he 'ran away before the shutter released. Coward.' (DR, 30) Although he fervently hoped to capture what he saw, 'the chaos and cruelty' of the incident remains invisible in his photographic work. Helmut's 'implicated gaze', the gaze of a proud Nazi who wants so fervently to document the *Führer's* glory, represents at once the systemic blindness and the visceral connection at the core of the postmemorial position. Marianne Hirsch and Leo Spitzer argue that Helmut's failed photographs are no accident. Rather, they capture the shortcomings of the belated gaze. The blind photographs

> illustrate the belatedness of photographic looking and the temporal disjunction be-
> tween the moment an image is taken and the moment it is developed and viewed – a
> disjunction that, paradoxically, is no less enormous within the very time frame of the
> scene in the narrative (no more than several hours) than it is for second-generation
> viewers like us. Helmut's photographs are destroyed; the most important ones in his
> act of witnessing are never taken.[23]

In other words, Helmut's heuristic failure to understand what went on before his very eyes captures the fact that we, ourselves, can never objectively read or understand in a straightforward way evidence that

23   Marianne Hirsch and Leo Spitzer, 'What's Wrong with This Picture?', *The Generation of Postmemory: Writing and Visual Culture after the Holocaust* (New York: Columbia University Press, 2012), 64.

has been left behind by history, whether witnessed directly or seen be-latedly. All stories in *The Dark Room* parse a foundational disconnect be-tween seeing and understanding; the 'evidentiary authority' of photog-raphy – its indexical trace – remains illegible. This becomes even more central in 'Micha', the third story of the collection. Micha, a *Kriegsenkel* born after the war in 1957, searches for evidence of his grandfather's in-volvement in the SS. Frustrated since he cannot see what he thinks he knows – and cannot reconcile the difference between the kind grand-father he knows and the Nazi perpetrator he seems to have been – he is reminded by his sister that family legends and historical reality never con-verge. 'They don't show anything, the pictures. They're family shots, you know? Celebrations. Always happy. You can't see anything.' (DR, 266)[24] 'Micha' chronicles the tenacious yet elusive search for the truth about a Nazi family history driven by the desires and anxieties of the third gen-eration. Despite the resistance of his family and his pregnant life partner, Micha wants to know whether and to what extent his grandfather had been involved in mass shootings of Jews. Yet when he travels to Belarus to interview eyewitnesses, he does not gain clarity but leaves with a sense of even greater undecidability. The eyewitness and, as it turns out, Nazi collaborator who he asks can only confirm what he already knew: 'most' Germans were involved in the shootings.

Due to her gender and her age, Lore, the protagonist of the middle story occupies a different subject position from Helmut and Micha. In marked contrast to the male protagonists we do not know her exact age, although it is clear the events take place after the German surrender in May 1945. No longer a child but not yet adult, Lore has to grow up quickly when she and her siblings are tasked with traversing the occupied country alone to find refuge with their grandmother. She feels both attracted to and repelled by Tomas, a young man whose tattoo and papers seem to identify him as Jewish and whose street-savviness helps them navigate the barriers between different occupation zones. Lore eventually gets her

---

24   This family album evokes the pictorial narrative that was on display in the 1995 *Wehrmacht* exhibit, 'War of Annihilation: Crimes of the German Army, 1941–1944', that is, snapshots of German soldiers relaxing at home or at various frontlines.

siblings to Hamburg but cannot reconcile the reality of a defeated country with her belief in the *Endsieg* [the final victory], the steadfast party-line reinforced by her parents. In the following analysis of 'Lore', I draw on three points that Michael Rothberg has made with respect to the nature and transgenerational transmission of historical violence: first, historical violence rarely offers clear distinctions between traumatized victims and traumatizing perpetrators; second, large and heterogenous collections of subjects who both enable and benefit from this violence often remain invisible; and third, insidious, structural and slow forms of violence are often ignored in favor of punctual, event-centred violence. Seiffert's aesthetic transcription of the *Kriegskind* contests delimiting subject positions. Lore – as victim and perpetrator, confused witness and accomplice – benefits from a system of violence and oppression without, however, bearing direct responsibility for it. Evoking the certainties of the fairy tale only to dispute them, the text delineates complicity in a manner that is less stylized, yet no less provocative than Elsner's rendering in *Fliegeralarm*. Like Elsner, but from a different generational perspective, Seiffert addresses the question of *Mitwisserschaft* [shared knowledge of a crime], one's emotional and psychological involvement in a violent past without being actively involved or responsible for its unfolding.

Almost a Fairy Tale

The text opens with an arrival that also marks a departure. Lore's father, a member of the SS, unexpectedly arrives home in the middle of the night and moves the family to a farmhouse to await what Lore assumes to be the *Endsieg*. Yet when both parents are arrested, the five children have to find their way from Southern Germany to their grandmother in Hamburg. Their picaresque sojourn across a devastated landscape is not only a journey through space but also a journey *within*, which radically challenges and ultimately refutes their childhood beliefs. Their familial identity becomes a liability, contradicted by everything they see and hear. Not only are they forced to lie in order to reach their destination and resort to previously unthinkable acts of immorality, but Lore and her oldest sister are also deeply confused by the change from a firmly ingrained victor's perspective to the reality of shame and humiliation after total defeat. The children's journey becomes even more complicated when they meet Tomas, whose papers and tattoo identify him as a Jewish survivor of Buchenwald. He temporarily adopts them as his siblings, but he is not who he claims to be, neither Jewish nor a camp survivor. For a brief moment the deal, met with ambivalence by Lore, seems simple: he has papers that allow easier movement across a country divided into different military zones; they, in turn, contribute Lore's youngest sibling, a baby, which allows them easier access to food and shelter. While crossing the Russian zone one of the twin brothers is shot dead, presumable by a Russian soldier; yet without time for mourning, they flee onwards and eventually make it to Hamburg. As the children settle into a routine at their grandmother's house, Tomas stays in one of the numerous ruins, only to suddenly disappear when he thinks Lore has discovered his deceitful use of a Holocaust victim's identity.

On the plot level, the text modulates the tropes of fairy tales: there are evil outside forces that lead to a sudden departure from the family home; encounters with villains and helpers in the woods; and there is a happy ending that allows the children to find a safe home. Similar to the classic German fairy tale, the protagonists are closely identified by their social status, in this case as children of high-ranking Nazi parents. Furthermore, the text mimics the flat register of the classic fairy tale, which defines most protagonists through their actions without offering their thoughts or feelings. The narrating voice is restrained and exceedingly sober; dialogues are sparse and interior monologues are kept to a minimum and often difficult to attribute. This narrative register fuses the exteriority of actions and circumstance with the interiority of thought and perception. The reader is kept at a distance from both the characters and the unfolding events. Lore's inner struggles come to light through plot twists, dialogues, sparse auctorial comments and interspersed interior monologues. The story's implausible finale also bears fairy-tale elements. The children make their way through various occupation zones without access to vital resources; almost all of them survive and miraculously manage to find their grandmother in Hamburg, a city devastated by a firestorm in 1943.[25] That said, in stark contrast to the simplicity of the classic fairy tale, which insists on clear boundaries between good and evil and seeks to establish order and justice in the face of social violence, there is no redeeming symmetry in 'Lore'. Although the characters are no longer who they were when they started out, their miraculous 'arrival' is not celebrated in the manner of a miraculous fairy-tale ending. Rather, they must realize that the simple truths they used to live by, both externally and internally, have collapsed into confusing ambivalence.

Before Lore sets off with her siblings, she has to assist her mother with burning incriminating evidence of her family's support of participation in Hitler's project.

> Lore works through the morning, watching their clothes and papers burn, balancing logs around the chimney to dry for later. The photo album burns badly at first, too thick and full for the flames to catch hold. The blue linen cover browns and curls and Lore's eyes dry in the heat from the open stove. (DR, 57)

Later, during their perilous journey to Hamburg, Lore is shocked when confronted with photographic evidence of the Holocaust publicly displayed by the American Allies. As the daughter of Nazi parents, the wall of photos literally 'sticks to her': 'The pictures are of skeletons. Lore can see that now, pulling her hands back, tugging her sleeves down over her glue-damp palms. [...] Lore holds her breath, looks away, sees the next picture: hair and skin and breasts. She takes a step back, trapped by the wall of the crowd.' (DR, 76–77) This clueless young witness is framed, if not 'trapped' by an anonymous collective of viewers, 'the wall of the crowd', without being able to make sense of what she sees. Initially she gladly accepts speculations that this photographic evidence is fake, nothing but American propaganda, but when she repeats this rumour while riding the tram in Hamburg, she is harshly rebuked by strangers sitting next to

---

25   For more on the fairy-tale motif see María Jesús Martínez-Alfaro, 'The Estrangement Effect in Three Holocaust Narratives: Defamiliarizing Victims, Perpetrators and the Fairy Tale Genre', *Atlantis. Journal of the Spanish Association of Anglo-American Studies* 42/1 (June 2020): 37–56.

her, 'They're Jews. Lore flushes. The dark-haired woman is angry. "Look at them. They're not acting, they're dead."' (DR, 146) The '[p]ictures of men in uniform. Clear-eyed portraits: SS, SA, Gestapo' force her to realize that the soldiers pointing guns at civilians 'wear Vati's uniform' (DR, 146).

Since the whole story unfolds as a recalibration of the father–daughter relationship, it has oedipal undertones. Premised on the father's sudden arrival and followed by his inexplicable disappearance, he remains a ghost-like presence, manifest in photographs depicting Nazi officers in his likeness executing prisoners. Lore's realization that her father may be a murderer constitutes a familiar trope in representations of child witnesses of catastrophic events. Like Micha, she has to reconcile two contradictory realities: fond childhood memories of her father and photographic traces that show him in a brutally different light. When focalized through a child witness, recognition of and inadvertent complicity in crimes of the Nazi period mark the end of childhood innocence – analogous to the foundational story about expulsion from paradise. The transition from innocent child to historical subject rests on the Judeo-Christian premise of the human subject born into a fundamental alienation and has become a central memory trope often used in films centred on children as witnesses of historical trauma: to become fully human and subject to history means to irrevocably fall from grace and into despair.[26]

Blurred Evidence

As discussed above, photographs play a central role in *The Dark Room*. They remind the reader of the larger framework of history – albeit always as decontextualized and discontinuous fragments. In 'Lore', historical

---

26   See for instance Louis Malle's *Au Revoir les Enfants* (1987) and Marianne Rosenbaum's *Peppermint Frieden* (1983). For more on this see Karen Lury, *The Child in Film: Tears, Fears, and Fairy Tales* (New Brunswick, NJ: Rutgers University Press, 2010).

reality comes into view in photos that are detached (torn out of the family album and buried), forcefully exhibited as (part of the American re-education campaign), and lost, fragmented or stolen (like the Jewish victim's papers used by Tomas). No longer intact, this family is dislocated, the parents imprisoned, the children *en route* to a new destination. Marked by the burning of select family photos, the abrupt departures of father and mother necessitate a rushed dismantling of the family history followed by further acts of concealment. Lore instinctively conceals her parentage when she buries rather than burns photos of her father. This leaves open the possibility of a later discovery and suggests that what (she) was can never be completely hidden. Her attempt to hide incriminating evidence evokes the figure of the palimpsest: traces of the past, while ostensibly erased, remain witnesses, forever legible, if only faintly. However, Lore's decision to burn the last remaining trace of the Jewish victim, whose papers Tomas had used to gain passage across different occupation zones, is a decisive act of violence that evokes the emergent culture of collective denial and obfuscation. This last act of destroying (photographic) evidence – in this case an identity card – in effect murders the Jewish victim a second time: 'The charred edges fold over the thin face in the photo, and when they fall away again the dead man is gone.' (DR, 151)

Many critics have called attention to the pivotal role photographs play in *The Dark Room* (as indicated by the suggestive title).[27] The dark room is not only the room where Helmut attempts and fails to capture, with his photographs, the reality of Nazi crimes and violence, but also a space

27   See Pascale Tollance, 'Freezing Emotion: The Impersonality of 'Photographic Writing' in Rachel Seiffert's *The Dark Room*', in Christine Reynier and Michel Ganteau, eds, *Impersonality and Emotion in Twentieth-Century British Literature* (Montpellier: Publications Montpellier III, 2005), 287–98; Silke Horstkotte, 'Transgenerational Mediations of Identity in Rachel Seiffert's *The Dark Room* and Marcel Beyer's *Spies*', in Silke Horstkotte and Esther Peeren, eds, *The Shock of the Other: Situating Alterity* (Amsterdam: Rodopi, 2007), 149–60; and Cristina Pividori, 'Out of the Dark Room: Photography and Memory in Rachel Seiffert's Holocaust Tales', *Atlantis. Journal of the Spanish Association for Anglo-American Studies* 30/2 (2008): 79–94.

of belated mediation and undecidability. Pascale Tollance has argued that
photography plays both a fictional and a metafictional role in 'Lore'. Since

> it mediates the character's changing perspective of the world, photography becomes
> the means to reflect on art itself. The impersonality of photography can be seen as
> the instrument of two opposing aesthetics – one that seeks closure and an escape
> from emotions, and another that exposes the viewer or the reader to fragmentation,
> uncertainty and lets emotions loose.[28]

These opposing forces correspond to two kinds of photographs: those
that convey a sense of familial belonging and stability, framed, displayed
or archived in the family album, and those that are detached, lost, fragmented and displaced. The fact that the children's departure from their
home is prefaced by burning parts of the family album suggests that,
cut off from a reassuring familial frame, they are forced to reframe their
identity. And Lore must re-interpret herself against the backdrop of fragmented and detached photos depicting Jewish victims who haunt her on
her journey and in her nightmares. In that sense the use of photography
does indeed denote a 'process of depersonalization and a questioning of
identity', as Tollance claims. It 'marks the release from a number of fictions, myths or lies', but it also has a destabilizing effect insofar as 'the uncertainties produced by conflicting images create an emotional confusion
which risks ending once again in paralysis'.[29]

As in the works discussed previously, the reader witnesses a *Kriegskind*
witnessing. Caring and confused, yet also proud and defiant, Lore is tasked
with the role of an adult and has to take on maternal responsibilities. She is a
young Nazi who, at first obediently and then proactively, destroys incriminating evidence. After her journey through a devastated country, she is forced
to come to terms with a war of annihilation and murder but reassured by
her unreformed grandmother that her parents 'did nothing wrong' (DR
152). Thus, she remains at a loss about what to believe. As mentioned above,
her conscious and unconscious acts of denial mirror the emergent culture
of resistance to the truth of the Third Reich. From the perspective of the

---

28   Tollance, 292.
29   Ibid.

twenty first century, and beyond the diegetic framework of the text, her acts, statements and thoughts anticipate a larger postwar culture which knows only German victims. The last passage of the text describes Lore and her siblings on an excursion in Hamburg in the winter of 1945. It is Lore's birthday and the beginning of a new time; 'more than half a year since the end of the war' (DR 154) has passed, and a new era of oblivion and erasure is about to begin. As the children take note of the ruined and bombed-out city, Lore reassures them that 'they are going to build houses there. On top of where the rubble is now.' (DR, 155) Again they are in transit, this time waiting for a ferry to take them home. Lore briefly steps away from her siblings, seemingly lost in thoughts while taking in the destroyed city. 'She looks forward to when there will be no more ruins, only new houses, and she won't remember anymore how it was before.' (DR, 156) Battered and thoroughly chilled by the elements, 'she stands on her own and the wind claws at her skin, tears through her clothes' (DR, 156). She is filled with a desire for a new beginning: 'Lore doesn't look down at the water, faces the far shore ahead. She unbuttons her coat and lets the wind rip it open, pounding in her ears. She stretches her mouth wide, lets the winter rush down past her lungs and fill her with bitter chill.' (DR 156) Her state of mind evokes the collective German mindset of the time, a 'derealization' that shuts out details of the past and remains trained on the present and future. In this instance derealization does not connote the sense advanced by Margarete and Alexander Mitscherlich, that is, a psychological strategy for managing the loss of Hitler as an internalized ego ideal. To the contrary, it suggests a lingering and distinct awareness of what went before, countered by a transactional desire to forget and rebuild. Battered by the headwinds, Lore seems emotionally empty but also hyper-perceptive and vulnerable. At once rooted in the present moment and unable to gain traction, she is battered by circumstances beyond her control yet not defeated: 'Lore hears and tastes and feels only air. Her eyes are closed, seeing nothing, streaming brittle tears.' (DR, 156)

How, then, can the reader relate to a protagonist like Lore who cannot easily be located on the victim–perpetrator imaginary? Like *Der Verlorene*, *The Dark Room* deploys the *Kriegskind* perspective in a meta-reflexive way when it evokes the German *Kriegskind* in close proximity to the Jewish victim. In 'Micha' this proximity is critiqued as a ploy to 'identify with the survivors, with the victims' (DR, 206). German students, Micha notes,

> are being taught that there are no perpetrators, only victims. They are being taught like it just happened, you know, just out of the blue people came along and did it and then disappeared. Not the same people who lived in the same towns and did the same jobs and had children and grandchildren after the war. (DR, 207)

Questioning familiarizing strategies that underlie the genrefication of the Holocaust, 'Lore' reveals the self-serving blind spots of this victimology. The text not only urges the reader to look more carefully at nuances and gradations that shade every subject position, but also brings up questions Hunter poses in her probing of historical subject positions vis-à-vis the Holocaust.

> How can we position ourselves in relation to a historical event in which [...] there are infinitesimal layers of guilt and innocence? When we gaze at the mirror provided by the Holocaust, with whom or what are we able to identify? We reject an identification with the perpetrators of atrocity outright, as to acknowledge this would be to admit that our own culture, indeed ourselves, are capable of the same.[30]

These queries return us to my initial considerations of the recent shift to perpetrator figures in literary memory work. The Lore character, framed by a flat auctorial voice and defined by inadvertent entanglements between various subject positions, does not offer what Crownshaw describes as the kind of 'absolute innocence that art attributes to its subjects', nor does the text invite an escape into 'fantasies of over-identification or rescue'.[31] To what degree, then, can this fiction of memory represent a critical intervention in apologetic recalibrations of history without relying on 'idiopathic identification' – an inadvertent identification between character and reader that conflates self and other?[32] In conclusion I examine whether 'Lore' is yet another form of Holocaust Kitsch, as one reviewer has decried, that deploys childhood 'innocence' to bracket

---

30　Hunter, 16.
31　Crownshaw, 76.
32　Hirsch, 155–77.

various degrees of implication[33] or critical memory work in the sense described by Susannah Radstone, that is, an open narrative space that moves the reader 'through fantasy identification with perpetration as well as with victimhood'.[34] Does the story illuminate transgenerational and 'infinitesimal layers of guilt and innocence'?[35] And finally, how does the text address and implicate the reader?

Writing Implication

The aesthetic tectonics of 'Lore' are markedly twofold: there is a disconnect between the staging of the characters and the staging of the plot. While the reader has only sparse access to the inner life of the characters, the plot is extremely detail-oriented, the pronounced lack of access to the characters' interiority contrasts with minute descriptions of their actions and experiences. Seiffert's bare and pragmatic style may be particularly obvious in the river-crossing episode, which loosely evokes another fairy-tale trope: the final passage into safety aided by a magical helper. When the children come to a river and realize that the bridge across has been destroyed, Lore is challenged: she must find a way to get her siblings over this body of water and thus has to trust Tomas to assist them. Although Tomas had just proven helpful when Lore was too sick to care for her

---

33   See for instance Carole Angier's review of *The Dark Room*, 'Sins of the Fathers', *The Spectator*, 28 September 2001, <http://archive.spectator.co.uk./article/29th-september-2001/40/sins-of-the-fathers>, accessed 12 August 2021.

34   Susannah Radstone, 'Social Bonds and Psychical Order: Testimonies', *Cultural Values* 5/1 (2009): 61.

35   For more on the transgenerational legacy of the Holocaust see Werner Bohleber's early study, 'Das Fortwirken des Nationalsozialismus in der zweiten und dritten Generation', *Babylon* 7 (1990): 70–83, Gabriele Schwab, *Haunting Legacies: Violent Histories and Transgenerational Trauma* (New York: Columbia University Press, 2010), and most recently Angelika Bammer's powerful personal meditation *Born After: Reckoning with the German Past* (London, Oxford, New York: Bloomsbury, 2019).

siblings, because of his tattoo Lore regards him with great ambivalence and suspicion. Framed by an impersonal narrator, the whole episode spans seven pages and rests on Lore's surveillance of Tomas. I quote an extensive excerpt to illustrate the narrative choreography of the text.

> Tomas takes off his boots and ties the laces together. He drapes them round his neck, buttons his jacket, and wades out into the water with his raft. When he is just waist deep he starts swimming, holding the stocking between his teeth, pulling the bag after him to the first pillar. When he gets there, he stands up out of the water and pulls the raft over. He turns to them and waves. Water streams out of his sleeves in an arc, and the twins both laugh and wave back. They run to the water's edge, but Lore calls them back.
>
> —Yes, wait. I'll go across and then I'll come and help you.
>
> Tomas steps off the ledge into the water and swims to the next pillar. The boys crouch at the water's edge, watching, tying their bootlaces together as Tomas had done. Lore squeezes Liesl's hand and tells her to take her boots off, too.
>
> Tomas is past the middle of the river now. Still swimming. He hasn't looked back again, and Lore wonders absently if he will come back and help them. She calculates what is in the bag. Food and clothes. The last tin of meat. But no money, no valuables. No great loss. Tomas wades out onto the far shore, pulling the bag behind him. He doesn't look back or wave. He walks up onto the road, out of sight. The twins both stand up and turn to look at Lore. She shrugs, makes a mental list. The tin of meat, the half loaf, three blankets, and Liesl's coat. (DR, 106)

Like the text as a whole, this sober description mimics the experiential reality of May 1945. It underscores the extent to which this particular historical moment was shaped by the constant struggle for survival in a country ravaged by bombings and occupied by the Allies. The search for food and shelter, lost children and relatives, and ways to travel through various military zones dominated each day. 'Lore' conveys this struggle with forensic acuity. The few reflective passages and brief inner mono-logues are mostly focused on planning the next move; dialogues are reduced to brief orders or curt explanations. May 1945, as experienced through the lens of this *Kriegskind*, is marked by the psychological dis-orientation brought about by the collapse of the Nazi world view and physical disorientation caused by the extensive destruction of the infra-structure. There are no authority figures who offer the children guidance, there is no one to explain a reality that no longer makes sense, no one to explain photographs that contradict what previously seemed indisputable, no one to explain a character like Tomas, no one to explain the danger of crossing different occupation zones.

In order to understand how the Lore character articulates the ambivalent position, moral ambiguity and inadvertent implication of any bystander or witness to histories of violence – including in this case the reader – I believe we need to expand Tollance's point that Seiffert's 'photographic writing' corresponds 'to the disappearance of a voice that could explain, connect, certify', leaving only images in its stead.[36] 'Lore' underscores the fact that rather than intentional actors, we are more often unwitting participants in histories not of our own making, histories beyond our immediate reach or experience. Despite its seemingly neutral register, however, the text does not offer an impartial perspective which becomes most evident after Tomas joins the group and Lore's perpetrator bias is brought into sharper focus and leads the reader. Beginning with their first encounter, as mentioned above, Lore is caught between attraction and repulsion; she simply cannot clearly locate him on the friend-or-foe-spectrum. And since Lore's perspective focalizes the story, the reader cannot help but wonder with Lore what to make of Tomas. Who is he? How did he survive the camps he seems to have escaped?

Tomas, his very presence and his past, his identity and his character, both contrast with and ground the detailed description of the children's journey through a defeated wasteland. Nonetheless, he remains a figure whose background is never fully explained or revealed. We eventually find out that he was in a German prison or concentration camp and did forced labour; we also learn that he 'stole from people. Money. Names, too' (DR, 114). But his past and identity remain largely unexplained; like all the characters he is defined by any given moment. Lore wonders about the numbers on his arm and the papers that allow them to travel across occupation zones. (The text does not explain if or why Lore understands these numbers to be connected to Holocaust victims.) 'She doesn't trust the man. Doesn't want to pretend he is her brother. Lies piled on lies. Hard to keep

36   Tollance, 293.

track.' (DR, 97) Avoiding physical contact with him, she refuses to take his helpful but tattooed arm when crossing the river. 'Lore hesitates; eyes fixed on the reaching arm; on the blue smudge below the greenish skin; the tattoo halfway between wrist and elbow. Numbers. Blurred. As if the river water has seeped under the skin and smeared the ink.' (DR, 109) Lore's ambivalence is based on her half-knowledge and her Nazi upbringing and anti-Semitic prejudice. And while his tattooed arm is enough to cause a man at a train station to spit at him, an act of anti-Semitism (DR, 123), the tattoo ultimately turns out to be evidence of his duplicity. Yet even the information that he has stolen papers and 'used those things to pretend' (DR, 151) still allows for the possibility that he *is* a Jewish survivor using another victim's paper because his own were lost – leaving the reader at a loss, too, about this character. Jennifer Kapczynski has argued that the ambiguity of this character is a salient feature of a trope in Holocaust representations. Tomas is the 'singular Jew', a sole, disconnected individual who stands in for the fate of German Jewry as such. The 'singular Jew' remains somewhat 'hazy, strangely specific (insofar as it is reduced to one character) and yet vague (to the extent that the historical particularities of the Holocaust are skipped over or referenced only obliquely)'.[37] Tomas insistently asks Lore, 'What do you want from me?' This question reveals his anxiety over having been found out as a fraud, and it preoccupies Lore's thoughts as well. She continuously asks herself the same questions. (DR, 148, 151) Tomas both represents and preserves 'Germany's secret'. His ruse at once evokes the memory of state-sanctioned mass murder and its subsequent collective denial, reflecting a postwar memory culture that relies on appropriating and (in some cases) usurping the identity of Holocaust victims.

Lore's ambivalence towards Tomas shifts to suspicion when her initial disbelief about 'the skeleton people' is rebuked. But, as María Jesús Martínez-Alfaro notes, she never gains certainty, since her 'attempts to understand always clash with the silence of those close to her. The effect of the public secret extends from what was known about what was happening

---

37   Jennifer Kapczynski, 'The Singular Jew: Representing National Socialism's Jewish Victims in Recent Historical Cinema', in Oleksandr Kobrynskyy and Gerd Bayer, eds, *Holocaust Cinema in the Twenty-First Century: Memories, Images, and the Ethics of Representation* (New York: Wallflower Press, 2015), 151.

during the war to the knowledge of what had happened once it was publicly exposed.'[38] By extension, we can say that Tomas represents the collective ambivalence that continues to keep the Holocaust at once firmly anchored and suspended in German cultural memory. He remains a vaguely defined figure – seemingly a Holocaust victim but also a magical helper who is met with resentment by Lore and other anonymous citizens. But he is also a savvy survivor, a young German and petty criminal who uses the identity of a Jewish victim because, as he himself puts it, 'it didn't matter. The man was a Jew, you see. He was dead already.' (DR. 150) The ambiguity of this character, or rather the way this character makes ambiguous what is historical fact, reflects not only the grey zones of May 1945, but also grey zones of identity and accountability for those who come after. Like Lore, we cannot read him clearly; the authority of historical facts, this character shows, is all too often obscured by savvy manipulation and convenient adaptations.

All three stories of *The Dark Room* foreground photographic evidence that fails to reveal the truth of the historical moment, indicating, as Hirsch and Spitzer put it, the temporal and semantic disjunction between the full depth of the historical past and its legibility in the present. In 'Lore', this 'failure of the archive' becomes apparent when Tomas is gone. All that remains of him are the worn identity papers he had used. Although Lore carefully scrutinizes the photo of the cardholder, she is unable to decipher his name and is left rehearsing Tomas's claim that this man was 'dead already'. 'Lore hasn't stopped looking into the face. The gaunt features, the fine lips, eyes downcast, lids almost closed. *Dead already*. Lore studies the paper, but the name has disappeared in a crease, lost in the nervous folding and refolding.' (DR, 150–51) Even though she now realizes that Tomas was an impostor, she still does not know who this man was whose death had saved them. Lore decides to resolve her confusion by destroying the trace of this stranger and burns the last remaining evidence until, finally, 'the dead man is gone' (DR, 151).

38   Martínez-Alfaro, 49.

What Do You Want from Me? What Do We Want from Him?

The memorial perspective represented in 'Lore' is distinctly different from that of the other work discussed previously. Seiffert's staging of the encounter between a young German girl, raised as a fervent Nazi, and Tomas, a young German who abuses the identity of a Jewish victim to survive, reflects the role of the Jewish victim within Germany's cultural memory more than half a century after the end of the Second World War: an exculpatory abstraction used manipulatively to obscure various gradations of collective implication. Seiffert's text makes clear that by the turn of the millennium, the Jewish victim has become a figure of great ambivalence. Appropriated as the invisible 'other' of German history, those persecuted under Hitler continue to trigger unresolved feelings of attraction and repulsion. In the text, this configuration is brought into focus by Tomas's repeated question 'What do you want from me?', a question which haunts the final segment of the story and preoccupies the protagonist. Uttered by the impostor of a Jewish victim, it addresses the reader as well: what do we want from him? Put differently, from the vantage point of our belated perspective we also demand to know who is guilty and who is not, who knew and who did not know about 'the skeleton people'. Yet the text frustrates this desire for clear demarcations, leaving us caught – like the protagonist – between unstable boundaries of empathy and identification, rejection and dismissal, perpetration and victimization. As her grandmother reminds her, 'Everything has changed. But your father is still a good man.' (DR, 152) Lore feels increasingly frustrated in her attempts to figure out the new reality that surrounds her. She cannot stop thinking about Tomas, who had posed as her 'other' brother to ensure their safe passage, and who had cautioned her that 'people are angry now, so it's safer to be a different person' (DR, 151). Thus, she keeps returning to the question:

> *What do you want from me?* She tries to unravel Tomas and prisons and skeleton people; lies and photographs; Jews and graves; tattoos and newspapers and things not being as bad as people say. In the middle of this all are Mutti and Vati and the badges in the bushes and the ashes in the stove and the sick feeling that Tomas was both right and wrong; good and bad; both at the same time. (DR, 151–52)

In these final reflections, the text draws attention to the impurity of any subject position, an intrinsic impurity that Tomas exploited to ensure his survival. He was, it seems, aware of and probably complicit in acts of perpetration. Yet at the same time, he and Lore are framed as victims to circumstances beyond their control. Lore and the reader realize that suspicions about Tomas are at once unfounded and founded, that he used the persecuted 'other' to their mutual advantage, that they all benefitted from those who were murdered, and hence are implicated. In simple pared-down language, the passage above asks what it means, as Seiffert wrote in 2017, to be 'on the wrong side of history'. Lore increasingly wonders, what does it mean to be simultaneously right and wrong, good and bad? In short, the reader is forced to confront, along with the protagonist, distinct but unstable degrees of complicity and implication.

As the last case study in this book, Seiffert's work presents an example of literary memory work that, as noted above, deploys the blind spots of child focalizers in order to explore historical subject positions beyond the victim–perpetrator imaginary. On the plot level and the level of character configuration, Lore and Tomas model gradations of complicity which, as Sanyal has argued, 'requires us to consider our at times contradictory position within the political fabric of a given moment, as victims, perpetrators, accomplices, bystanders, witnesses, or spectators'.[39] Seiffert's aesthetic register – based on forensically detailed action and vaguely explained characters – keeps the reader at once drawn in and at a distance. Thus, it evokes the more archaic connotation of complicity as a 'state of being complex or involved' (*OED*).[40] Both Lore and Tomas demonstrate that the fusion of contradictory subject positions can have divergent effects: 'It might illuminate convergences between self and other, past and present, here and elsewhere. But it can also convert difference into sameness or conflate the extreme and the everyday.'[41] In this case, the interaction between a young Nazi and a German using Jewish identity papers unfolds what it may mean to be born into 'atrocity-producing-situations'. Lore and

---

39   Debarati Sanyal, *Memory and Complicity: Migrations of Holocaust Remembrance* (New York: Fordham University Press, 2015), 1.
40   Sanyal, 10.
41   Ibid.

Tomas are implicated subjects, aligned with power and privilege based on a racist ideology, but they are not direct agents of harm. Without having actively contributed to the violence that surrounds them, these *Kriegskinder* nonetheless inhabit, inherit and, most importantly, benefit from it.[42] Their identity evolves in light of an internalized discriminatory belief system and in the tension of defiant denials, a collective silence simultaneously bounded and obscured by photographic evidence of Nazi perpetration. The survival of the *Kriegskind*, at that historical moment, rested on exploiting and symbolically killing a Holocaust victim a second time. Even after the end of the war, this and subsequent generations continue to benefit from a system of discrimination and murder: violent histories, as Rothberg notes, inevitably 'trouble the distinction between a "fully absent past" and a fully "present" present […]. [T]here is neither strict continuity between past and present nor a clean break between the two temporal dimensions. Rather, implication emerges from an ongoing, uneven, and destabilizing intrusion of irrevocable pasts into an unredeemed present.'[43]

To return to the questions introduced in the previous section of this chapter: unlike Forte, Seiffert does not rehearse the trauma of a *Kriegskind* by relying on inadvertent identifications between character and reader that conflate self and other. Her text questions the metanarrative of the Holocaust, in particular the naturalizing tendencies of any fiction of memory propped up by familiar tropes and metaphors. Probing what Crownshaw has called a 'more nuanced and gradated sense of trauma and historical affect, particularly in the face of confluence of histories not necessarily our own', *The Dark Room* demands an awareness of the possibility and the limits of our experiential participation in this history.[44] 'Lore', then, negotiates mitigating screen memories – not in a redemptive sense but as an exploration of unresolved questions about incremental layers of guilt and innocence. By exposing fragments of historical truths that simultaneously *hide and reveal* not only state-sanctioned mass murder but also central tenets of German cultural memory, the text delineates appropriations

---

42   Michael Rothberg, *The Implicated Subject: Beyond Victims and Perpetrators* (Stanford: Stanford University Press, 2019), 1.
43   Rothberg, *Implicated Subject,* 9.
44   Quoted in Sanyal, 9.

of the Holocaust victim, and provocatively challenges the reader to recognize their own curative desires. From the perspective of belatedness, it
soberly examines that which has been and that which came of it, while
keeping open a space for what may still come of it. In that sense, Seiffert's
'writing the child' echoes Bachmann's conviction that 'die Wahrheit ist
dem Menschen zumutbar' [we can bear the truth], 'dass man ent-täuscht
und das heißt ohne Täuschung zu leben vermag'[45] [that one can live disappointed, dis-illusioned, and that means without illusions].

45   Ingeborg Bachmann, *Werke*, Christine Koschel et al., eds, 4 (Munich, Zurich: Piper,
      1982), 277.

Memory in a Moment of Danger

The child is never just a child, I claimed in the introduction. Examined here as a memory icon deployed in German postwar literature, it holds open the need to look and the desire to look away, the need to know and the desire of not wanting to know, the need to question and the desire to remain indifferent, the need to remain curious and the desire to ignore the shadow of a history of enduring consequences. In other words, the voice of the child carries for the reader the weight of a history that is difficult to hold. Dispatched to traverse a space of unanswered questions and unacknowledged accountabilities, the child has become a delegate for generations who still remember and for those who have come after. Expressing traumatic unresolve, deployed as aesthetic resistance, stylized to radical critique, reinhabited with humour and irony, and observed with sober intensity, it has made legible abiding postwar victimologies. While the work examined here does not present a linear progression towards a shared perspective or critique, there are nonetheless notable commonalities and differences which extend to more recent fictions of memory worth sketching out in closing.

Towards Ironic Complicity

Dieter Forte's *Der Junge mit den blutigen Schuhen* – representative of the ascent of the *Kriegskind* generation – celebrates a new, reluctant but insightful hero of postwar German memory. 'The boy' speaks for war-traumatized Germans whose experiences could not find entrance into a perpetrator memory. Permanently injured, yet determined to give testimony, he resides in a space of knowing innocence which obfuscates foundational incompatibilities between Hitler's victims and Germans victimized by their own war. In contrast to Forte's text that naturalizes the process of remembering, Günter Grass's *Die Blechtrommel*, published decades earlier, highlights the manipulative and distorting force of remembering. The novel's childlike narrator, an intricately layered figure of memory, reveals the degree to which the 1950s are permeated by phantasmagoric residues of the Nazi past. Centred on affectations of ignorance and powerlessness, his defiant stance mimics a postwar collective bound together by acts of denial and acts of faux-contrition. Gisela Elsner's satire *Fliegeralarm* is also based on autobiographical experiences of the (air) war yet relies neither on the voice of a traumatized child nor on the voice of a childlike figure to assert the authority of the eyewitness. Her child protagonists are savvy wartime actors, fluent in the mimicry of innocence and victimhood, well-versed in the kind of German exceptionalism promoted by National Socialism. Sardonically distorted, they do not invite identification with a violated childhood self but deftly assert the reality of collective *Mittäterschaft*. In contrast to Forte, who deploys a faintly heroic and innocent child and Grass, who presents a knowing child, obscured behind a performance of confession and denial, Elsner provokes the reader with the implicated child whose half-knowledge betrays the reality of collective implication. When seen in dialogue, this body of postwar literature both mirrors and critically examines shifts in the German conversation about the Nazi past: from ubiquitous gestures of confessions of guilt in the postwar era underscored by Grass, to strategies of normalization and guilt reversal in the Kohl era described by Elsner, and finally a language of deflection and exculpation presented by Forte.

Part II showed that subsequent generations of authors have deployed the child witness in a more self-reflexive manner. No longer interested in the tectonics of history, their work traces reverberations of Nazi history as manifest in received stories of parental war wounds. Now, fictions of memory weave autobiographical details, private family legends and historical facts into increasingly multifaceted memory pastiches. Born to parents traumatized by war or *Kriegskind* parents, Treichel and Seiffert use the child perspective in ways that are more self-deprecating and more impassive than in earlier texts. Based on irony, humour and a form of stripped-down writing, their texts deconstruct the story of Nazi history from the perpetrator perspective. Treichel's child narrator represents a symptomatic site of wounding yet not of a wound culture. Equipped with dry humour, he relays the futile struggle to locate a stable or coherent sense of identity in the shadow of emergent family stories. His voice navigates impasses of a memory culture permeated by identification *with* and *as* Hitler's victims, a liminal space which also comes into view in Rachel Seiffert's story 'Lore'. Both *Der Verlorene* and 'Lore' articulate a perspective of (temporal, generational and conceptual) belatedness. Both draw attention to indexical traces of perpetration captured in photos that have been preserved in or torn out of the family album, visual traces of a past which were intentionally destroyed or strategically exhibited as icons of collective shame. As silent witnesses to the Nazi past they remain obscure for characters and readers alike. Treichel's and Seiffert's fictions of memory travel across victim and perpetrator fantasies and move the reader multidirectionally through various subject positions. Eschewing the closure of rescue or redemption, they reveal the boundaries between victims and perpetrators to be porous. While the voice of Treichel's laconic narrator keeps the reader at a distance, Seiffert's prose, stripped bare of auctorial support, goes even further and orphans the reader. Bound together in unsavoury ways, the young adults in 'Lore' expose the degree to which the Jewish victim has been and continues to be appropriated in the texture of Germany's cultural memory. In summary, postmemorial fictions of memory move away from concepts of guilt and increasingly explore contours of implication. Drawing on ironic complicity, a postmodern mode of production/reception that initiates a dialogue between an unredeemable past and an unredeemed present, they don't leave space for a reassuring identification with traumatized characters.

'Writing the child' became legible as a form of imaginative travel between different points in time and space that relies on a lexis of critical self-reflection and brings into relief our responsibilities as *secondary* witnesses to violent legacies. 'Writing the child' narrates historical identity less as a fixed ontological framework than as a multidirectional and intersectional configuration in constant flux. Thus, this kind of memory work mobilizes the meaning of fiction in the double sense described by Nünning: it uses fictional memory stories to reveal the framework of suppositions underlying the collective fiction of cultural memory. 'Writing the child', then, is instructive in Benjamin's sense:

> *A writer who does not teach other writers teaches nobody.* The crucial point, therefore, is that a writer's production must have the character of a model: it must be able to instruct other writers in their production, and secondly it must be able to place an improved apparatus at their disposal. This apparatus will be better the more consumers it brings in contact with the production process – in short, the more readers or spectators it turns into collaborators.[1]

Increasingly, reading (the past) has to become an act of meta-reflective collaboration across time and space, a challenge to rethink historical identity outside of reassuring but nonetheless false and unproductive binaries. In conclusion, I want to briefly return to the discursive backdrop of my discussion of fictions of memory, the *Kriegskind* narrative, in light of more recent memory work of the *Kriegsenkel*.

Intergenerational Conversations

As a generalized concept seldom inscribed by historical or autobiographical nuance, the *Kriegskind* represents a useful subject of German cultural memory. Ennobled through suffering but modest in his or her claims, the *Kriegskind* belongs to the last living witnesses of the Third Reich and speaks for the exemplary German victim. While numerous psychological symptoms align the *Kriegskind* with the Jewish survivor child, a divided history keeps them forever apart – a foundational difference most adequately captured in texts that keep a space for the silenced other of German history. In *Der Junge mit den blutigen Schuhen*, this space collapses into a generalized suffering; in *Die Blechtrommel*, this space is barely implied in form of the voice of the drums obtained from a Jewish toyshop; in *Fliegeralarm*, it exists only obliquely through collective fantasies

---

1   Walter Benjamin, 'The Author as Producer', in Anna Bostock, trans., *Understanding Brecht: Walter Benjamin* (London, New York: Verso, 1989), 98.

that produce the Jewish other; in *Der Verlorene*, it emerges as troubling correspondences between German and Jewish 'replacement children'; in 'Lore', it reveals fraught appropriations of the Jewish victim post-1945. In more recent family novels, this space opens towards increasingly heterogenous and more nuanced explorations of historical accountability.

Two decades into the twenty-first century, the *Kriegsenkel* document or imagine conversations with their (dead or dying) parents about their family history. More determined than ever to break the generational 'Schweigekartell' [cartel of silence], texts like *Tagesanbruch* [*Dawn*] (2016) by Hans-Ulrich Treichel, *Heimat. Ein deutsches Familienalbum* [*Heimat: A Family Album*] (2018) by Nora Krug, *Wie kommt der Krieg ins Kind* [*How Does War Enter the Child*] (2019) by Susanne Fritz and *Sieben Heringe* [*Seven Herrings*] (2021) by Jürgen Wiebicke tenaciously overwrite this silence. The *Kriegsenkel* look back with an increased rigour, less to creatively fill in the blanks than to take a more sober look at a mnemonic web made of the legendary and the real. With ever greater personal urgency, their work delineates spaces of *Mitwisser-* and *Mittäterschaft* [the shared but tacit knowledge of the accomplice or co-perpetrator] contained in parental gaps, silences and resistance. While listening to family stories of trauma, the *Kriegsenkel* hear stories about familial complicity without lecturing those they listen to about the historical facts. In their imagination the *Kriegsenkel* converse with grandfathers and grandmothers they never met, letting the previous generation know that their presence was all too palpable at the family table. Premised on the desire 'die eigene Familiengeschichte nicht schön[zu]schreiben, wichtiger Vorsatz'[2] [to embellish nothing, important intention], these fictions of memory are as relentless as they are insistent, as uncompromising as they are accepting. This kind memory work ties in with a larger framework of collective remembrance Aleida Assmann calls 'dialogic memory'. Dialogic memory seeks to navigate intersections of factual historical knowledge and differing family memories; it parses the impact of shifting positions of perpetrators and victims within a shared history of traumatic violence across the boundaries of generations and

---

2   Jürgen Wiebicke, *Sieben Heringe. Meine Mutter, das Schweigen der Kriegskinder und das Sprechen vor dem Tod* (Cologne: Kiepenheuer & Witsch, 2021), 52.

nations. Still evolving, it responds to a shared history of trauma that has affected two or more nations and is based on efforts of mutually shared stories and empathic listening.[3]

Framed by the war generation's mantra of silences maintained and secrets kept, *Tagesanbruch* dramatizes the persistence of unspoken war secrets within the family. It is centred on a moment of confessional honesty between a mother holding her son who has just died of cancer, one last time. The mother, a modern pietà, reveals to an impassive listener not only that his father was probably a Russian soldier who raped her but also that she owes her life to another Russian soldier who allowed her and her husband to escape. The enemy, it seems, was not always a violent foe. These maternal confessions are framed by obsessively repeated defences, 'man muss nicht alles bereden. Schon gar nicht mit dem eigenen Kind'[4] [one does not have to discuss everything. Certainly not with one's child]. While they move towards an increasing willingness to speak 'man muss alles aussprechen'[5] [one has to talk about everything], they remain unable to integrate this knowledge into the larger story of perpetration. *Sieben Heringe*, a conversation between a son and his dying mother, expresses the resolve to counter historical discontinuity with narrative continuity. The text patiently parses the grammar of silence and suffering (both experienced and witnessed) and thus reveals the effects of socio-psychic violence beyond the abstractions of innocence and culpability. As a whole, these continued fictions of memory reckon with the legacy of war violence in a sober yet empathic way but refuse to contribute to the exculpatory wound culture. From the perspective of belatedness, they attempt to find a space of identity in a new 'house', a house made of intersecting, imagined and received (his)stories described by the voice of the narrator in *Wie kommt der Krieg ins Kind* as, 'Ein Papierhaus. Ein Buchstabenhaus. Ein Traumhaus aus dem Alptraumhaus: viel Geschichte auf wenig Quadratmetern. Deutsche Geschichte. Polnische Geschichte. Deutsch-polnische Geschichte.

3   Aleida Assmann, *Das neue Unbehagen an der Erinnerungskultur. Eine Intervention* (Munich: Beck, 2013), 195–203.
4   Hans-Ulrich Treichel, *Tagesanbruch* (Berlin: Suhrkamp, 2016), 10.
5   Treichel, 83.

Europäische Geschichte.'[6] [A house made of paper. A house made of letters. A dream house from the nightmare house: lots of history spanning just a few square feet. German history. Polish history. German-Polish history. European history.] Beyond the clichés, the savvy packaging and the exploitations of traumatized victims by the media industry, these fictions of memory know only too well: 'Es gab keinen Frieden' (DV, 132) [There was no peace]; the war has not ended.

Memory in a Moment of Danger

Not surprisingly, as I mentioned in the preface, the work on this book also challenged me to reflect on the question of how this war has crossed my own life, how its legacy has shaped me – a white German woman, born thirteen years after the end of the war.[7] I am the daughter of a father who was born one year before the First World War and who wore Hitler's uniform in the Second World War (allegedly as a medic), but only yelled incoherently in response to my questions about more details. I am also the daughter of a *Kriegskind* mother who, born two years after Hitler came to power, never spoke about her war childhood, at least not in so many words. I came to the United States in my late twenties as an exchange student but stayed on, grateful for the opportunities afforded to me here. But what kind of 'barbarism', to use Benjamin's phrase, do these advantages ultimately rest on? For the past three decades, I have lived and worked in a country whose national myths bracket the murderous

6   Susanne Fritz, *Wie kommt der Krieg ins Kind* (Munich: btb, 2019), 155.

7   In many ways, this book became 'personal' in the way Susan Neiman's study *Learning from the Germans: Confronting Race and the Memory of Evil* is personal. Neiman's perspective of German history is premised on the paradoxical intersections that have shaped her life. Her upbringing in the American South left indelible imprints that have informed her exploration of how the personal and the collective converge in her – a Jewish women who was born in the US, lived and worked in Israel, but ultimately decided to settle in Berlin. I have to thank the reviewer of the manuscript for pointing this out.

dispossession of indigenous people, as well as the 'slow trauma' of the legacy of slavery. While I grew up in a country marked by a shameful history obscured by postwar prosperity, I have lived most of my adult life in a country whose prosperity rests on adjacent histories of racial domination and exploitation. Hence, I not only inherited but also benefited from related systems of oppression: the advantages of white supremacy mitigated by insidious forms of patriarchal domination shaped and continue to shape my own subject position, implicating me in contradictory ways in systemic forms of historical injustice. Writing this book has forced me to acknowledge these entanglements. It forced me to appreciate the violent facts of German history in a more nuanced and integrated way. But it has also reminded me of the power of literature to lead the reader into spaces of painful indeterminacy, into open spaces of incomplete knowledge and fragmentary insights, spaces that refuse to provide any one answer while nonetheless offering invaluable questions. I realized once again, not unlike myths which are centred around unresolved and enduring questions, literature can open new possibilities of thinking about the past beyond the certainties of historical facts. It can offer what Krista Tippet has called a 'muscular hope': an imaginative leap that, while resting on a careful exploration of what was, refuses to accept that the world has to be this way.[8]

To reflect on refractions of identity that shape our lives and inform our fictions of memory is all the more important when we find ourselves living in what Benjamin has called 'a moment of danger': a moment defined by bombs raining down on civilians in Ukraine, by the sound of Ukrainian air raid sirens already haunting the next generation of *Kriegskinder*. This moment allowed US nationalists like Richard Spencer to repeat the ethnocentric vitriol of National Socialism with impunity. It is also a moment when German alt-right representatives like Christian Lüth can declare that migrants, while advantageous for the party, 'could still be shot later [...] or gassed'; a moment when AfD politicians like Alexander Gauland

8   David Marchese, 'Krista Tippet Wants You ro See All the Hope That's Being Hidden', *New York Times Magazine*, 1 July 2022, <https://www.nytimes.com/interactive/2022/07/05/magazine/krista-tippett-interview.html>, accessed 5 July 2022.

can trivialize the Holocaust as 'a speck of bird shit'.⁹ In moments like these, memory (writing) becomes a form of contestatory empowerment. Because, as Benjamin reminds us, '[t]o articulate the past historically does not mean to recognize "the way it really was" (Ranke). It means to seize hold of a memory as it flashes up in a moment of danger.'¹⁰ This kind of empowerment rests on the power of the imagination to offer a new sense of the future, not yet tested yet potentially emancipatory possibilities to reside in history. The child is never just a child: it keeps offering illusive but constantly emerging new truths about history through images 'we never saw prior to recalling them'.

9   'AfD leaders and their most offensive remarks', DW, <https://p.dw.com/p/2Xyln>, accessed 3 March 2022.

10   Walter Benjamin, 'Theses on the Philosophy of History', in Hannah Arendt, ed. and trans., *Illuminations* (New York: Schocken, 1985), 255.

Bibliography

Primary Literature

Elsner, Gisela, *Fliegeralarm* (Berlin: Verbrecher Verlag, 2009).

Forte, Dieter, *Der Junge mit den blutigen Schuhen* (Frankfurt a.M.: Fischer, 2003).

____, *Das Muster* (Frankfurt a.M.: Fischer, 2003).

Fritz, Susanne, *Wie kommt der Krieg ins Kind* (Munich: btb, 2019).

Grass, Günter, *Beim Häuten der Zwiebel* (Göttingen: Steidel, 2007).

____, *Die Blechtrommel*, Volker Neuhaus, ed., *Werkausgabe in zehn Bänden*, II (Darmstadt, Neuwied: Luchterhand, 1987).

Krug, Nora, *Heimat. Ein deutsches Familienalbum* (Munich: Penguin Verlag, 2018).

Treichel, Hans-Ulrich, *Tagesanbruch* (Berlin: Suhrkamp, 2016).

____, *Lost*, Carol Brown Janeway, trans. (New York: Vintage, 2000).

____, *Der Verlorene* (Frankfurt a.M.: Suhrkamp, 1999).

____, *Heimatkunde* (Frankfurt a.M.: Suhrkamp, 1996).

Seiffert, Rachel, *The Dark Room* (New York, Pantheon, 2001).

Walser, Martin, *A Gushing Fountain,* David Dollenmayer, trans. (New York: Arcade, 2015).

____, *Ein springender Brunnen* (Frankfurt a.M.: Suhrkamp, 1998).

Wiebicke, Jürgen, *Sieben Heringe. Meine Mutter, das Schweigen der Kriegskinder und das Sprechen vor dem Tod* (Cologne: Kiepenheuer&Witsch, 2021).

Secondary Literature

Adorno, Theodor W., 'The Meaning of Working Through the Past', in Henry W. Pickford, trans., *Critical Models: Intervention and Catchwords* (New York: Columbia University Press, 1998), 89–103.

____, 'Was bedeutet Aufarbeitung der Vergangenheit', in Rolf Tiedemann, ed., *Adorno. Kulturkritik und Gesellschaft*, 10-2 (Frankfurt a.M.: Suhrkamp, 1997), 555–72.

_____, 'Zur Bekämpfung des Antisemitismus heute', in Rolf Tiedemann, ed., *Adorno. Vermischte Schriften I*, 20–1 (Frankfurt a.M.: Suhrkamp, 1997), 360–83.

_____, 'Commitment', Francis McDonagh, trans., <https://unhistoricactsdotnet. files.wordpress.com/2015/01/adorno–commitment.pdf>.

Alberti, Bettina, *Seelische Trümmer. Geboren in den 50er und 60er Jahren: Die Nachkriegsgeneration im Schatten des Kriegstraumas* (Munich: Kösel, 2010).

Alsen, Raimo, *Wandlungen der Erinnerungskultur. Gibt es eine "neue deutsche Opfergeschichte"?* (Hamburg: Diplomica Verlag, 2011).

Anderson, Benedict, *Imagined Communities* (London, New York: Verso, 1983).

Arendt, Hannah, 'Collective Responsibility', in Jerome Kohn, ed., *Responsibility and Judgment.* (New York: Schoken, 2003), 147–58.

_____, 'On Humanity in Dark Times: Thoughts about Lessing', in Clara and Richard Winston, trans., *Men in Dark Times. Hannah Arendt* (San Diego, New York, London: Harvest, 1995), 3–31.

_____, *Karl Jaspers Correspondence 1926–1969*, Lotte Köhler and Hans Saner, eds, Robert and Rita Kimber, trans. (New York: Harcourt Brace Jovanovich, 1992).

_____, 'Rede zur Verleihung des Lessingpreises 1959', <https://www.derstandard.at/ story/2617038/der–holocaust–laesst–sich–nicht–bewaeltigen>.

Ariès, Phillipe, and Robert Baldick, trans., *Centuries of Childhood: A Social History of Family Life* (New York: Vintage Books, 1962).

Assmann, Aleida, and Sarah Clift, trans., *Shadows of Trauma: Memory and Politics of Postwar Identity* (New York: Fordham University Press, 2016).

_____, *Das neue Unbehagen an der Erinnerungskultur. Eine Intervention* (Munich: Beck, 2013).

_____, 'On the (In)Compatibility of Guilt and Suffering in German Memory', *German Life and Letters* 59/2 (April 2006): 187–200.

_____, 'Limits of Understanding: Generational Identities in Recent German Memory Literature', in Dagmar Wienroder-Skinner and Laurel Cohen-Pfister, eds, *Victims and Perpetrators 1933–1945: Representing the Past in Post-unification Culture* (Berlin: De Gruyter, 2006), 29–48.

_____, *Generationsidentitäten und Vorurteilsstrukturen in der neuen deutschen Erinnerungsliteratur* (Wien: Picus, 2006).

_____, and Ute Frevert. *Geschichtsvergessenheit, Geschichtsversessenheit. Vom Umgang mit deutschen Vergangenheiten nach 1945* (Munich: dva, 1999).

Assmann, Jan, 'Communicative and Cultural Memory', in Astrid Erll and Ansgard Nünning, eds, *A Companion to Cultural Memory Studies* (Berlin, New York: de Gruyter, 2010), 109–18.

Baackmann, Susanne. 'Reconfiguring the Witness of the Holocaust: The Child as a Lieu de Mémoire in Marianne Rosenbaum's Film Peppermint Frieden', *Seminar* 40/1 (February 2004): 19–34.

____, *Erklär mir Liebe. Weibliche Schreibweisen von Liebe in der Gegenwartsliteratur* (Hamburg: Argument Verlag, 1995).

Bach, Jonathan, and Benjamin Nienass, 'Introduction: Innocence and the Politics of Memory', *German Politics and* Society 39/1 (Spring 2021): 1–12.

Bachmann, Ingeborg, *Werke*, 3 and 5, Christine Koschel, ed. (Munich, Zurich: Piper, 1982).

Bal, Mieke, 'Introduction', in Mieke Bal, Jonathan Crewe and Leo Spitzer, eds, *Acts of Memory: Cultural Recall in the Present* (Hannover, London: University Press of New England, 1999), vii–xvii.

Bammer, Angelika, *Born After: Reckoning with the German Past* (London, Oxford, New York: Bloomsbury, 2019).

Barthes, Roland, Richard Howard and Annette Lavers, trans., *Mythologies* (New York: Hill and Wang, 2012).

____, Richard Howard, trans., *Camera Lucida*: *Reflections on Photography* (New York: Hill and Wang, 2010).

Bartov, Omer, '"Seit die Juden weg sind ...": Germany, History, and Representations of Absence', in Scott Denham, Irene Kacandes and Jonathan Petropoulos, eds, *A User's Guide to German Cultural Studies* (Ann Arbour: University of Michigan Press, 1997), 209–26.

Baumgartl, Annette, *'Auf das Opfer darf sich keiner berufen'. Zur Dekonstruktion von Opferfiguren bei Ingeborg Bachmann und Barbara Duden* (Marburg: Tectum Verlag, 2008).

Benjamin, Walter, 'Aus einer kleinen Rede über Proust, an meinem vierzigsten Geburtstag gehalten', in Rolf Tiedemann and Hermann Schweppenhäuser, eds, *Walter Benjamin. Gesammelte Schriften*, II–3 (Frankfurt a.M.: Suhrkamp, 1991), 1064–65.

____, 'Berliner Kindheit um neunzehnhundert', in Rolf Tiedemann and Hermann Schweppenhäuser, eds, *Walter Benjamin. Gesammelte Schriften*, VII–1 (Frankfurt a.M.: Suhrkamp, 1989), 385–482.

____, 'Theses on the Philosophy of History', in Hannah Arendt, ed. and trans., *Illuminations*: *Walter Benjamin: Essays and Reflections* (New York: Schocken, 1985), 253–67.

____, 'On Some Motifs in Baudelaire', in Harry Zohn, trans., *Illuminations: Walter Benjamin Essays and Reflections* (New York: Schocken, 1968), 155–200.

Beyersdorf, H. F., 'The Narrator as Artful Deceiver: Aspects of Narrative Perspective in *Die Blechtrommel*', *Germanic Review* 55/4 (Fall 1980): 129–38.

Blasberg, Cornelia, 'Geschichte als Palimpsest. Schreiben und Lesen über die Kinder der Täter', *Deutsche Vierteljahresschrift* 3 (2002): 464–95.

Bode, Sabine, *Kriegsenkel. Die Erben der vergessenen Generation* (Stuttgart: Klett-Cotta, 2009).

____, *Die deutsche Krankheit – German Angst* (Munich, Zurich: Piper, 2008).

____, *Die vergessene Generation. Die Kriegskinder brechen ihr Schweigen* (orig. pub. 2004) (Munich, Zurich: Piper, 2010).

Bohleber, Werner, 'Transgenerationelles Trauma, Identifizierung und Geschichtsbewußtsein', in Jörn Rüsen and Jürgen Straub, eds, *Die dunkle Spur der Vergangenheit* (Frankfurt a.M.: Suhrkamp, 1998), 256–74.

Bormann von, Alexander. 'Besetzt war sie durch und durch'. Traumatisierung im Werk von Anne Duden, in Stephan Braese, Hoger Gehle, and Doron Kiesel eds, *Deutsche Nachkriegsliteratur und der Holocaust*, 6 (Frankfurt a.M., New York: Campus, 1998), 245–67.

Bos, Pascale, 'Positionality and Postmemory in Scholarship on the Holocaust', in *Women in German Yearbook* 19 (2003): 50–74.

Braese, Stephan, 'Bombenkrieg und literarische Gegenwart. Zu W. G. Sebald und Dieter Forte', *Mittelweg* 36/1 (2002): 4–24.

Braun, Michael, 'Die Wahrheit der Geschichte(n). Zur Erinnerungsliteratur von Tanja Dückers, Günter Grass, Uwe Timm', in Judith Klinger and Gerhard Wolf, eds, *Gedächtnis und kultureller Wandel. Erinnerndes Schreiben – Perspektiven und Kontroversen* (Tübingen: Niemeyer Verlag, 2009), 97–111.

____, 'Günter Grass und die Rolle der Literatur in der deutschen Erinnerungsliteratur', *Der Deutschunterricht* 58/6 (2006): 87–91.

Brockhaus, Gudrun, 'Kontroversen um die 'Kriegskindheit'', *Forum Psychoanalyse* 26 (2010): 313–24.

Bude, Heinz, 'Die Achtundsechziger im Familienroman der Bundesrepublik', in Helmut König, ed., *Vertuschte Vergangenheit: der Fall Schwerte und die NS-Vergangenheit der deutschen Hochschulen* (Munich: Beck, 1997), 287–300.

Cohen-Pfister, Laurel, 'The Suffering of the Perpetrators: Unleashing Collective Memory in German Literature of the Twenty-First Century', *Forum of Modern Language Studies*, 4 1/2 (2005): 123–35.

Cosgrove, Mary, 'Narrating German Suffering in the Shadow of Holocaust Victimology: W. G. Sebald, Contemporary Trauma Theory, and Dieter Forte's Air Raid Epic', in Stuart Taberner and Karina Berger, eds, *Germans as Victims in the Literary Fiction of the Berlin Republic* (Rochester, NY: Camden House, 2009), 162–76.

Craig, Robert, ' "Ist die Schwarze Köchin da? Jajaja...": Mimesis and Günter Grass's *Die Blechtrommel*', *Monatshefte* 108/1 (Spring 2016): 99–119.

Crownshaw, Richard, 'Perpetrator Fictions and Transcultural Memory', *Parallax* 17/4 (2011): 75–89.

Curran, Jane V., and Steve Dowden, 'Ostwestfalen ist überall. Gespräch mit Hans-Ulrich Treichel', *Colloquia Germanica* 37 3/4 (2004): 307–31.

Diner, Dan, 'Zwischen Aporie und Apologie. Über Grenzen der Historisierung des Nationalsozialismus', *Gewerkschaftliche Monatshefte* 3 (2018): 153–59.

_____, 'Negative Symbiose. Deutsche und Juden nach Auschwitz', in Dan Diner, ed., *Ist der Nationalsozialismus Geschichte? Zu Historisierung und Historikerstreit* (Frankfurt a.M.: Fischer, 1987), 185–97.

Dörr, Margarete, *Der Krieg hat uns geprägt. Wie Kinder den Zweiten Weltkrieg erlebten* (Frankfurt a.M.: Campus, 2007).

Echternkamp, Jörg, 'Von der Gewalterfahrung zur Kriegserinnerung – über den Bombenkrieg als Thema einer Geschichte der deutschen Kriegsgesellschaft', in Dietmar Süss, ed., *Deutschland im Luftkrieg. Geschichte und Erinnerung* (Munich: Oldenbourg Verlag, 2007), 13–26.

Eckstaedt, Anita, *Nationalsozialismus in der 'zweiten Generation'. Psychoanalyse von Hörigkeitsverhältnissen* (Frankfurt a.M.: Suhrkamp, 1989).

Eigler, Friedericke, *Gedächtnis und Geschichte in Generationenromanen seit der Wende* (Berlin: Erich Schmidt, 2005).

_____, 'Zur Historisierung des Heimatbegriffs im Generationenroman. Dieter Fortes Trilogie *Das Haus auf meinen Schultern*', *The Germanic Review* 83/2 (2004): 83–106.

Elsner, Gisela, *Gisela Elsner. Flüche einer Verfluchten. Kritische Schriften* I and II, Christine Künzel, ed. (Berlin: Verbrecher Verlag, 2011).

Epstein, Helen, *Children of the Holocaust. Conversations with Sons and Daughters of Survivors* (New York: Penguin, 1979).

Erll, Astrid, and Sara B. Young, trans., *Memory in Culture* (New York: Palgrave Macmillan, 2011).

Ermann, Michael, 'Kriegskinder in Psychoanalysen', Farewell lecture given in Munich on 20 March 2009, <https://studylibde.com/doc/2146360/abschiedsvorles ung>, accessed 10 October 2021.

_____, 'Wir Kriegskinder', *Forum der Psychoanalyse* 20 (2004): 226–39.

_____, Diana Pflichthofer, and Harald Kamm. 'Children of Nazi Germany 60 Years On', *International Forum of Psychoanalysis* 18 (2009): 225–36.

Eshel, Amir, *Futurity: Contemporary Literature and the Quest for the Past* (Chicago, London: University of Chicago Press, 2013).

_____, 'Die Grammatik des Verlusts: Verlorene Kinder, verlorene Zeit in Barbara Honigmanns *Soharas Reise* und in Hans-Ulrichs *Der Verlorene*', in Hartmut Steinecke and Sander Gilman, eds, Beiheft zur *Zeitschrift für deutsche Philologie. Deutsch–jüdische Literatur der neunziger Jahre: Die Generation nach der Shoah* (Berlin: Erich Schmidt, 2002), 59–74.

Faimberg, Haydée. 'Apres-coup', *The International Journal of Psychoanalysis* 86/1 (2005): 1–13.

_____, *The Telescoping of Generations: Listening to the Narcissistic Links between Generations* (New York: Routledge, 2005).

Felman, Shoshan, and Dori Laub, *Testimony: Crises of Witnessing in Literature, Psychoanalysis, and History* (New York, London: Routledge, 1992).

Finkler, Heinrich, *Der Schrei der Kriegskinder. Eine Kindheit im Zeichen von Angst, Schwermut und Hunger* (Frankfurt a.M.: Fischer, 2014).

Forte, Dieter, Volker Hage, ed., *Schweigen oder Sprechen* (Frankfurt a.M.: Fischer, 2002), 45–68.

Frei, Norbert, *1945 und wir. Das Dritte Reich im Bewußtsein der Deutschen* (Munich: Beck, 2005).

____, *Adenauer's Germany and the Nazi Past*, Joel Golb, trans. (New York: Columbia University Press, 2002).

Freud, Sigmund, 'Screen Memories' (orig. pub. 1899), in James Strachey, ed., trans., *The Standard Edition of the Complete Psychological Works of Sigmund Freud*, III (London: The Hogarth Press, 1964), 302–21.

____, 'Childhood and Concealing Memories' (orig. pub. 1914), *Psychopathology of Everyday Life* (London: Ernest Benn Limited, 1914), 55–68.

____, 'Constructions in Analysis' (orig. pub. 1937), in James Strachey, ed., trans., *The Standard Edition of the Complete Psychological Works of Sigmund Freud*, XXIII (London: The Hogarth Press, 1964), 257–69.

Friedlaender, Saul, 'History, Memory, and the Historian: Facing the Shoah', in Michael S. Roth and Charles G. Salas, eds, *Disturbing Remains: Memory, History, and Crisis in the Twentieth Century* (Los Angeles: Getty Research Institute, 2001), 271–81.

____, Thomas Weyr, trans., *Reflections of Nazism: An Essay on Kitsch and Death* (Bloomington: Indiana University Press, 1993).

Friedrich, Jörg, *Der Brand. Deutschland im Bombenkrieg 1940–1945* (Berlin: List, 2004).

Frizen, Werner, 'Blechmusik. Oskar Matzeraths Erzählkunst', *Etudes Germanique* 42/1 (1987): 129–38.

Frosh, Paul, 'Telling Presences: Witnesses, Mass Media, and the Imagined Lives of Strangers', in Paul Frosh and Amit Pinchevski, eds, *Media Witnessing: Testimony in the Age of Mass Communication* (Houndmills, Basingstoke, Palgrave Macmillan, 2009), 49–72.

Fuchs, Anne, *Phantoms of War in Contemporary German Literature, Films, and Discourse: The Politics of Memory* (Houndmills, Basingstoke: Palgrave Macmillan, 2008).

____, 'Towards and Ethics of Remembering: The Walser-Bubis Debate and the Other of Discourse', *The German Quarterly* 75/3 (2002): 235–46.

Gaus, Günter, *Wo Deutschland liegt. Eine Ortsbestimmung* (Hamburg: Hoffmann Campe, 1983).

Grass, Günter, 'Jungbürgerrede: Über Erwachsene und Verwachsene' (1970), in Volker Neuhaus and Daniela Hermes, eds, *Günter Grass, Essays, Reden,*

Briefe, Kommentare. Werkausgabe in zehn Bänden, IX (Darmstadt und Neuwied: Luchterhand, 1987), 429–39.

_____, 'Sisyphos und der Traum vom Gelingen. Günter Grass im Gespräch mit Johann Strasser and Oskar Negt (1985)', *Werkausgabe in zehn Bänden*, X (Frankfurt a.M.: Büchergilde Gutenberg, 1987), 325–33.

Grazzini, Serena, 'Erinnerte Vergangenheit und subjektive Wahrnehmung: Hans-Ulrich Treichels *Der Verlorene*', in Manuel Maldonado-Alemán and Carsten Gansel, eds, *Literarische Inszenierungen von Geschichte. Formen der Erinnerung in der deutschsprachigen Literatur nach 1945 und 1989* (Stuttgart: Metzler, 2018), 71–81.

Gwyer, Kirstin, 'Beyond Lateness? 'Postmemory' and the Late(st) German Language Family Novel', *New German Critique* 42/2 (2015): 137–53.

Hage, Volker, *Zeugen der Zerstörung. Die Literaten und der Luftkrieg* (Frankfurt a.M.: Fischer, 2003).

_____, 'Rückblick mit Oskar. Was heißt hier Nachkriegsliteratur?', in *Propheten im eigenen Land. Auf der Suche nach der deutschen Literatur* (Munich: dtv, 1999), 324–34.

Hartmann, Christian, Johannes Hürter and Ulrike Jureit, eds, *Verbrechen der Wehrmacht. Bilanz einer Debatte* (Munich: Beck, 2005).

Hegener, Wolfgang, *Schuld-Abwehr. Psychoanalytische und kulturwissenschaftliche Studien zum Antisemitismus* (Gießen: Psychosozial Verlag, 2019).

Heinl, Peter, *'Maikäfer flieg, dein Vater ist im Krieg.' Seelische Wunden aus der Kriegskindheit.* (Munich: Kösel, 1994).

Heinlein, Michael, *Die Erfindung der Erinnerung. Deutsche Kriegskinder im Gedächtnis der Gegenwart* (Bielefeld: transcript, 2010).

Herf, Jeffrey, 'Legacies of a Divided Memory for German Debates about the Holocaust in the 1990s', *German Politics and Society* 17/3 (Fall 1999): 10–34.

Higonnet, Anne, *Pictures of Innocence: The History and Crisis of Ideal Childhood* (London: Thames & Hudson, 1998).

Hirsch, Marianne, *The Generation of Postmemory: Writing and Visual Culture after the Holocaust* (New York: Columbia University, 2012).

_____, 'The Generation of Postmemory', *Poetics Today* 29/1 (Spring 2008): 103–28.

_____, 'Surviving Images: Holocaust Photographs and the Work of Postmemory', *Yale Journal of Criticism* 14/1 (2001): 5–37.

_____, *Family Frames. Photography, Narrative and Postmemory* (Cambridge, London, Harvard University Press, 1997).

Historikerstreit. Die Dokumentation der Kontroverse um die Einzigartigkeit der nationalsozialistischen Judenvernichtung (Munich, Zurich: Piper, 1988).

Hoffman, Eva, *After Such Knowledge: Memory, History, and the Legacy of the Holocaust* (New York: Public Affairs, 2004).

Horstkotte, Silke, 'Transgenerational Mediations of Identity in Rachel Seiffert's *The Dark Room* and Marcel Beyer's *The Spies*', in Silke Horstkotte and Esther Peeren, eds, *The Shock of the Other: Situating Alterity* (Amsterdam: Rodopi, 2007), 149–60.

Hunter, Anna Claire, '"To tell the Story': Cultural Trauma and Holocaust Metanarrative', *Holocaust Studies* 25 1/2 (2019): 12–27.

Huyssen, Andreas, *Present Pasts. Urban Palimpsests and the Politics of Memory* (Stanford: Stanford University Press, 2003).

Jenkins, Henry, 'Introduction: Childhood Innocence and Other Modern Myths', in Henry Jenkins, ed., *The Children's Culture Reader* (New York, London: New York University Press, 1998), 1–37.

Jones, Sara, *The Media of Testimony: Remembering the East German Stasi in the Berlin Republic* (Houndmills, Basingstoke: Macmillan Palgrave, 2014).

Judt, Tony, *Postwar. A History of Europe since 1945* (New York: Penguin, 2005).

Jureit, Ulrike, 'Generationen Gedächtnis. Überlegungen zu einem Konzept kommunikativer Vergesellschaftung', in Lu Seegers, ed., *Die 'Generation der Kriegskinder': Historische Hintergründe und Deutungen* (Giessen: Psychosozial Verlag, 2009), 125–37.

——, and Christian Schneider, *Gefühlte Opfer. Illusionen der Vergangenheitsbewältigung* (Stuttgart: Klett–Cotta, 2011).

Kaes, Anton, *From Hitler to Heimat: The Return of History as Film* (Cambridge, MA: Harvard University Press, 1989).

——, *Deutschlandbilder. Die Wiederkehr der Geschichte als Film* (Munich: edition text+kritik, 1987).

Kantsteiner, Wulf, *in Pursuit of German Memory: History, Television, and Politics after Auschwitz* (Athens, OH: Ohio University Press, 2006).

Kapczynski, Jennifer, 'The Singular Jew. Representing National Socialism's Jewish Victims in Recent Historical Cinema', in Oleksandr Kobrynsky and Gerd Bayer, eds, *Holocaust Cinema in the Twenty-First Century: Memories, Images, and the Ethics of Representation* (New York: Wallflower Press, 2015), 117–40.

Kershaw, Ian, *Hitler, the Germans, and the Final Solution* (New Haven, London: Yale University Press, 2008).

Kettenacker, Lothar, ed. *Ein Volk von Opfern? Die neue Debatte um den Bombenkrieg 1940–45* (Berlin: Rowohlt, 2003).

Kincaid, James R., *Child–Loving: The Erotic Child and Victorian Culture* (New York: Routledge, 1992).

Kleindienst, Jürgen, and Ingrid Hantke, eds, *Kriegskinder erzählen. 1939–1945* (Berlin: Zeitgut Verlag, 2013).

Knittel, Susanne C., and Sofia Forchieri, 'Navigating Implication: An Interview with Michael Rothberg', *Journal of Perpetrator Studies* 3/1 (2020): 6–19.

Koselleck, Reinhardt, 'Die Diskontinuität der Erinnerung', *Deutsche Zeitschrift für Philosophie* 47/2 (1999): 213–22.

Krimmer, Elisabeth, '"Ein Volk von Opfern?" Germans as Victims in Günter Grass's *Die Blechtrommel* and *Im Krebsgang*', *Seminar: A Journal of Germanic Studies* 44/2 (May 2008): 272–90.

Kuhn, Annette, *Family Secrets: Acts of Memory and Imagination* (London, New York: Verso, 2005).

Künzel, Christine, '"Ohne einen Anflug von Mitgefühl". Der Generationendiskurs als "Gegenfluch". Monströse Kriegskinder in Gisela Elsners Roman *Fliegeralarm*', in Jan Süselbeck, ed., *Familiengefühle. Generationengeschichte und NS-Erinnerung in den Medien* (Berlin: Verbrecher Verlag, 2014), 107–25.

——, '*Ich bin eine schmutzige Satirikerin*'. *Zum Werk Gisela Elsners 1937–1992*. (Taunus: Ulrike Helmer, 2012).

——, 'The Most Dangerous Presumption: Women Authors and the Problems of Writing Satire', in Beate Neumeier, ed., *Gender and Humour II: Reinventing the Genres of Laughter, Gender Forum* 35 (2011): 47–68.

——, 'Einmal im Abseits, immer im Abseits? Anmerkungen zum Verschwinden der Autorin Gisela Elsner', in *Die letzte Kommunistin. Texte zu Gisela Elsner* (Hamburg; Konkret, 2009), 7–20.

LaCapra, Dominick, *History in Transit: Experience, Identity, Critical Theory* (Ithaca, NY: Cornell University Press, 2004).

——, *History and Memory after Auschwitz* (Ithaca, NY: Cornell University Press, 1998).

Landsberg, Alison, *Prosthetic Memory: The Transformation of American Remembrance in the Age of Mass Culture* (New York: Columbia University Press, 2004).

Latzel, Klaus, 'Kriegskinder, Kriegsopfer und kriegskompetente Mädchen', in Hans-Heino Ewers, ed., *Erinnerungen an Kriegskindheiten: Erfahrungsräume, Erinnerungskultur und Geschichtspolitik unter sozial- und kulturwissenschaftlicher Perspektive* (Weinheim: Juventa, 2006), 207–18.

Lau, Jörg, 'Auf der Suche nach der verlorenen Normalität', in *Nachkrieg in Deutschland*. (Hamburg: Hamburger Edition, 2001), 498–520.

Leggewie, Claus, and Erik Meyer, *Ein Ort, an den man gerne geht: Das Holocaust Mahnmal und die deutsche Geschichtspolitik nach 1989* (Munich: Hanser, 2005).

Leinemann, Jürgen, *Höhenrausch. Die wirklichkeitsleere Welt der Politiker* (Munich: Karl Blessing, 2004).

Lessing, Hellmut, ed., *Kriegskinder* (Frankfurt a.M.: Extra Buch, 1984).

Levine, Michael G., *The Belated Witness* (Stanford: Stanford University Press, 2006).

Lohre, Matthias, *Das Erbe der Kriegsenkel. Was das Schweigen der Eltern mit uns macht* (Gütersloh: Gütersloher Verlagshaus, 2016).

Lorenz, Hilke, *Kriegskinder. Das Schicksal einer Generation* (Berlin: List, 2007).

Lury, Karen, *The Child in Film* (New Brunswick, NJ: Rutgers University Press, 2010).

Maguire, Nora, *Childness and the Writing of the German Past: Tropes of Childhood in Contemporary German Literature* (Oxford: Peter Lang, 2013).

Malchow, Timothy B., *Günter Grass and the Gender of German Memory: From the Tin Drum to Peeling the Onion* (Rochester, NY: Camden House, 2021).

Marcuse, Harold, *Legacies of Dachau. The Uses and Abuses of a Concentration Camp* (Cambridge, NY: Cambridge University Press, 2008).

Markovits, Andrei S., and Simon Reich, *The German Predicament: Memory and Power in the New Europe* (Ithaca, NY: Cornell University Press, 1997).

Martínez-Alfaro, María Jesús, 'The Estrangement Effect in Three Holocaust Narratives: Defamiliarizing Victims, Perpetrators and the Fairy Tale Genre', *Atlantis. Journal of the Spanish Association of Anglo-American Studies* 42/1 (June 2020): 37–56.

McGlothlin, Erin, and Jennifer M. Kapczynski, eds, *Persistent Legacy: The Holocaust and German Studies* (Rochester, NY: Camden House, 2016).

Meyer, Mathias, 'Gisela Elsner und die Kommunisten', in Christine Künzel, ed., *Gisela Elsner. Flüche einer Verfluchten. Kritische Schriften I* (Berlin: Verbrecher Verlag, 2011), 375–94.

Moeller, Robert G., *War Stories: The Search for a Usable Past in the Federal Republic of Germany* (Berkeley: University of California Press, 2001).

Morag, Raya, 'On the Definition of the Perpetrator: From the Twentieth to the Twenty-First Century', *Journal of Perpetrator Research* 2/1 (2018): 13–19.

Natov, Roni, *The Poetics of Childhood* (New York, London: Routlege, 2003).

Naumann, Klaus, 'Die Neunziger Jahre, ein nervöses Jahrzehnt. Deutsche Kriegsbilder am Ende der Nachkriegszeit, in Ursula Heulenkamp, ed., *Schuld und Sühne? Kriegserlebnis und Kriegsdeutung in deutschen Medien der Nachkriegszeit (1945–1961)* (Amsterdam: Rodopi, 2001), 801–11.

Neiman, Susan, *Learning from the Germans: Confronting Race and the Memory of Evil* (New York: Farrar, Strauss, Giroux, 2019).

Neumann, Birgit, 'The Literary Representation of Memory', in Astrid Erll and Ansgar Nünning, eds, *A Companion to Cultural Memory Studies* (Berlin, New York: De Gruyter, 2010), 333–43.

Niven, Bill, *Facing the Nazi Past: United Germany and the Legacy of the Third Reich* (London: Taylor & Francis, 2001).

Nolan, Mary, 'Germans as Victims during the Second World War. Air Wars, Memory Wars', *Central European History* 38/1 (2005): 7–40.

Nünning, Ansgar, 'Editorial: New Directions in the Study of Individual and Cultural Memory and Memorial Culture', *The Journal for the Study of British Cultures* 10 1/3 (2003): 3–9.

Olick, Jeffrey K., 'What Does It Mean to Normalize the Past? Official Memory in German Politics since 1989', *Social Science History* 224 (Memory and the Nation) (Winter 1998): 259–88.

O'Neill, 'Patrick, '*Die Blechtrommel*: Implications of Unreliability in Günter Grass's *Die* Blechtrommel', in *Acts of Narrative. Textual Strategies in Modern German Fiction* (Toronto: University of Toronto Press, 1996), 97–116.

Parry, Christoph, 'Die Rechtfertigung der Erinnerung vor der Last der Geschichte. Autobiographische Strategien bei Timm, Treichel, Walser und Sebald', in *Grenzen der Fiktionalität und der Erinnerung* (Munich: Iudicum, 2007), 98–111.

Peiter, Anne D., 'Erlebte Vorstellung' versus 'den Vorstellungen abgezogene Begriffe'. Überlegungen zum Shoah–Kitsch', in Inge Stephan and Alexander Tacke, eds, *Nachbilder des Holocaust* (Cologne, Weimar, Berlin: Böhlau, 2007), 66–76.

Peter, Nina, '"Märchen, Nazipropaganda und kindliche Unwissenheit". Märcheneinsatz als Ideologiekritik in Gisela Elsners *Fliegeralarm* (1989)', in Michael Peter Hehl and Christine Künzel, eds, *Ikonisierung, Kritik, Wiederentdeckung* (Munich: edition text+kritik, 2014), 159–76.

Peters, John Durham, 'Witnessing', *Witnessing, Media, Culture, Society* 23/6 (2001): 707–23.

Pividori, Cristina, 'Out of the Dark Room: Photography and Memory in Rachel Seiffert's Holocaust Tales', *Atlantis. Journal of the Spanish Association for Anglo-American Studies* 30/2 (2008): 79–94.

Radebold, Hartmut, *Spurensuche eines Kriegskindes* (Stuttgart: Klett–Cotta, 2015).

____, Werner Bohleber and Jürgen Zinnecker, eds, *Transgenerationelle Weitergabe kriegsbelasteter Kindheiten. Interdisziplinäre Studien zur Nachhaltigkeit historischer Erfahrungen über vier Generationen* (Weinheim, Munich: Juventa, 2008).

Radstone, Susannah, 'Social Bonds and Psychical Order: Testimonies', *Cultural Values* 5/1 (2009): 59–78.

____, 'Memory Studies: For and Against', *Memory Studies* 1/1 (2008): 31–39.

____, 'Working with Memory: An Introduction', *Memory and Methodology* (Oxford, Berg, 2000), 1–24.

Rauschning, Hermann, *Gespräche mit Hitler* (Zurich, Vienna, New York: Europa Verlag, 1940).

Raczymow, Henri, 'Memory Shot Through with Holes', *Yale French Studies* 85 (1994): 98–105.

Röckemann, Tanja, 'Die 'Wiedervereinigungsflickschusterei'. Zur Rezeption von Gisela Elsners Roman *Fliegeralarm* in den deutschen Verhältnissen von 1989/2000', *undercurrents. Forum für linke Literaturwissenschaft* (October

2013), <https://undercurrentsforum.com/index.php/undercurrents/article/view/37>.

Rose, Jacqueline, *The Case of Peter Pan or The Impossibility of Children's Fiction* (Philadelphia: The University of Pennsylvania Press, 1992).

Rothberg, Michael, *The Implicated Subject: Beyond Victims and Perpetrators* (Stanford: Stanford University Press, 2019).

____, 'Trauma Theory, Implicated Subjects, and the Question of Israel/Palestine." *Profession*, 2 May 2014, <https://profession.commons.mla.org/2014/05/02/trauma-theory-implicated-subjects-and-the-question-of-israelpalestine/>.

____, *Multidirectional Memory: Remembering in the Age of Decolonization* (Stanford: Stanford University Press, 2009).

Rubin Suleiman, Susan, 'The 1.5. Generation: Thinking About Child Survivors and the Holocaust', *American Imago* 59/3 (Fall 2002): 277–95.

Rumpf, Hans, Edward Fitzgerald, trans., *The Bombing of Germany* (New York, Chicago: Holt, Rinehardt and Winston, 1962).

Salzborn, Samuel, *Kollektive Unschuld. Die Abwehr der Shoah im deutschen Erinnern* (Berlin, Leipzig: Hentrich & Hentrich, 2020).

____, 'Opfer, Tabu, Kollektivschuld. Über Motive deutscher Obsession', in *Erinnern, Verdrängen, Vergessen. Geschichtspolitische Wege ins 20. Jahrhundert* (Giessen: Netzwerk für politische Bildung, Kultur und Kommunikation, 2003), 17–41.

Santner, Eric, 'History beyond the Pleasure Principle', in Saul Friedlaender, ed., *Probing the Limits of Representation* (Cambridge, MA: Harvard University Press, 1992), 143–54.

____, *Objects. Mourning, Memory, and Film in Postwar Germany* (Ithaca, NY: Cornell University Press, 1990).

Sanyal, Debarati, *Memory and Complicity: Migrations of Holocaust Remembrance* (New York: Fordham University Press, 2015).

Schilling von, Klaus, *Schuldmotoren: Artistisches Erzählen in Günter Grass Danziger Trilogie* (Bielefeld: Aisthesis, 2002).

Schmitz, Helmut, '"Postmemory": Erbe und Familiengedächtnis bei Hanns-Joseph Ortheil, Thomas Medicus, Wibke Bruns, Uwe Timm and Dagmar Leupold', in *Autobiographie und historische Krisenerfahrung* (Heidelberg: Universitätsverlag, 2010), 259–76.

____, ed. *A Nation of Victims? Representations of German Wartime Suffering from 1945 to the Present* (Amsterdam: Rodopi, 2007).

____, '"Fire and sulphur fall from the sky" – Dieter Forte's *Der Junge mit den blutigen Schuhen'*, in *On Their Own Terms: The Legacy of National Socialism in Post–1990 German Fiction* (Birmingham: The University of Birmingham Press, 2004), 241–61.

Schneider, Christian, 'Der Holocaust als Generationsobjekt', *Mittelweg* 36/13 (2004): 56–73.

____, 'Deutsche als Opfer? Über ein Tabu der Nachkriegsgeneration', in Lothar Kettenacker, ed., *Ein Volk von Opfern? Die neue Debatte um den Bombenkrieg 1940–1945* (Berlin: Rowohlt, 2003), 158–65.

Schödel, Katrin, 'Radikale Umkehrungen von Gedächtnisdiskursen und das politisch Subversive in Gisela Elsners Roman *Fliegeralarm*', in Ari Sepp and Gunther Martens, eds, *Gegen den Strich, das Subversive in der deutschsprachigen Literatur nach 1945* (Berlin: Lit Verlag, 2017), 9–21.

Schwab, Gabriele, *Haunting Legacies: Violent History and Transgenerational Trauma* (New York: Columbia University Press, 2010).

Sebald, W. G., 'Air War and Literature', in Anthea Bell trans., *On the Natural History of Destruction* (New York: Random House, 2003), 1–104.

____, *Luftkrieg und Literatur* (Munich: Hanser, 1999).

Silverman, Maxim, *Palimpsestic Memory: The Holocaust and Colonialism in Francophone Fiction and Film* (New York, Oxford: Berghahn, 2013).

Sontag, Susan, *Regarding the Pain of Others* (New York: Picador, 2003).

Spiegelman, Art, *Maus II. A Survivor's Tale: And Here My Troubles Began* (New York: Pantheon, 1991).

Stargardt, Nicholas, *Witnesses of War. Children's Lives under the Nazis* (New York: Vintage, 2007).

Steedman, Carolyn, *Strange Dislocations: Childhood and the Idea of Human Interiority, 1780–1930* (Cambridge, MA: Harvard University Press, 1995).

Stölzl, Jürgen, and Jürgen Tietz, eds, *Die Neue Wache Unter den Linden: Ein deutsches Denkmal im Wandel der Geschichte* (Berlin: Scheibel, 1995).

Stopka, Katja, 'Vertriebene Erinnerung: Transgenerationelle Nachwirkungen von Flucht und Vertreibung im literarischen Gedächtnis am Beispiel von Hans-Ulrich Treichels *Der Verlorene*', in Wolfgang Hartwig and Erhardt Schutz, eds, *Keiner kommt davon: Zeitgeschichte in der Literatur nach 1945* (Göttingen: Vandenhoeck & Ruprecht, 2008), 166–84.

Straub, Jürgen, 'Psychology, Narrative and Cultural Memory', in Astrid Erll and Ansgar Nünning, eds, *A Companion to Cultural Memory Studies* (Berlin, New York: De Gruyter, 2010), 215–28.

Stürmer, Michael, *Historikerstreit. Die Dokumentation der Kontroverse um die Einzigartigkeit der nationalsozialistischen Judenvernichtung* (Munich, Zurich: Piper, 1988).

Süselbeck, Jan, 'Verfluchung einer Kriegskinderbiografie. NS–Geschlechtsbilder und Generationenkritik in Gisela Elsners Roman *Fliegeralarm*', in Christian Poetini, ed., *Gender im Gedächtnis. Geschlechtsspezifische Erinnerungen in der deutschsprachigen Gegenwartsliteratur* (Bielefeld: Aisthesis, 2015), 201–16.

Taberner, Stuart, 'Hans–Ulrich Treichel's *Der Verlorene* and the Problem of Wartime Suffering', *The Modern Language Review* 97/1 (January 2002): 123–34.

Ticktin, Miriam, 'A World without Innocence', *American Ethnologist* 44/4, (2017): 577–90.

Tollance, Pascale, 'Freezing Emotion: The Impersonality of 'Photographic Writing' in Rachel Seiffert's *The Dark Room*', in Christine Reynier and Michel, eds, Ganteau *Impersonality and Emotion in Twentieth–Century British Literature* (Montpellier: Publications Montpellier III, 2005), 287–98.

Treichel, Hans-Ulrich, 'Das Autobiographische', *Allmende* 26/78 (2006): 7–11.

____, 'Lebenserfahrungen sind Leseerfahrungen': Gespräch mit Hans-Ulrich Treichel, in David Basker, ed., *Hans-Ulrich Treichel* (Cardiff: University of Wales Press, 2004), 12–27.

____, *Der Entwurf des Autors. Poetikvorlesungen* (Frankfurt a.M.: Suhrkamp, 2000).

Ulrich, Bernd, ed., *Besucher einer Ausstellung: Die Ausstellung 'Vernichtungskrieg: Verbrechen der Wehrmacht 1941–1944'. Interview und Gespräch* (Hamburg: Hamburger Institut für Sozialforschung, 1998).

Vees-Gulani, Susanne, 'The Language of Trauma: Dieter Forte's Memories of Air War', in Laurel Cohen-Pfister and Dagmar Wienroeder-Skinner, eds, *Victims and Perpetrators: 1933–1945: (Re-)Presenting the Past in Post-Unification Culture* (Berlin, Boston: De Gruyter, 2006), 114–35.

Venken, Machteld, and Maren Röger, 'Growing Up in the Shadow of the Second World War: European Perspectives', *European Review of History* 22/2 (2015): 199–220.

Weigel, Sigrid, '"Generation" as a Symbolic Form: On the Genealogical Discourse of Memory since 1945', *Germanic Review* 77/4 (Fall 2002): 264–77.

Weissman, Gary, *Fantasies of Witnessing* (Ithaca, NY: Cornell University Press, 2004).

Welzer, Harald, 'Re–narrations: How Pasts Change in Conversational Remembering', *Memory Studies* 3/1 (2010): 5–17.

____, Sabine Moller and Karoline Tschuggnall, eds, *Opa war kein Nazi. Nationalismus und Holocaust im Familiengedächtnis* (Frankfurt a.M.: Fischer, 2002).

____, 'Die Nachhaltigkeit historischer Erfahrungen. Eine sozialpsychologische Perspektive', in Hartmut Hartmut, Werner Bohleber and Jürgen Zinnecker, eds, *Transgenerationale Weitergabe kriegsbelasteter Kindheiten: Interdisziplinäre Studien zur Nachhaltigkeit historischer Erfahrungen über vier Generationen* (Weinheim, München: Juventa 2002), 75–93.

Williams, Rhys W., '"Leseerfahrungen sind Lebenserfahrungen": Gespräch mit Hans-Ulrich Treichel', in David Basker, ed., *Hans-Ulrich Treichel* (Cardiff: University of Wales, 2004), 12–27.

Winterberg, Yury, and Sonya, *Kriegskinder. Erinnerungen einer Generation* (Berlin: Rotbuch, 2009.

Wittlinger, Ruth, 'Taboo or Tradition? The 'Germans as Victims' Theme in the Federal Republic until the mid–1990s', in Bill Niven, ed., *Germans as Victims. Remembering the Past in Contemporary Germany* (New York: Palgrave Macmillan, 2006), 62–75.

Wüstenberg, Jenny, *Civil Society and Memory in Postwar Germany* (Cambridge, UK: Cambridge University Press, 2017).

Index

CULTURAL MEMORIES

SERIES EDITOR

Katia Pizzi
Director, Italian Cultural Institute, London

Cultural Memories is the publishing project of the Centre for the Study of Cultural Memory at the Institute of Modern Languages Research, University of London. The Centre is international in scope and promotes innovative research with a focus on interdisciplinary approaches to memory.

This series supports the Centre by furthering original research in the global field of cultural memory studies. In particular, it seeks to challenge a monumentalizing model of memory in favour of a more fluid and heterogeneous one, where history, culture and memory are seen as complementary and intersecting. The series embraces new methodological approaches, encompassing a wide range of technologies of memory in cognate fields, including comparative studies, cultural studies, history, literature, media and communication, and cognitive science. The aim of *Cultural Memories* is to encourage and enhance research in the broad field of memory studies while, at the same time, pointing in new directions, providing a unique platform for creative and and forward-looking scholarship in the discipline.

Vol. 1   Margherita Sprio
          Migrant Memories: Cultural History, Cinema and the Italian Post-War
          Diaspora in Britain
          2013. ISBN 978-3-0343-0947-9

Vol. 2   Shanti Sumartojo and Ben Wellings (eds)
          Nation, Memory and Great War Commemoration: Mobilizing the
          Past in Europe, Australia and New Zealand
          2014. ISBN 978-3-0343-0937-0

Vol. 18   Susanne Baackmann
          Writing the Child:
          Fictions of Memory in German Postwar Literature
          2022. ISBN 978-1-78707-722-5

Printed by
CPI books GmbH, Leck